Mortuary Practices and Social Differentiation at Casas Grandes, Chihuahua, Mexico

ANTHROPOLOGICAL PAPERS OF
THE UNIVERSITY OF ARIZONA
NUMBER 49

Mortuary Practices and Social Differentiation at Casas Grandes, Chihuahua, Mexico

John C. Ravesloot

THE UNIVERSITY OF ARIZONA PRESS
TUCSON
1988

About the author

JOHN C. RAVESLOOT first became interested in the prehistory of the Casas Grandes region of northern Chihuahua in 1974 while working in the Mimbres Valley, southwestern New Mexico. His Master's thesis, written in 1979, considered the relationship between the Animas phase, a post-Classic Mimbres phenomenon, and the development of Casas Grandes. Since that time he has participated in and directed archaeological field work in southwestern and south central New Mexico and throughout Arizona. Currently his research interests include a reanalysis and evaluation of the Casas Grandes temporal sequence and the study of prehistoric Hohokam organization in southern Arizona. He received his doctoral degree in Anthropology from Southern Illinois University, Carbondale in 1984. Dr. Ravesloot is an Assistant Curator at the Arizona State Museum, University of Arizona.

Cover: Ramos Polychrome jars that contained secondary burials from the Mound of the Offerings at Casas Grandes, Chihuahua, Mexico. Height of front vessel is 46.8 cm. (Photographs courtesy of the Amerind Foundation, Inc., Dragoon, Arizona; see Figs. 4.3, 4.5*a*, and 4.5*b*.)

Publication of this book was made possible in part by a generous grant from the Provost's Fund, University of Arizona.

THE UNIVERSITY OF ARIZONA PRESS

This book was set in 10/12 Times Roman
Manufactured in the U.S.A.

Library of Congress Cataloging-in-Publication Data

Ravesloot, John C., 1952–
    Mortuary practices and social differentiation at Casas Grandes,
Chihuahua, Mexico / John C. Ravesloot.
p. cm.—(Anthropological papers of the University of
Arizona; no. 49)
    Bibliography: p.
    Includes index.
    ISBN 0-8165-1048-2 (alk. paper)
    1. Casas Grandes Site (Mexico) 2. Indians of Mexico—Chihuahua
(State)—Mortuary customs. 3. Indians of Mexico—Chihuahua (State)—
Antiquities. 4. Chihuahua (Mexico: State)—Antiquities.
5. Mexico—Antiquities. I. Title. II. Series.
F1219.1.C3R38 1988   88-15385
393.1'097216—dc19   CIP

British Library Cataloguing in Publication data are available.

For Pat and Brian

Contents

FIGURES

TABLES

Preface

Twenty years have passed since Charles Di Peso (1968a, 1968b) first reported on his excavations of Casas Grandes. The multiple volume report (1974) provided a detailed description of the material culture and lifeways of the Casas Grandes people. However, much work remains to be done with this important data set. Di Peso's conclusions regarding the temporal sequence of the site, regional chronology, and the role and nature of Mesoamerican influence are still subjects of considerable controversy, and they need to be further evaluated with the Casas Grandes archaeological data.

It is generally accepted that Casas Grandes society achieved a level of sociopolitical complexity unparalleled by most prehistoric Southwestern societies, although its position within the regional interaction sphere is still unclear. Yet, the current debate among archaeologists concerning levels of social complexity suggested to have been attained by some southwestern puebloan societies is based on far less evidence than the Casas Grandes case and on questionable data sets. Much of the complexity controversy centers around contrasting interpretations of the social correlates of ranking as marked by differential burial treatments. A first step toward a resolution of this issue may be achieved by studies of mortuary practices from societies that represent varying degrees of social complexity.

It was to this end that this analysis of Casas Grandes mortuary practices during the Medio period (A.D. 1200 to 1450) was directed. The research discussed in this volume attempts to provide a descriptive model of the Casas Grandes mortuary program and to test for the presence of vertical social differentiation or ranking. The results of this analysis of social ranking should serve as an important case study for cross-cultural comparisons with other studies of social complexity that use mortuary data. Furthermore, this volume supplements previous studies of Casas Grandes and demonstrates the potential of this data set for addressing a wide range of research issues currently of interest to archaeologists.

Chapter 1 introduces the problem addressed in this study, briefly describes Casas Grandes, and provides a summary of previous interpretations of social complexity for the site. A brief historical introduction to the archaeological study of social organization is presented in Chapter 2, which focuses on the use of ethnographic concepts by archaeologists, specifically evolutionary typological models to classify prehistoric societies and to make generalizations about cultural change. The problems with such an approach are summarized and several alternative approaches to the study of prehistoric societies, specifically hierarchically organized ones, are outlined. This chapter also considers the concept of "an organization" and defines the properties of hierarchically structured organizations. The theoretical perspectives behind archaeological studies of mortuary patterning are then summarized in Chapter 3, emphasizing various approaches that have been used to identify social ranking from mortuary data. In Chapter 4, the hypothesis of ascriptive ranking and its test implications are summarized. The Casas Grandes burials are described in terms of the architectural contexts in which they were found. This discussion attempts to distinguish units and specific rooms where religious activities occurred by describing the distribution and frequency of ritual paraphernalia. The hypothesis of ascriptive ranking is evaluated in Chapter 5 through a univariate analysis of a 43 variable data set. Frequency tabulations for the variables of burial treatment identified and the cross-tabulation of these variables with age, gender, and spatial distinctions are presented. The results of this analysis are then used to prepare a descriptive model for the Medio period mortuary program. The hypothesis is further evaluated in Chapter 6 through a multivariate analysis of the data set. The results of the research described herein and their implications for the organization of Casas Grandes are further considered in Chapter 7.

Acknowledgments

The fine and detailed reporting of the Casas Grandes excavations by Charles Di Peso made this study possible. His support and enthusiasm for this work during its initial stages are greatly appreciated. I hope he would have been pleased with the results.

The research and analyses in this monograph were part of my doctoral dissertation, completed at Southern Illinois University at Carbondale under the direction of George Gumerman, David Braun, Lewellyn Hendrix, Bruce MacLachlan, and Carroll Riley. Financial support was provided by the Graduate School at Southern Illinois University through a Dissertation Research Award during the 1982 to 1983 academic year. The Department of Sociology and Anthropology at New Mexico State University at Las Cruces provided computer time for the statistical analyses.

The publication of this monograph would not have been possible without the support and interest of two individuals at the Arizona State Museum, University of Arizona: Raymond H. Thompson, Director, and Paul Fish, Curator of Archaeology. Dr. Fish urged me to consider revising the dissertation for publication. His guidance during the preparation of this volume is acknowledged.

John Speth, Ken Kvamme, Stephanie Whittlesey, and two anonymous reviewers read an early draft of this manuscript and provided valuable comments. Every effort was made to address the suggestions offered by these reviewers. The staff of the Amerind Foundation, in particular the Director, Anne Woosley, provided access to unpublished field notes and allowed me to reproduce the photographs herein.

I particularly would like to thank my wife, Patricia Spoerl, for her support and encouragement during the preparation of my dissertation and this manuscript. The final results have been greatly enhanced by her comments on countless drafts and through numerous discussions.

Special thanks go to Carol Gifford, editor of the *Anthropological Papers of the University of Arizona,* for technical and organizational assistance. Charles Sternberg drafted the illustrations; Annette Cvitkovich and Rose Slavin typed the References and Appendix A. Appreciation is expressed to Carmen Prezelski, of the Arizona State Museum, for providing the Spanish translation of the Abstract.

Mortuary Practices and Social Differentiation at Casas Grandes, Chihuahua, Mexico

Figure 1.1.   Location of Casas Grandes within the Greater Southwest.

CHAPTER ONE

Prehistoric Social Complexity at Casas Grandes

Variability in the treatment of the dead has been increasingly used by archaeologists to model aspects of prehistoric social organization. The use of mortuary data to reconstruct past social systems is based on ethnographically tested assumptions concerning the relationship of social organization to variability in burial treatment. Mortuary rituals function as systems of symbolic communication that convey information about the social standing or status of the deceased and the size and composition of the groups recognizing social obligations to the deceased.

Studies of prehistoric social organization through analyses of mortuary data are rare in the Greater Southwest. Large and representative burial collections necessary for such analyses are generally unavailable. The few burial collections that do exist have not been reported in sufficient detail for thorough mortuary analyses. Specific archaeological data (for example, mode of interment and associated grave goods) and osteological data (such as age and gender) seldom have been described for each burial. Notable exceptions are burials reported from the Carter Ranch site (Longacre 1970), Grasshopper Pueblo (Clark 1967; Griffin 1967; Whittlesey 1978), Arroyo Hondo Pueblo (Palkovich 1980), Gran Quivira (Hayes 1981), Rainbow Bridge-Monument Valley Expedition site RB 568 (Crotty 1983), Sinagua settlements (Hohmann 1983), and Chaco Canyon settlements (Akins 1986). Some of these studies are based on composite burial samples from a series of settlements rather than single sites. In most cases, with the exception of Grasshopper Pueblo and Gran Quivira, these burial populations are small in size, numbering less than two hundred individuals.

Excavations at Casas Grandes (Fig. 1.1) by the Amerind Foundation recovered a burial series consisting of 576 individuals, one of the largest and best documented collections known for the Greater Southwest. This study attempts to gain a better understanding of the ways in which Casas Grandes society was organized by determining the manner and degree to which Casas Grandians were socially differentiated. This goal is accomplished by testing the hypothesis that Casas Grandes society was organized on the principles of ascriptive or hereditary inequality, a societal characteristic that can be evaluated by testing for the presence of symbolic indicators of distinct offices of power and rank displayed by qualitative or categorical attributes of burial treatment.

This investigation of social ranking at Casas Grandes using mortuary data is based to a large extent on the so-called dimensional approach. This perspective views social organization as consisting of multidimensional social spaces (that is, identities or social positions) that are assigned to members based on the specific criteria that society has chosen to differentiate those positions. The dimensional perspective as applied to the study of mortuary data is based on the assumption that the criteria used to differentiate qualitatively different social positions or identities should be symbolized in a society's mortuary program by qualitative distinctions in burial treatment among individuals. These differences include the location of the burial facility, the size and the type of burial facility, methods and techniques of corpse processing and disposal, and the type of associated grave goods.

By viewing Casas Grandes society as a formal organization, it is possible to make use of concepts concerning the properties of hierarchically structured contemporary decision-making organizations. These concepts include vertical differentiation or ranking, status hierarchies, and levels of authority, concepts that can be behaviorally defined and inferred from archaeological data. This uniformitarian perspective of hierarchical organization provides an approach with which to model specific aspects of prehistoric social variation.

The burial collection recovered by the Amerind Foundation from Casas Grandes represents an exception to the recovery and the reporting of prehistoric burial collections from the Greater Southwest. Additional intensive and comprehensive analyses of this important burial collection can contribute to the theoretical and methodological approaches developed elsewhere for the identification of social ranking from mortuary data. Determining the level of organizational complexity reached by the Casas Grandes community is essential for a better understanding of ways in which this society interacted with other societies and ways in which the organization of this society may have affected other apparently less complex societies in the Greater Southwest. Furthermore, results of the analysis of social ranking at Casas Grandes can provide a baseline model for evaluating alternative interpretations that have been presented for sociopolitical complexity in the Greater Southwest in late prehistoric times. Some archaeologists maintain that certain societies were characterized by regional integration and social hierarchies, whereas others view a tribal level of organization as a more appropriate analog (Cordell 1984: 346).

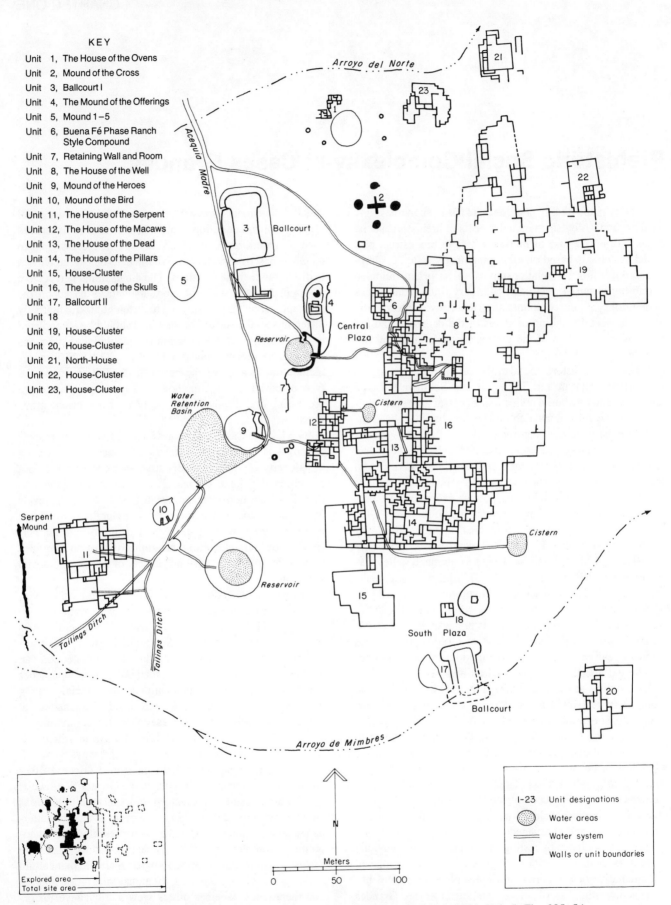

KEY

Unit 1, The House of the Ovens
Unit 2, Mound of the Cross
Unit 3, Ballcourt I
Unit 4, The Mound of the Offerings
Unit 5, Mound 1–5
Unit 6, Buena Fé Phase Ranch Style Compound
Unit 7, Retaining Wall and Room
Unit 8, The House of the Well
Unit 9, Mound of the Heroes
Unit 10, Mound of the Bird
Unit 11, The House of the Serpent
Unit 12, The House of the Macaws
Unit 13, The House of the Dead
Unit 14, The House of the Pillars
Unit 15, House-Cluster
Unit 16, The House of the Skulls
Unit 17, Ballcourt II
Unit 18
Unit 19, House-Cluster
Unit 20, House-Cluster
Unit 21, North-House
Unit 22, House-Cluster
Unit 23, House-Cluster

1-23   Unit designations
       Water areas
       Water system
       Walls or unit boundaries

Meters
0   50   100

Figure 1.2.   The Casas Grandes site. (Map adapted from Di Peso, Rinaldo, and Fenner 1974, Vol. 5, Fig. 285–5.)

Figure 1.3.   General scene of Casas Grandes and its central plaza, viewed from the top of Unit 16. (Photo courtesy of the Amerind Foundation, Inc., Dragoon, Arizona; Negative No. CG 583–14F.)

THE SITE AND ITS SETTING

Casas Grandes, also known as Paquimé, was partially excavated by the Amerind Foundation between 1958 and 1961 (Di Peso 1968a, 1968b, 1974). The site, located in Chihuahua, Mexico was constructed on a terrace above the Rio Casas Grandes. At one time it covered approximately 36 hectares, or 88 acres (Fig. 1.2), of which 37 acres (42.1%) were excavated (Di Peso, Rinaldo, and Fenner 1974, Vol. 4: 198). The excavations that focused on the western portion of the site defined multistoried domestic, public, and ceremonial architectural units, constructed primarily of puddled adobe and encompassing enclosed plazas and hundreds of rooms that were built around a large central plaza (Fig. 1.3). In addition, three ballcourts, numerous platform mounds, a mortuary complex, and an extensive city water system were identified. A detailed description of Casas Grandes has been published by Di Peso (1974, Vol. 1–3) and Di Peso, Rinaldo, and Fenner (1974, Vol. 4–8). Throughout this monograph, references to these publications are cited by volume number and page.

Casas Grandes was occupied primarily during the Medio period, divided by Di Peso into three phases: Buena Fé (A.D. 1060 to 1205), Paquimé (A.D. 1205 to 1261), and Diablo (A.D. 1261 to 1340). The beginning and ending dates for the Medio period have been the subject of controversy since they were originally proposed (Braniff 1986; Doyel 1976; LeBlanc 1980, 1986; Lekson 1984; Carlson 1982; Ravesloot 1979; Ravesloot and others 1986; Wilcox 1986; Wilcox and Shenk 1977). A reevaluation of the Casas Grandes tree-ring samples indicates that major episodes of building occurred in the 13th and 14th centuries, that the community was occupied in the 15th century, and that construction or repair activity lasted as late as A.D. 1470 (Ravesloot and others 1986). For this reason, the Medio period is considered herein to date between A.D. 1200 to 1450.

PREVIOUS INTERPRETATIONS

Excavations at Casas Grandes documented extensive changes in material culture between the Viejo period (A.D. 700–1060) and the later Medio period. These differences are inferred to represent changes in the social, economic, and political organization. Di Peso attributes the apparent shifts in organization features to an intrusion of Mesoamerican "pochteca" into the Casas Grandes region. He (Vol. 2: 290) proposed that ". . . sometime around the year A.D. 1060 a group of sophisticated Mesoamerican merchants came into the valley of Casas Grandes and inspired the indigenous Chichimecans to build the city of Paquimé over a portion of an older Viejo Period village." The evidence for this view includes the identification of numerous Mesoamerican features such as the plumed serpent motif, platform mounds, ballcourts, ceramic handdrums, a market exchange system, copper metallurgy, macaw aviculture, human sacrifice, and an elaborate mortuary complex. These merchants, or pochteca, presumably reorganized the indigenous population from an egalitarian society to a stratified urban society in which they served in a managerial capacity as overlords or rulers.

Di Peso (1968a, 1968b, 1974, 1976) and other proponents of the pochteca model (Frisbie 1978; Kelley 1966, 1980; Kelley and Kelley 1975; Reyman 1971, 1978) propose that long-distance traders or pochteca from Mesoamerican societies were responsible for, or at least greatly influenced, cultural development among some Southwestern groups between A.D. 1000 and 1400 through economic, religious, and political control. The pochteca concept is taken from Bernardino de Sahagún's description of the organization and operation of long-distance traders in 16th century Aztec society (Anderson and Dibble 1950–1955; Dibble and Anderson 1957–1969). These traders were an important component of Aztec economic policy; they served the needs of an expansionist political hierarchy that sought to control the source areas of needed raw materials and luxuries (Sanders and Price 1968; Driver 1961). Evidence presented in support of this model includes (1) the identification of archaeological sites within the Greater Southwest such as Chaco Canyon, New Mexico and Casas Grandes, Chihuahua, Mexico as Mesoamerican "outposts"; (2) the existence of Mesoamerican "traits" such as T-shaped doorways, platform mounds, copper bells, and macaws at Southwestern sites; (3) the identification at several sites of iconographic symbols or characteristics of Mesoamerican religious complexes; and (4) the discovery at a few sites of "high status" burials identified as the remains of pochteca traders (McGuire 1980: 4).

Casas Grandes, then, presumably was used by merchants as an outpost or base in a far-flung Mesoamerican-Southwestern exchange system through which large quantities of marine shell, ceramics, macaws, turquoise, and other items were imported and exported. Merchants controlled and exploited adjacent areas of the Greater Southwest for the primary purpose of acquiring turquoise, a highly valued commodity of the elite classes of Toltec society for which these merchants probably served.

Di Peso (Vol. 2: 293) suggested that about A.D. 1205 these merchants, in their position as leaders, reorganized the indigenous population of Casas Grandes in order to institute an urban renewal program. During the Paquimé phase (A.D. 1205–1261):

Casas Grandes was changed from a conglomerate of Buena Fé Phase, single-storied, ranch style house clus-

ters to a massive, multi-storied, high-rise apartment house covering some 36 hectares. The former were either razed, remodeled, or abandoned, and the earlier city water system was revamped to accommodate the remodeling, and the city planners surrounded this new housing complex with a ring of ceremonial structures including effigy mounds, ball courts, a market place, stately open plazas, and other specialized edifices (Di Peso 1974, Vol. 2: 313).

Hundreds of smaller communities also were located within the mountains and valleys of the Casas Grandes province during this period. These communities may have functioned as satellite villages that provided subsistence resources to support craft specialists and religious leaders at Casas Grandes. Intensive agriculture was practiced in addition to hunting and gathering. This city, and the market exchange system that operated from its confines, supposedly reached its height during the Paquimé phase. Following this phase Casas Grandes experienced a period of disintegration or stagnation until its demise about A.D. 1340 (Vol. 2: 293).

Evidence for the destruction of Casas Grandes consists of collapsed and blackened walls, suggesting the burning of the city; the presence of breeding turkeys and macaws left to die in their pens; unburied bodies found throughout the city; the discovery of broken altar stones and figures, particularly those found at the Mound of the Offerings; and the fully articulated remains of two individuals within the Mound of the Offerings who were interpreted as representing guards. Furthermore, Di Peso (Vol. 2: 321) commented:

It was equally obvious that no one remained to clean up the aftermath after the smoke of attack had cleared, save for scavenging animals which came to rummage and disperse the bodies of the unburied dead.

This collapse, as the rise, is explained mainly in relation to events taking place farther south in Mexico, particularly in Toltec society.

Di Peso's explanation for cultural changes at Casas Grandes, particularly those dealing with the construction and organization of the city, although based to a large extent on the pochteca model, is also based on Foster's (1960) donor-recipient frontier culture conquest model, on Wittfogel's (1957) model of semicomplex hydraulic societies, on Jacobs' (1969) concept of the economy of cities, and on evolutionary models of social complexity (Fried 1967; Service 1962, 1971). The interpretations of the social and religious organization during the Medio period are derived mainly from comparisons of the archaeological record with the writings of Sahagún. On the basis of Sahagún's description of the organization of long-distance traders or pochteca Di Peso argued that these merchants, in frontier contexts such as Casas Grandes, were led by a head merchant ("quappoyoultzin") whose office combined the authorities associated with military, religious, and mercantile activities (Vol. 2: 328–329). This merchant was responsible for coordinating these activities in the frontier town and for protecting the interests of the leader he served to the south in Mesoamerica.

The manner in which the pochteca and the indigenous population of Casas Grandes were organized under the "quappoyoultzin" is not entirely clear. Di Peso (Vol. 2: 476) suggested:

If these pochteca patterned their social organization after that of contemporary Mesoamerica, then nobility was determined by both birth and deed. Lesser nobles may have been distributed throughout the provincial population centers with the Casas Grandes sovereignty in order that they might better control the taxable commoners. The latter were perhaps subdivided into specific stratified groups such as free land holders, tenant farmers, and poor human pawns who were enslaved by raiding parties, wars, or by selling their own bodies or those of their progeny into servitude. Such a hierarchy would have brought the various townsmen and the rural populations under a unified political, economic, and social whole, with the central authority in the capital city of Paquimé.

Casas Grandes, therefore, is presumed to have been organized hierarchically on the basis of hereditary inequality where the founding merchants and their descendants occupied the most important social positions or statuses within the society. The individuals who formed this social group may have controlled the market complex, the agricultural land that surrounded the city, and its strategic resources. In particular, this group may have controlled the distribution of surface water rights through military enforcement (Vol. 2: 340).

The Casas Grandes population also may have been differentiated on the basis of occupation, since not all Casas Grandians were involved full-time in subsistence related activities. Di Peso (Vol. 2: 332) suggested that many of the inhabitants may have served in a guild system that produced finished goods for the city's market center. Occupational specialization (Vol. 2: 506–545, 598–602) may have included shell workers, lapidaries, coppersmiths, woodworkers, stone cutters, potters, weavers, bone workers, and aviculturists (macaw and turkey breeders).

Furthermore, a small number of the city's population may have served as priests since there are signs of the worship of the Mesoamerican gods Quetzalcóatl, Xiuhtecultli, Xipe, and Tláloc (Vol. 2: 546–573). Evidence for these religious complexes includes ceremonial mounds, sacred and public ballcourts, the plumed serpent motif, trophy heads, cannibalism, and human sacrifice. Di Peso (Vol. 2: 546) suggested:

Religion, the constant companion of every townsman, established a close relationship between the local parrot-headed plumed serpent image and other iconographic forms of the Mesoamerican god Quetzalcóatl. The related mass of gods permeated all aspects of their lives and was reflected in their music, games, funerary customs, acts of magic and curing, and priesthood practices.

Priestly orders may have been present at Paquimé for each of the religious complexes, assuming they were organized in a manner similar to contemporary ones in Mesoamerica.

These priests may have played an important role in the mortuary ritual of Casas Grandians, if funerary practices at Paquimé were similar to those described by Sahagún. Priests involved in burial of the dead may have resided and performed mortuary rituals in the so-called House of the Dead (Unit 13). This structure contained evidence for elaborate mortuary rituals, including the presumed use of the blood and heads of common turkeys and the playing and destruction of ceramic handdrums (Vol. 2: 575, 635).

Di Peso's interpretation of the social and religious complexity of Casas Grandes is the subject of considerable controversy. The validity of the pochteca model as an explanation for cultural change in the Greater Southwest, as well as its use as a general archaeological analogue for the social, religious, and economic organization of Casas Grandes during the Medio period, is seriously questioned. Numerous archaeologists have debated the appropriateness of using a description of historic Aztec society, particularly institutions such as the pochteca, to interpret earlier prehistoric periods in both Mesoamerica and the Greater Southwest (McGuire 1980; Plog, Upham, and Weigand 1982; Ravesloot 1979; Riley 1979, 1982; Weigand 1980; Mathien and McGuire 1986). Weigand (1980: 3) and others (Plog, Upham, and Weigand 1982: 11–12) also have argued that the use of the pochteca model to interpret the organization of long-distance trade for pre-Aztec times is inappropriate, because there is no discussion within the codices of Aztecan merchants engaging in exchange with groups to the north. Their activities were focused to the south of the basin of Mexico.

In addition, this interpretation, like numerous other archaeological attempts to model the social complexity of prehistoric Southwestern groups, depends to a large degree on evolutionary typological models (Service 1962; Fried 1967) as analogues for prehistoric ones. Ethnological concepts such as "ranking" and "stratification" are often used interchangeably with no clear distinction between the two. For example, Di Peso spoke of social stratification, ranked burial modes, overlords, rulers, freeland holders, tenant farmers, and human pawns. It is not entirely clear whether he was speaking of a society organized on the basis of ranked social positions as defined by Fried (1967) or a stratified social form that included social classes or castes. This distinction is important and needs to be clarified.

Alternative hypotheses must be formulated and evaluated through additional analyses of Casas Grandes archaeological data if we are to gain a better understanding of the nature of the social, economic, and political systems that linked this town with other communities. This study underscores the value of reexamining existing archaeological collections from alternative perspectives.

CHAPTER TWO

The Archaeological Study of Social Systems

For a long time archaeologists have tried to describe the organizational aspects of prehistoric societies based on only meagre evidence gathered from their excavations. Their concern with the social organization of early populations has been particularly evident in the Greater Southwest, where some of the first such studies involved the prehistoric Puebloan societies (V. Mindeleff 1891; C. Mindeleff 1897, 1900; Bandelier 1892; Cushing 1896; Fewkes 1896, 1900; Hewett 1905). Many of the generalizations regarding organizational aspects of prehistoric cultures that developed from these studies in the late 19th and early 20th centuries were considered useless speculation by the next generation of archaeologists. Most of them commonly assumed that the social and ideological aspects of prehistoric societies could not be observed in the archaeological record. In the majority of studies made in the mid 1900s, archaeologists emphasized chronological reconstructions and there were few notable attempts to infer the social, religious, and political structures of prehistoric cultures.

Not all archaeologists felt that reconstruction of the social and ideological components of prehistoric cultures was beyond the scope of archaeological studies. Taylor (1948), for one, criticized his colleagues for their preoccupation with cultural traits and chronological sequences and for their lack of concern for the less tangible parts of prehistoric cultures such as social organization and religious institutions. He proposed the use of a conjunctive approach to study prehistoric cultures that emphasized the interconnection of archaeological artifacts within their cultural contexts. This approach focused on the contextual relationships of all archaeological evidence such as architecture, technology, and nonartifactual materials to reconstruct the past lifeways of people and to describe the changes that occurred in their culture.

During the 1950s a number of archaeological publications in the United States included work dealing with organizational aspects of prehistoric societies. These studies included consideration of settlement patterns (Martin and Rinaldo 1950; Haury 1956; Willey 1956; Chang 1958), ceremonial structures (Sears 1954, 1958; Spaulding 1952), mortuary practices (Deuel 1952; Ritchie 1955), and craft specialization (Sears 1958). Sears (1961: 225), expressing the view of a number of archaeologists, suggested:

With the proper approach it should be possible to discover and document a great deal about social systems and the political and religious organization for most prehistoric North American cultures. There must be limits, kinds of information we cannot reconstruct, but until we have tried we shall not know where these limits are.

Binford (1962, 1965, 1968) also questioned the assumption that the nonmaterial or intangible components of prehistoric societies were beyond the scope of archaeological interpretation. He argued that, theoretically, the archaeological record possesses the data necessary to reconstruct most aspects of prehistoric cultures (Binford 1968: 22). What was lacking was a methodological approach with which to observe indirectly these components of past societies.

Binford formulated an approach for examining the archaeological record that incorporated cultural evolutionary theory, cultural ecology, a view of culture as a complex dynamic system, and hypothetico-deductive reasoning. This approach, he believed, would enable archaeologists to test formal hypotheses dealing with the ecological and social dimensions of culture and the nature of cultural change. Following White (1949), he proposed that culture should be viewed as a complex adaptive system that functions to adapt man to both his physical and social environment. This systemic perspective visualizes culture as composed of a number of interrelated subsystems (that is, technological, social, and ideological) of interacting variables that are constantly changing in response to internal and external factors. This view of culture recognizes the critical role that social systems play in the adaptation of human societies. Binford (1962) then outlined an approach to the study of prehistoric social systems that necessitated the examination of artifactual material in terms of the cultural context in which it functioned. He argued that three distinct classes of artifacts had to be defined: technomic artifacts, tools that functioned primarily to adapt man to his physical environment; sociotechnic artifacts, objects related to the social system; and ideotechnic artifacts, items that dealt with the ideological component of culture.

A major assumption of this systemic approach is that objects found at an archaeological site once functioned in a viable prehistoric cultural system. It is also assumed that artifacts occur in meaningful patterns in the archaeological record and that this patterning is potentially informative with regard to the cultural context with which these artifacts were utilized. Therefore, artifacts are more than material items; they are reflections of the manner in which a society was organized. Binford (1968: 23) argued:

> Granted we cannot excavate a kinship terminology or a philosophy, but we can and do excavate the material items which functioned together with those more behavioral elements within the appropriate cultural subsystems. The formal structure of artifact assemblages together with the between elements contextual relationships should and do present a systematic and understandable picture of the total extinct cultural system.

Following Binford, a number of archaeologists in the early 1960s focused their studies on the reconstruction of various aspects of prehistoric social subsystems. The classic studies of design elements on pottery (for example, Deetz 1965; Whallon 1968; Hill 1970; Longacre 1970) are good examples of the direction that archaeological studies of social organization took at the time. These writers utilized style or design interaction models in an attempt to reconstruct postmarital residence patterns. Numerous anthropologists have commented on the difficulties of applying ethnological concepts such as residence and descent to interpret organizational aspects of prehistoric societies (Barth 1967; Aberle 1968; Binford 1968; Harris 1968; Allen and Richardson 1971; Wobst 1978). A major difficulty outlined with the utilization of these concepts concerns problems with their definition and measurement (Aberle 1968; Allen and Richardson 1971; S. Plog 1976, 1978, 1980).

The archaeological study of prehistoric social organization has progressed considerably since the early studies of residence patterns. This progress is particularly evident within the Southwest, where archaeologists have attempted to describe and interpret various aspects of prehistoric Southwestern sociopolitical organization (Dean 1970; Vivian 1970; Di Peso 1974; F. Plog 1974; Braun and Plog 1982; Upham 1982; Lightfoot 1984).

Although major advances have been made in the archaeological study of social organization since the early 1960s, serious problems still exist with the theoretical and methodological approaches developed for that purpose. These include the misuse of ethnological concepts, the reliance on evolutionary typologies to classify and compare the social complexity of prehistoric societies, the failure to view the social dimension as one component of a complex organizational system, and the lack of a theoretical and methodological framework with which to measure variables of prehistoric organization that would facilitate the description and explanation of social variation observed in the archaeological record (Flannery 1972; F. Plog 1974; Tainter 1975, 1978; Johnson 1982; Synenki and Braun 1980).

SOCIAL EVOLUTIONARY TYPOLOGIES

For the most part, archaeologists studying social organization continue to rely on the evolutionary typologies of Service (1962, 1971) and of Fried (1967) to make generalizations about the social variation observed in the archaeological record rather than to explain that variability. The ethnologically defined societal types (that is, bands, tribes, chiefdoms, and states or egalitarian, ranked, and stratified) that comprise these typologies are generally used by archaeologists merely as analogs for prehistoric societies. The delineation of one or two of the characteristics presented for the defined types is usually considered sufficient to categorize a prehistoric society. This use of social evolutionary typologies by archaeologists is particularly evident in studies where they have attempted to identify ranked social statuses as reflected in differential burial treatment (Tainter 1978).

The use of these conceptual schemes for describing and explaining prehistoric sociopolitical organization may be criticized on a number of points: (1) the typological stages, as other ethnographically derived concepts, suffer from the spatial and historical biases of the ethnographic record; (2) the typologies are ideal models that in reality do not exist and are difficult to define and measure (Tainter 1975; Hill 1977; Synenki and Braun 1980); and (3) the typological approach is concerned with classifying social forms rather than measuring properties or variables of organization (Binford 1968; Harris 1968; Clarke 1972; Renfrew 1974; Tainter 1975; Hill 1977; Wobst 1978; Synenki and Braun 1980).

There has been some confusion among archaeologists using evolutionary models, specifically in studies that have dealt with the ranking of social statuses, regarding what these typologies of social complexity actually represent. Fried's (1967) typology was one of principles of political organization, whereas Service's (1962, 1971) model was concerned with the organization of social relations. Consequently, most archaeologists who applied Fried's (1967) concepts of egalitarian, ranked, or stratified to classify prehistoric societies used these concepts incorrectly, because few of them treated the concentration of authority as a scalar property.

Because the ultimate goal of studying prehistoric societies is to describe and explain social variation, it is necessary to view prehistoric societies as complex adaptive systems. Furthermore, viewing social adaptation as a dynamic process necessitates the development of a scale with which social variables can be measured rather than merely classified and described as aspects or attributes of these systems, as is the case with the typological approach. To be successful in describing and explaining social variation it is necessary to construct schemes with which to measure variables or properties of prehistoric social organization. Evolutionary typologies do not provide scales with which to measure variation and change.

ALTERNATIVE APPROACHES TO SOCIAL COMPLEXITY

A number of archaeologists have attempted to model and measure various aspects of prehistoric social and political complexity rather than to use the evolutionary typological approach (for example, Flannery 1972; Renfrew 1974; Tainter 1975, 1978; Wright and Johnson 1975; Steponaitis 1978, 1981; Johnson 1978, 1981; Plog and Upham 1979; O'Shea 1984). In their studies they have utilized settlement, ceramic, and mortuary data to model and measure organizational complexity. An emphasis on variables such as the centralization of authority or the degree to which the decision-making structure of a society is centralized could enhance our ability to describe and explain the processes responsible for the social variation observed in the archaeological record. Several of the more significant studies are briefly summarized.

Flannery (1972) was among the first to develop an approach for the study of the origins of complex societies, specifically the state, based on the principles of general systems theory. He argued that sociopolitical complexity can be measured in terms of two systemic processes: *segregation* (the amount of internal differentiation and specialization of subsystems) and *centralization* (the degree of linkage between the various subsystems and the highest-order controls in society). These two processes are considered to be universal in the evolution of complex organizations, as are the mechanisms that cause increasing segregation and centralization in societies. Flannery (1972: 413) proposed that *promotion* and *linearization* are two of the many evolutionary mechanisms responsible for changes in the above systemic processes.

> In promotion . . . an institution may rise from its place in the control hierarchy to assume a position in a higher level; it may in the process go from 'special-purpose' to more 'general-purpose.' Alternatively, a new institution, as the office of chieftainship, presumably arose out of the leadership role of the informal headman in a simpler society.
>
> . . . In linearization . . . lower-order controls are repeatedly or permanently bypassed by higher-order controls, usually after the former have failed to maintain relevant variables in range for some critical length of time (Flannery 1972: 413).

These evolutionary mechanisms are believed to be triggered by one variable, or a combination of variables, referred to as socioenvironmental stresses (for example, managerial requirements of irrigation systems, population growth, warfare, and trade). Socioenvironmental stresses vary in space and time, whereas evolutionary mechanisms such as promotion and linearization and the systemic processes of centralization and segregation are considered basic to the development of all societies. This approach, then, emphasizes the measurement of general processes of sociocultural evolution rather than specific developments such as trade in order to explain cultural change.

Wright and Johnson (1975), in examining early state formation in southwest Asia, proposed a model that emphasizes the organization of decision-making activities within a state rather than traditional characteristics such as governmental monopoly of force, formal law, or private landholding. They defined a state (Wright and Johnson 1975: 267) as a specialized decision-making organization that possesses at least three hierarchical levels of administrative organization. The number of hierarchical levels that a society possesses is determined by the number of activities for which information has to be processed. Consequently, the organizational complexity of societies can be classified on the basis of the number of administrative or decision-making levels. Wright and Johnson (1975) suggested that the hierarchical structure of societies may be inferred by examining the evidence provided from variability in site size, settlement patterns, and technological development.

Johnson (1978) offered a more comprehensive discussion of the above model. He argued that decision-making hierarchies permit the integration of a large number of organizational units and the coordination of activities that would be impossible in a society lacking this type of organization. Horizontal specialization (that is, increase in the number of decision making units) and vertical specialization (increase in the number of hierarchical levels) are the two processes responsible for increased complexity in these organizations. His examination of the development of decision-making organizations focused on the manner in which information sources are integrated.

In addition, Johnson (1978: 100–104) suggested that the development of an ascriptive ranking system may coincide with the vertical specialization of a decision-making organization. There are a number of problems involved in decision-making in vertically organized societies for which a system of regular status inheritance can provide solutions. Such problems include the recruitment and training of personnel for decision-making positions and the implementation of decisions.

Synenki and Braun (1980) presented an outline for an analytical approach to the study of social processes that was designed to resolve some of the difficulties encountered in describing and explaining social variation observable in the archaeological record. They argued that archaeologists are

> . . . handicapped by the lack of a perspective which recognizes the uniformitarian character of social processes and which emphasizes the analytical measurement of properties or variables of organization rather than organizational events (Synenki and Braun 1980: 1).

Their approach to the study of social processes is based on two major premises. The first premise deals with the importance of adopting a uniformitarian view of social organizational processes. This view enables the application of perspectives on the properties of self-organizing systems from disciplines such as systems theory, theoretical ecology, and organizational theory to archaeological problems. They also argued that the application of abstract organizational variables to the study of prehistoric social variation enables archaeologists to construct models that possess testable arguments of plausibility. In addition, they suggested that the use of concepts developed for the study of self-organizing systems will improve the investigation of the processes of social adaptation, because system theorists have studied the effects that environmental variables have on the stability of complex adaptive systems (Synenki and Braun 1980: 9–14).

Johnson (1982), in an article entitled "Organizational Structure and Scalar Stress," also suggested that the archaeological study of social variation and change will benefit from a uniformitarian approach. He argued that viewing social systems as organizations will provide a set of concepts for the study of the general properties of hierarchical structured organizations. The justification for this approach is that all organizations have to deal with similar problems, one of which is scalar stress. Johnson (1982: 32) indicated that the development of simultaneous hierarchies are ". . . responses to scalar-communication stress and degrading decision performance with increasing organizational scale." The initial occurrence in the archaeological record of status differentiation, elite access to certain resources, and differential power and authority are believed to be related to the development of the general properties of hierarchically structured organizations. Therefore, it is argued that the archaeological study of social variation and change should investigate the general properties of contemporary hierarchical organizations to interpret changes in organizational size and structure in prehistoric societies.

Thus, there are numerous approaches currently in use to describe and explain prehistoric social variation and change. Traditionally archaeologists have merely used evolutionary typologies as analogs for prehistoric societies. An inherent problem with the use of typologies is that they limit the study of prehistoric social variation to the variability defined by types. Consequently, gradations within social dimensions such as ranking are not measurable when typological scales are used. Recent alternative approaches to evolutionary typologies have stressed the uniformitarian view of prehistoric social systems as organizations and the quantitative measurement of specific organizational variables. This approach could strengthen the ability of archaeologists to model past social systems, because a uniformitarian view of social organizational processes makes available perspectives on the properties of formal organizations from a wide range of disciplines. In addition, the use of abstract organizational variables emphasizes the measurement rather than the classification of social variables.

This study follows the general uniformitarian view of social organization and focuses on variables or properties of organizational complexity to describe the organizational structure of Casas Grandes. Organizational theorists and sociologists have examined a number of different variables to describe and explain variability in the structural dimensions of hierarchically integrated organizations. The following discussion briefly examines the concept of an organization, defines the structural dimensions or properties of hierarchically structured organizations, and presents the logic for the way in which hierarchical complexity is conceptualized in this study.

PROPERTIES OF HIERARCHICALLY STRUCTURED ORGANIZATIONS

Hierarchically integrated organizations have been studied from a number of perspectives, each of which has resulted in important knowledge regarding their structural characteristics and the manner in which they function. Some reports include examinations of the processes of social interaction whereas others emphasize comparisons between different organizations in order to explain structural variability.

The Concept of an Organization

One of the major difficulties in discussing organizational theory is arriving at a clear definition of an organization. An organization consists of a group of people who engage in regular sets of activities and interrelationships. Sociologists distinguished two general types of organizations: informal and formal. Informal organizations consist of families, friendship cliques, and the like that are coordinated usually on the basis of birth and voluntarism. They normally lack specific objectives that are visible to a nonmember. Formal organizations, on the other hand, traditionally have been defined as the mechanisms for accomplishing the explicit goals and objectives of a group (Scott 1961; Litterer 1963, 1965). There are, however, numerous other definitions of formal organizations. Litterer (1963: 3) has defined an organization ". . . as a product of rational thought concerned with coordinating tasks through the use of legitimate authority." Organizations are also defined as complex decision-making structures (Simon 1957; March and Simon 1958). Champion (1975: 1) suggested:

> A formal organization is a predetermined arrangement of individuals whose interrelated tasks and specialties enable the total aggregate to achieve goals. It is further characterized by provisions for the replacement of members who resign, transfer, die, or retire; a system of rewards and benefits, which accrue to each member in return for his services; a hierarchy of authority which allocates power and delegates duties to be performed by the membership; and a communication system which transmits information and assists in the coordination of the activities of the members.

A systemic view of organizations as living systems has been presented by Miller (1978: 595):

> Organizations are systems with multiechelon deciders whose components and subsystems may be subsidiary organizations, groups, and (uncommonly) single persons. In my conceptual system they are concrete living systems with components that are also concrete living systems rather than abstracted systems whose units are

actions or roles (see page 19). Organizations are subsystems, components, or subcomponents of societies, sometimes of more than one society (see page 910).

As the above examples indicate, presenting a general definition of a formal organization is not an easy task, particularly since the field of organizational theory lacks a single perspective or strategy with which to view formal organizations. In simple terms, organizations may best be viewed as social systems of interaction. Different organizational forms are created through the processes of social interaction (Olsen 1968).

Models of Organizations

A number of different models or classificatory schemes have been formulated to study the behavior, structure, and processes of organizations. They are used by theorists to describe and explain structural variability within and between formal organizations and they include bureaucracy, goal, decision, equilibrium, natural system, and open-system schemes. Each emphasizes a different dimension or characteristic of an organization such as decision-making power, organization size, or centralization of authority (Scott 1961, 1975; Litterer 1963; Scott and Mitchell 1972; Haas and Drabeck 1973; Champion 1975). Many of these models overlap to a considerable extent, because they are derivatives and modifications of others (Champion 1975: 25). Consequently, no single model of organization is universally accepted among researchers.

The various theoretical models used to study organizations may be examined from the perspective of whether they are open or closed schemes (Katz and Kahn 1966: 19). Open-system models (natural system and open-system) focus on the interrelations of organizations with their environments, whereas closed-system schemes stress the processes within organizations to explain organization behavior.

Decision and Open-system Models

Some researchers view organizations as decision-making structures (Simon 1944, 1947, 1957; March and Simon 1958). A decision may be defined as an organization's response to a problem. Decision-making organizations are considered to be closed-rational systems that serve to solve problems confronting them. Decisions are considered rational when the problem solver has selected the best alternative action or strategy available from several to reach a goal or objective.

> Organization involves a 'horizontal' specialization of work and a 'vertical' specialization in decision-making, the function of the latter being to secure coordination of the operative employees, expertness in decision-making, and responsibility to policymaking agencies (Simon 1944: 29).

Simon (1957) has suggested that the structural dimensions of organizations such as hierarchy of authority and specialization of work are designed to ensure rational decision-making within organizations. For example, the hierarchy of authority exists in order to delineate the role or position that an individual plays in the problem-solving processes of an organization.

The open-systems approach conceptualizes organizations as dynamic fluctuating entities rather than as static ones. This perspective, as applied to human organizations, developed from the work of general systems theorists (Ashby 1962; Miller 1965, 1978; Bertalanffy 1968) who attempted to formulate a conceptual approach for the discovery of general principles of systems (that is, biological, physical, and social).

The systems perspective applied to human organizations is best illustrated from the work of Miller (1965, 1978), Katz and Kahn (1966), Lawrence and Lorsch (1967), and Crozier (1964). These theorists and others who use this perspective emphasize the following general properties of organizations: organizations are viewed as systems within systems, these systems are open rather than closed, organizations possess boundaries that differentiate them from their environments, organizations as open systems possess complex feedback and regulatory mechanisms that enable adaptive responses to environmental variation, variability in an organization's environment necessitates variation in the structure of an organization, interaction within and between organizations reflects differing layers of autonomy and control (Miller 1965, 1978; Thompson 1967; Scott and Mitchell 1972; Haas and Drabeck 1973).

In summary, the decision model assumes a static or unchanging structural arrangement of organizations, whereas the open-systems perspective provides a framework with which to conceptualize the dynamic processes of interaction, stability, and change within organizations. Both of these perspectives provide important insights concerning the structure and operation of complex organizations that can be used to study prehistoric societies.

For purposes of this study, an organization is viewed as a complex problem-solving and decision-making structure. Through various feedback processes, decision-making organizations are capable of providing solutions or strategies with which to respond to variation and stress. These solutions are not always principally concerned with maintaining the structure of organizations; they are also adaptive and may involve structural changes. Adaptive changes in an organization include not only the evolution to a higher level of structural complexity such as increased differentiation or specialization in decision-making but also maladaptive changes.

Structural Dimensions of Organizations

Organizational theorists have examined a number of different variables in an attempt to describe and explain variability in the structural dimensions or characteristics of complex organizations. The variables they have selected to measure are those that they believe reveal an organization's efforts to deal with differentiation and integration (Jackson and Morgan 1978: 88), including organization size, complexity or differentiation, formalization, control, administrative component, bureaucratization, centralization, and levels of authority (Lawrence and Lorsch 1967; Pugh and others 1968; Blau and Schoenherr 1971; Champion 1975; Jackson and Morgan 1978). The study of these structural dimensions of organizations has resulted in an understanding and a description of the general properties of hierarchically structured organizations. Two of these organizational concepts, differentiation and levels of authority, are particularly relevant to the study of hierarchical organization at Casas Grandes.

The structural complexity of an organization refers to the number of differentiated elements or components that must be coordinated and integrated for an organization to function as a unit (Blau and Schoenherr 1971; Jackson and Morgan 1978). The concept of differentiation has been defined by Lawrence and Lorsch (1967: 4) as:

> . . . the state of segmentation of the organizational system into subsystems, each of which tends to develop particular attributes in relation to the requirements posed by its relevant external environment.

The degree of differentiation within an organization can be measured by determining the number of subunits or positions and hierarchical levels present (Blau and Schoenherr 1971).

Social differentiation refers to the differential distribution of an organization's members among different social positions (Linton 1936; Blau 1970). Individual members of an organization are socially differentiated on the basis of a number of distinct sets of criteria (or "dimensions") that determine the structure of differentiation. The division of labor based on criteria of sexual differences is probably the most commonly recognized social difference within organizations and societies (Durkheim 1933). Blau (1970: 301) has defined a dimension of differentiation as:

> . . . any criterion on the basis of which the members of an organization are formally divided into positions, as illustrated by the division of labor; or into ranks, notably managerial levels; or into subunits such as local branches, headquarters divisions, or sections within branches or divisions.

There are two general forms within which all varieties of differentiation may be subsumed: heterogeneity and inequality (Blau 1977: 8). Heterogeneity or horizontal differentiation is the distribution of a population among a society's social groups. This refers to those groups not hierarchically ranked, although recruitment to the groups may be determined by an individual's placement in the status hierarchy. Inequality or vertical differentiation refers to the

hierarchical ranking of social positions in terms of dimensions of status (Blau 1977: 45). Status is defined as all social positions that vary by gradation (in terms of graduated parameters) such as wealth, prestige, power, and administrative authority (Blau 1977: 46).

The concept of status hierarchy or hierarchical system refers to an organization in which subsystems or social positions are structured vertically in terms of levels or gradations. A hierarchical system is defined by Simon (1962: 267) as ". . . a system that is composed of interrelated subsystems, each of the latter being, in turn, hierarchic in structure until we reach some lowest level of elementary subsystem." Hierarchical structures are frequently encountered when studying organizations because they simplify the management of coordination of these systems (Simon 1944; Sutherland 1975). Gardner and Moore (1963: 176) have noted that an almost universal characteristic of status hierarchies is that as one ascends the hierarchy certain rights and privileges accompany high status positions that are denied to individuals in subordinate positions. Many of these rights and privileges are indicated by specific symbols of status and authority (Gardner and Moore 1963; Litterer 1965).

Two basic methods are used to assign, allocate, or recruit individuals to different social roles within a status hierarchy: ascription and achievement. Ascribed social positions are assigned on the basis of characteristics over which an individual has no control, such as the status of the family into which he or she is born (Linton 1936; Litterer 1965). Allocation of social roles on the basis of achievement are open to choice, individual effort, and competition. Further, all complex organizations possess hierarchies of authority that involve social interactions between individuals in subordinate and superordinate positions (Urwick 1956; Litterer 1965; Blau 1968, 1977; Champion 1975; Jackson and Morgan 1978).

The term "levels of authority," which includes "span of control," has been designated by organizational theorists as an important structural dimension of organizations. "Levels of authority" refers to the degree to which an organization is vertically differentiated, and the concept of levels refers to layers of different social positions. The concept of "span of control" is defined as the number of individuals or units in an organizational hierarchy that are subordinate or under the direct control of a supervisor (Urwick 1956; Litterer 1965; Blau 1968; Champion 1975; Mintzberg 1979). Litterer (1965: 308) noted that:

> To coordinate the efforts of a large number of people, it becomes necessary to divide the work to be supervised among a number of managers and, in turn, to have their efforts coordinated by a higher level of managers who also have their span of control limited by their work capacity.

Studies of the span of control in organizations have concluded that the number of individuals directly controlled by a supervisor should not exceed six, but in fact they usually do (Urwick 1956; Litterer 1965; Pugh and others 1968). The span of control is an important element that determines the shape of an organization's managerial hierarchy. A "tall" structure, which contains relatively small units or groups at each level in the hierarchy, has narrow spans of control whereas a "flat" structure has few levels and a wide span of control (Litterer 1965; Carzo and Yanouzas 1969; Blau and Schoenherr 1971; Scott and Mitchell 1972; Mintzberg 1979).

Centralization and decentralization refer to the two different ways in which the power over decision-making is delegated within hierarchically structured organizations. Power is defined as an individual's ability to influence another individual or other individuals to carry out orders (Parsons 1951: 121). An organization is considered to possess a centralized authority structure when the power for decision-making resides in the hands of one individual or a very small group of individuals at a single point in the organization (Litterer 1965; Pugh and others 1968; Jackson

and Morgan 1978; Mintzberg 1979; Osborn and others 1980). This point is usually at the apex of the organizational hierarchy (Litterer 1965: 379). A decentralized structure exists when the decision-making power is dispersed among many individuals and is carried out at the lowest levels in the organizational hierarchy.

In sum, the properties of formal organizations and several of their structural dimensions provide a basis for investigating certain organizational variables with archaeological data. Investigating properties of social ranking and recruitment to ranked social positions archaeologically commonly involves the study of burial practices. An appreciation of the potential of mortuary data for reconstructing social systems is evident by the numerous attempts to model aspects of prehistoric social organization from analyses of burial populations (for example, Peebles 1971, 1974; Peebles and Kus 1977; Brown 1971, 1979; Tainter 1975, 1978; Buikstra 1976; Goldstein 1976; Braun 1977, 1979; Whittlesey 1978; Rothschild 1979; Palkovich 1980; Chapman, Kinnes, and Randsborg 1981; O'Shea 1984; Milner 1984).

CHAPTER THREE

The Archaeological Analysis of Mortuary Patterning

The archaeological analysis of mortuary ritual is based on the assumption that there is a consistent relationship between the differential treatment received in life and the burial ritual treatment received in death (Binford 1971; Peebles 1971). This assumption provides archaeologists with a way to link social organization to the variability observed in mortuary treatment. The range of mortuary practices available to a society when one of its members dies may be viewed as a system of ritual procedures referred to as a mortuary program (Brown 1971; Buikstra 1976). Components or variables of a society's mortuary program consist of single attributes or sets of burial attributes that are observed to differentiate mortuary ritual acts.

Arthur Saxe (1970) and Lewis Binford have presented the basic theoretical arguments on which the sociological analysis of mortuary practices are based. The elements of anthropological role theory, particularly the concepts developed by Linton (1936) and Goodenough (1965) to define principles of social interaction, provide the basis of the framework developed by Saxe and Binford to reconstruct social status differences.

Ralph Linton (1936), in his classic examination of the concepts of status and role, defined status as simply a collection of rights and duties associated with a particular social position. Individual members of a society occupy a number of different social positions (in different groups) during their life and, therefore, possess more than a single status. All persons occupy positions in more than one group, thus acquiring a series of statuses. An individual's *total status* in a society is a function of the sum total of all of the roles and associated statuses a person occupies. When an individual ". . . puts the rights and duties which constitute the status into effect, he is performing a role" (Linton 1936: 114). Linton considered a role to represent the dynamic aspect of a status. There is a role for every status that dictates the appropriate behavior for a particular social interaction just as there is a status for every role.

There are two different ways in which individual members of a society are socially assigned statuses (Linton 1936: 115). An ascribed status is one assigned to an individual at birth without regard to innate abilities. An achieved status is acquired on the basis of special qualities or abilities.

Goodenough (1965) elaborated on the conceptual view presented by Linton (1936) concerning the organization of social roles and statuses within any system of social inter-

action. He developed three concepts to define elements of social interaction: social identity, identity relationships, and social persona.

Social identity refers to a social position or status and is defined as ". . . an aspect of self that makes a difference in how one's rights and duties distribute to specific others" (Goodenough 1965: 3).

In any given social interaction, there are a number of social identities available to an individual. Appropriate matching identities must be selected by each individual involved in an interaction if a social relationship is to develop. A social relationship that involves two or more matching social identities is referred to as an *identity relationship* (Goodenough 1965: 6–7). The composite of several identities selected as appropriate to a given interaction comprises the *social persona* selected by the individual for a specific social relationship. The selection by an individual of what he considers the appropriate social persona for a particular social interaction is determined by the organization of the society to which the individual belongs.

Saxe (1970) used Goodenough's (1965) consideration of status and role and the techniques of componential analysis to test a number of hypotheses dealing with mortuary symbolism.

> When archaeologists excavate a set of burials they are not merely excavating individuals, but a coherent personality who not only engaged in relationships with other social personalities but did so according to rules and structural slots dictated by the larger social system (Saxe 1970: 4).

Saxe's major goal was to develop a methodology that could be used to interpret the social phenomena represented in mortuary ritual. He formulated a set of eight hypotheses that linked burial treatment to social complexity. These hypotheses can be placed into two distinct groups. Hypotheses 1 through 4 pertain to the manner in which ". . . social personaè are differentially represented within disposal remains," and hypotheses 5 through 8 are ". . . concerned with the way different social structures are differentially represented among different disposal domains" (Saxe 1970: 65). These hypotheses were then tested by examining mortuary practices in three ethnographically documented societies (the Kapauku Papuans of New Guinea, the Ashanti of West Africa, and the Bontoc Igorot of Luzon). Some hypotheses that Saxe (1970) proposed were supported by the ethnographic data, whereas others were not. One hypothesis (Number 8) supported by all three societies stated:

> *To the Degree that Corporate Group Rights to Use and/or Control Crucial but Restricted Resources are Attained and/or Legitimized by Means of Lineal Descent from the Dead (i.e., Lineal Ties to Ancestors), Such Groups Will Maintain Formal Disposal Areas for the Exclusive Disposal of Their Dead, and Conversely* (Saxe 1970: 119).

This specific hypothesis received additional support through the studies of Goldstein (1976, 1980, 1981), who tested it using thirty ethnographic cases.

Saxe (1970: 7–8) noted that the organizational complexity of societies dictates the number of different identity relationships that different social identities may have. Therefore, if an analysis of mortuary data suggests that some infants have a larger social persona than some adults, the principle of social ranking by hereditary ascription is indicated. On the other hand, in egalitarian societies, infants should have few identities when compared to the number some adults may have acquired. Mortuary programs of egalitarian societies display graduated differences in the number of social identities from infants to adults representing achieved statuses.

Binford's (1971) study of mortuary practices, like Saxe's (1970), attempted to account for the variability in burial treatment observed among individuals belonging to the same or different societies. He argued that two components of social interaction must be evaluated in any attempt to understand the social phenomena symbolized in a burial. The first component is that of the social persona (Goodenough 1965: 7) of the deceased, which consists of a ". . . composite of the social identities maintained in life and recognized as appropriate for consideration at death" (Binford 1971: 17). The second component defined is ". . . the composition and size of the social unit recognizing status responsibilities to the deceased" (Binford 1971: 17).

Two propositions that relate mortuary ritual to social organization (complexity) were tested by Binford through a cross-cultural survey of mortuary treatment from a sample of ethnographically documented societies. The first proposition stated that ". . . there should be a high degree of isomorphism between (a) the complexity of the status structure in a sociocultural system and (b) the complexity of mortuary ceremonialism as regards differential treatment of persons occupying different status positions" (Binford 1971: 18). The second proposition stated that the dimensions of age, sex, and personal achievement will serve as the major dimensions of status in societies organized on an egalitarian level, and status positions in more complex or hierarchically structured societies will be defined by abstract characteristics related to the organization of the society. Binford (1971: 23) concluded that generally the form and structure of mortuary ritual are conditioned by the form and complexity of the organizational characteristics of a society.

The results of the cross-cultural ethnographic surveys of mortuary practices by Binford and Saxe demonstrated that ". . . both the structure and the organization of social systems, as well as the status positions occupied by members of such systems, are symbolized through acts of mortuary ritual" (Tainter 1975: 16). More specifically, these studies indicated that the variables of a society's mortuary program ". . . collectively differentiate burials into distinct subsets or burial types that represent different social personae" (Braun 1977: 223). In other words, different burial attributes symbolize different social identities, but taken collectively these variables represent what may have been distinct social personalities or social personae. The components of the total mortuary program ". . . constitute the material correlates of social identities that in various combinations represent the social personae extant in that system's practices of the disposal of the dead" (Saxe 1970: 16).

THE INVESTIGATION OF SOCIAL RANKING

Based on the research of Saxe (1970) and Binford (1971), archaeologists used mortuary data to test hypotheses concerning social complexity in prehistoric societies. In most of their studies of burial treatment they have attempted to demonstrate the presence of ascriptive ranking based on inheritance. Mortuary data also have been studied to investigate age-based and sex-role differentiation, corporate group affiliation, kinship and ceremonial organization, and regional differentiation.

Three approaches used by archaeologists to investigate properties of ascriptive social ranking with mortuary data are the energy expenditure approach (Tainter 1975, 1978), the symbols of authority approach (Peebles 1971, 1974; Braun 1977, 1979) and the demographic structure approach (Buikstra 1976, 1977). Brown (1981) has provided an extensive summary of these approaches. The first two approaches are briefly reviewed because various aspects of each are used in this study to test hypotheses concerning the hierarchical organization of power and authority at Casas Grandes.

The energy expenditure approach is best exemplified in the work of Tainter (1975, 1977, 1978, 1980, 1983; Tainter and Cordy 1977). Tainter proposed that the vertical dimension of differentiation can be measured by determining the amount of energy expended in interment.

Energy expenditure should in turn be reflected in such features of burial as size and elaborateness of the interment facility, method of handling and disposal of the corpse, and the nature of grave associations. Reversing this reasoning, when sets of mortuary data cluster into distinctive levels of energy expenditure it signifies distinctive levels of social involvement in the mortuary act and reflexively indicates distinctive grades or levels of grading (Tainter 1978: 125).

This approach to delineating ranking or social hierarchy originates from Binford's (1971: 17) observation that ". . . the form of a mortuary ritual will be determined by, among other factors, the size and composition of the social aggregate recognizing obligatory status responsibilities to the deceased." Tainter proposed that the higher the social rank of the deceased individual the greater the amount of energy expended in burial treatment, because the deceased will be entitled to a larger amount of corporate involvement in the act of interment. A determination of the relative size and number of vertical levels in a society can be attained by ordering burials according to the inferred amounts of energy expended.

This approach for investigating social complexity with mortuary data is based on two major assumptions, and the validity of their application has been questioned by Braun (1981: 410–411). These assumptions are that relative differences in energy expenditure in burial treatments always reflect discrete status distinctions and that the monitoring of structural differentiation along the vertical dimension may be used as an index of the overall complexity of an organization. Various aspects of this approach, however, offer considerable potential for the study of social differentiation using mortuary data when these difficulties are recognized.

Peebles (1971, 1974; Peebles and Kus 1977) presented an alternative way to order burials in hierarchical levels and to test for the presence of ascriptive ranking that also utilizes the concept of an energy scale to interpret differences in mortuary treatment (Peebles 1974: 45–46). He suggested that a society was organized on the basis of hereditary rank when symbols of authority (that is, high cost artifacts) placed with burials and other attributes of burial treatment cross-cut age and gender distinctions. Measures of mortuary differentiation also are considered the most effective way in which to establish the presence of any form of social ranking in a prehistoric society (Peebles and Kus 1977: 431). For example, most identifications of ascriptive ranking from mortuary data have been based on the following assumption:

> In such societies, we can expect some children to have objects signaling a higher rank because they are part of an ascribed status system and hence have inherited their positions. Finally, it is expected that there will be greater differences in wealth, rank, and energy expenditure seen among individuals and groups (Rothschild 1979: 661).

Peebles and Kus (1977: 431) suggested that ". . . the test for ranking is not merely the presence of richly accompanied child or infant burials," as has been commonly accepted (Saxe 1970; Binford 1971; Tainter 1975). Rather, they argued, the test for ascriptive ranking must demonstrate the presence of two independent dimensions of social persona.

Peebles (1971, 1974; Peebles and Kus 1977) proposed that the delineation of qualitative differences in mortuary ritual treatment, such as the cost of artifact accompaniments and burial facilities as measured in terms of energy expenditure, and differences in the location of burial facilities will define a hierarchy consisting of two distinct ranking dimensions: the superordinate and subordinate.

The superordinate dimension consists of an ordering of burials that ". . . is based on symbols, energy expenditure, and other variables of mortuary ritual, and which is not simultaneously ordered on the basis of age and sex" (Peebles and Kus 1977: 431). Recruitment to this rank level is based on genealogical ascription and is indicated by status-specific symbols of rank. Individuals belonging to this rank have access to elaborate burial facilities along with rare or high cost artifactual accompaniments, as measured in terms of the energy expenditure concept.

> Almost all the artifacts which define the first dimension are either made from imported raw materials or seem to have been imported as finished products. Many of these artifacts show great skill and long hours of work in their production (Peebles 1974: 46).

The subordinate dimension also is defined on the basis of an ordering of symbols and burial treatment and, like the superordinate one, has a pyramid of individuals ranked according to the energy cost of associated accompaniments and burial treatment. However, variability in mortuary treatment in this dimension is ordered on the basis of age and sex. Access to the most costly accompaniments and treatment is acquired through personal achievement rather than through ascription. The highest ranked individuals in this dimension have less energy expended in their burial treatment than the lowest ranked individuals associated with the superordinate dimension, and they are denied access to the status-specific artifactual symbols of the superordinate dimension (Peebles 1974: 56; Peebles and Kus 1977: 431–432).

Braun's (1977, 1979, 1981) approach to determining the presence of ascriptive rank using mortuary data incorporates aspects of Peebles work. This so-called dimensional approach views social organization as consisting of multidimensional social spaces (that is, social identities or positions) that are assigned to a society's members (see Whittlesey 1978 for another application of the dimension approach using burial data from Grasshopper Pueblo, Arizona). These positions are differentially distributed within a society on the basis of a number of criteria. Braun (1977) defined a dimension of differentiation following Blau (1970) as any criterion a society utilizes to differentially distribute its members among different social positions or ranks.

The dimensional perspective has been applied to the study of mortuary practices by viewing mortuary ritual as an aspect of the ritualization of social relations (Braun 1979). Braun (1977, 1979) argued that any criterion a society utilizes to differentiate significant social identities or positions generally should be symbolized in mortuary rites as a dimension of differentiation in ritual treatments. A dimension of ritual differentiation is perceived as consisting of a single variable or a group of variables that differentiate burial treatment among individuals within a society. These variables seldom consist of single attributes of burial treatment, but rather of sets of covarying attributes that are symbolized in burial types (Braun 1977: 236). This approach, then, views a society's mortuary program as consisting of dimensions of variation in mortuary treatment among individual burials that indicate the dimensions of status differentiation operating within that society.

Braun, like Peebles, suggested that symbolic indicators of social rank indicating inherited power and authority can be delineated from mortuary data by evaluating the relative cost of qualitative attributes of burial treatment. Braun (1979: 67) stated:

. . . as one moves up the rank gradient within the rank dimension of differentiation in burial treatments, the relative cost in terms of availability, means of procurement, extent of labor input in manufacture or construction, and/or size of accompanying artifacts, corpse processing techniques, and burial facilities will generally increase from lowest to highest rank grade (Tainter 1975: 48–61; cf, Peebles 1974: 44–47, 181–182; Peebles and Kus 1977).

Artifact accompaniments, however, that may represent symbols or badges of authority must be evaluated not only in terms of energy cost (for example, availability of material and manufacturing requirements), but also in terms of their distribution within the overall archaeological record in order to understand their meaning within the social system (Braun 1979: 67; Braun 1981: 412; and Orser 1980: 41–42). The distribution of high cost artifacts definable as symbols of authority should be restricted primarily to burial contexts or contexts associated with the production and use of those artifacts (Schiffer 1972).

Most archaeologists who have tested for the presence of ascriptive ranking have assumed that in hierarchically organized societies rare or costly grave accompaniments will be found associated with individuals or groups that cross-cut age and gender categories. The test for ranking has been the presence of children or infants associated with high cost artifactual accompaniments indicative of an ascribed status system and inherited social positions. Braun (1979: 68) argued that archaeologists who made this assumption failed to take into account the importance of the role that rites of passage play in the social recognition of maturing individuals. Surveys of the ethnographic literature indicate that infants and children usually are not recognized within the adult social sphere until after these rites of passage are performed.

Braun (1977, 1979) expected the following conditions to be met in a dimensional analysis of mortuary data if a society was organized on the basis of ranked social positions where the principles of ascription operated. First, the society's mortuary program will possess qualitative attributes of burial treatment (such as type of burial facility, location of the burial facility, processing of the body, and artifactual accompaniments) that may be interpreted as symbols of authority associated with the positions of power the deceased held or was eligible to hold in the society. Second, qualitative attributes representing symbols of authority will covary and

define a dimension of variation in mortuary treatment that operated within the society's mortuary program. Third, this dimension will be found to cross-cut age, gender, and personal ability.

BASIC DIMENSIONS OF MORTUARY ANALYSIS

Regardless of the approach used in a mortuary study, it is important not to limit analysis to one dimension or to emphasize one dimension over another, but to examine the total mortuary program of the society being investigated. In numerous studies people have assumed that a society was integrated on the basis of ascriptive social ranking when substantial variation in the quantity and quality of grave goods among individual burials could be demonstrated (Clark 1967; Stickel 1968; King 1970, 1978; Rathje 1970, 1973; Randsborg 1975; Rothschild 1979). The validity of such reconstructions of social organization based primarily on the artifact accompaniment dimension, however, has been questioned (Tainter 1975, 1978). As Tainter (1978: 119) succinctly noted, these studies have

. . . neglected the diversity of symbolic forms which may be employed in mortuary ritual, and have assumed instead that the most significant information may be derived from one data class: grave associations.

A number of variables of mortuary treatment should be given equal consideration in any analysis. These variables are listed in Table 3.1. However, any archaeological investigation of hierarchical differentiation is obviously limited by the behavioral dimensions of mortuary ritual that result in material residue.

One dimension of mortuary patterning that has not been adequately investigated by analyses of mortuary practices is the spatial component (Goldstein 1976, 1980, 1981; Chapman and Randsborg 1981). The relatively few people who have investigated the spatial aspect have emphasized the patterning of graves with formal disposal areas such as cemeteries, whereas the location of cemeteries within settlements on a regional scope has been basically ignored (Chapman and Randsborg 1981). Goldstein's studies of the spatial dimension within mortuary sites that are based on Saxe's Hypothesis 8 are one exception.

Because mortuary practices are reflections of interpersonal and inter- and intragroup relationships, as well as a reflection of the organization of the society as a whole, examination of the spatial component can yield information on at least two broad levels: 1) the degree of structure and spatial separation and ordering of the disposal area itself may reflect organisational principles of the society as a whole; and 2) the spatial relationship to each other of the individuals within a disposal area can represent status differentiation, family groups, descent groups, or special classes, dependent upon the correlation of these spatial relationships with other dimensions of study (Goldstein 1981: 57).

Table 3.1. Variables of Mortuary Treatment (from Binford 1971; Goldstein 1981)

Treatment of the body	Differential preparation of the facility in which the body is placed	Artifactual accompaniments within the grave	Demographic profile
Form of disposal (primary inhumation, secondary, etc.)	Form of the facility (simple pit, elaborate tomb, variation in materials used for construction, or architectural variability)	Form and quantity of grave goods	Age
Number of individuals per burial pit (single, multiple)		Placement of accompaniments within the facility in relation to the burial	Gender
Degree of articulation of the skeleton (articulated, rearticulated, disarticulated, disturbed)	Orientation of the facility (oriented with respect to some established reference point such as cardinal directions or topographic feature)		Evidence for disease and nutritional status of the burial
Position (extended, semiflexed, flexed, etc.)	Location of the burial facility within the site (are there spatially differentiated disposal areas)		
Deposition (back, face, side left or right, sitting)	Form of the disposal area within which the burial facility is placed (cemetery, mortuary complex such as a tomb or mound, with habitation areas, etc.)		
Orientation of body			

In sum, a society's mortuary program must be considered as a multidimensional one and an analysis of all dimensions of burial treatment is necessary to form a model of burial treatment and to understand the organization of the society reflected by such treatment. The investigation of organizational complexity, specifically ascriptive social ranking, using mortuary data is based on ethnographically tested assumptions concerning the relationships of social structure and organization in burial treatment. The identification of ranked social roles and recruitment (that is, ascribed and achieved) to these roles is based on the delineation of qualitative and quantitative differences in burial treatment. Qualitative distinctions in burial treatment are usually associated with qualitative differences in the social identities represented and quantitative ones apparently represent differences in the degree of importance within a category of social identity (Saxe 1970; Binford 1971; Braun 1977). Qualitative differences, thus, can be used as indicators of symbols of rank and authority and quantitative differences in burial treatment are indicators of differential access to wealth and prestige. Therefore, qualitative differences in burial treatment should be used first to test for ascriptive ranking. The organization concepts and the mortuary approaches to ranking summarized herein provide the basic framework and rationale for testing the hypothesis of the hierarchical organization of power and authority at Casas Grandes.

CHAPTER FOUR

The Medio Period Burial Collection at Casas Grandes

One way to study the manner and degree in which Casas Grandes society was hierarchically structured during the Medio period is to describe and analyze the variability in mortuary practices. A major purpose of such an analysis is to test the hypothesis that the Casas Grandes community was organized on the basis of ranked social positions and that symbolic indicators of social ranking are evident in the mortuary remains. The presence of such indicators, or so-called symbols of authority and power, should lead to the delineation of the number of levels or extent of gradation of social ranking that may have existed. In addition, the analysis provides a view of the manner in which Casas Grandians were enrolled in or recruited to various social positions within the organizational hierarchy, that is, whether recruitment to such positions was based on principles of ascription.

The identification of ranked social roles and of recruitment to these roles is based on qualitative differences in mortuary treatment. It is also valuable to determine if quantitative differences in mortuary treatment that are indicative of differential access to wealth and prestige occur in both male and female burials. The approach to this examination of mortuary data is based on the properties of hierarchically structured decision-making organizations and the assumptions of mortuary analysis discussed in Chapters 2 and 3. The assumptions of mortuary theory suggest that burials may be ordered according to their relative positions within a social hierarchy on the basis of both univariate (Chapter 5) and multivariate (Chapter 6) differences and similarities in burial treatment.

Prior to presenting the general hypothesis that is tested in this study, it is helpful to review the concepts of status, status hierarchy, and ranking and to discuss the term 'ranked society' as used herein. The concept of status is defined as all social positions that vary by gradation such as wealth, prestige, power, and administrative authority. A status hierarchy refers to a decision-making organization in which the social positions are structured vertically in terms of levels or gradations. Rights and privileges that accompany specific social positions within the hierarchy are indicated by symbols of status and authority. The term ranking is defined after Blau (1970) as managerial levels within formal decision-making hierarchies. A 'ranked society', therefore, is viewed as a complex, decision-making organization in which an individual's social position or rank is related to his in-

fluence, power, or administrative authority within the society.

Social status differences are often used in organizations to structure the decision-making hierarchy when it serves an integrative function. The higher the social status of an individual within the status hierarchy the larger role he or she plays in managerial decisions of the community. Furthermore, an individual's relative position or placement in a decision-making organization is often symbolized by differential access to certain rights and privileges that are denied to individuals in subordinate positions in the hierarchy. Differential access to space and to local and nonlocal resources are usually present in societies integrated on the basis of hierarchical organization.

HYPOTHESIS

If Casas Grandes society was organized hierarchically on the basis of ascriptive ranking during the Medio period, such social ranking should be reflected in the mortuary treatment observed among the deceased members of its population. Four expectations arise from this hypothesis.

1. To be able to identify one or more qualitative attributes of burial treatment within the mortuary program that can be interpreted as representing symbols of distinct offices of power and authority. These qualitative attributes in mortuary ritual treatment are defined by the presence or absence of discrete differences in burial treatment among individual burials and include: the location of the burial facility, the type and size of the grave facility, methods used in the processing and disposal of the corpse, and the accompaniments interred with the deceased. Furthermore, the relative cost of these attributes of burial treatment as defined in terms of the energy expended in the construction of grave facilities, labor involved in the processing of the corpse, and the accessibility of raw material and labor expended in the manufacture of artifactual accompaniments should decrease significantly from the apex to the bottom of the social hierarchy.

2. To recover artifactual accompaniments that presumably functioned as symbols of rank or authority from primarily burial contexts or contexts associated with their production, storage, or use.

3. To determine that the qualitative attributes or sets of attributes interpreted as symbols of authority or social rank are redundant or covary within the society's mortuary pro-

gram and to define on the basis of those attributes distinct dimensions of status differentiation in burial treatment.

4. To find that access to the qualitative hierarchical distinctions of power and authority in status differentiation crosscuts not only the biological categories of age and gender, but also any dimensions of the society's rites of passage from child to adolescent to adult status.

CASAS GRANDES BURIALS

A total of 576 individuals was recovered from Medio period contexts at Casas Grandes (Vol. 8: 355–410). Of these individuals, 447 were thought by the excavators to represent deliberate interments, and they were classified according to nine major types and numerous subtypes of burial treatment. These types and subtypes were formulated on the basis of the following characteristics: construction of the grave facility, location of the grave (that is, room or plaza), whether the grave was sealed or unsealed, whether the burial was an articulated (primary) inhumation or a disarticulated (secondary) burial, and whether the grave contained a single or

multiple burial (Vol. 8: 229–337). Burial frequencies and percentages for the defined types and subtypes of mortuary treatment are provided in Table 4.1.

The other 129 individuals were classified as Type 2 or unburied bodies (126), Type 9 or accidental deaths (2), Type 13 or random bones, and one unidentified type. The Type 2 remains are believed to have been individuals killed when Casas Grandes was attacked and destroyed at the end of the Diablo phase. These unburied bodies were found in the fill of rooms mixed in rooffall and scattered on room floors (Vol. 8: 337).

Data on the 447 individuals representing deliberate or purposely buried interments were used by the excavators to determine crude death rates and age and gender ratios for the site, and to describe variation in body position, orientation, and associated grave goods by burial type, phase, and excavation unit. Therefore, their description of Casas Grandes mortuary treatment is presented mainly in terms of burial frequencies and percentages for each of these types (Vol 8: 355–410).

Table 4.1. Classification of Casas Grandes Burials*
(after Di Peso and others 1974, Vol. 8: 360–361, Fig. 358–8)

Type	Form	No.	%	Type Total	Type %
1	SUBFLOOR ROOM BURIALS IN SEALED PITS			229	51.2
1a	Single articulated body	87	19.4		
1b	Multiple articulated bodies	100	22.4		
1c	Single disarticulated (secondary) bodies	2	0.5		
1d	Multiple disarticulated (secondary) bodies	10	2.2		
1e	Multiple articulated and disarticulated bodies	23	5.1		
1f	Body removed	1	0.2		
1g	Multiple articulated bodies with extra articulated body parts	4	0.9		
1h	Single articulated body with parts removed	2	0.5		
3	SUBFLOOR PLAZA BURIALS IN SEALED PITS			130	29.1
3a	Single articulated body	73	16.3		
3b	Multiple articulated bodies	55	7.8		
3d	Multiple disarticulated (secondary) bodies	15	3.4		
3e	Multiple articulated and disarticulated bodies	3	0.7		
3g	Single articulated body parts	1	0.2		
3h	Multiple articulated bodies with extra body parts	3	0.7		
4	SUBFLOOR ROOM BURIALS IN SEALED TOMBS			18	4.0
4a	Single articulated body	2	0.5		
4b	Multiple articulated bodies	4	0.9		
4e	Multiple articulated and disarticulated	12	2.6		

Table 4.1.
(continued)

Type	Form	No.	%	Type Total	Type %
5	SECONDARY URN BURIALS IN SURFACE TOMBS			3	0.7
6	NONSEPULCHERED SECONDARY URN BURIALS			2	0.4
7	BURIALS SUPERIMPOSED ON OLDER, ABANDONED ARCHITECTURE			19	4.3
7a	Single articulated body	13	2.9		
7b	Multiple articulated bodies	6	1.4		
8	HUMAN SACRIFICES			10	2.2
8a	Single articulated body	2	0.5		
8b	Multiple articulated bodies	5	1.1		
8e	Multiple articulated and disarticulated bodies	3	0.7		
11	SUBFLOOR ROOM BURIALS IN UNSEALED PITS			31	7.0
11a	Single articulated body	2	0.5		
11b	Multiple articulated bodies	22	4.9		
11d	Multiple disarticulated (secondary) bodies	4	0.9		
11e	Multiple articulated and disarticulated bodies	2	0.5		
11f	Body removed	1	0.2		
12	SUBFLOOR PLAZA BURIALS IN UNSEALED PITS			5	1.1
12a	Single articulated body	5	1.1		
	Total	447			

*Type 2 Unburied Bodies and Type 9 Accidental Deaths not included.

Burials were placed within the phase sequence developed for the site on the basis of their stratigraphic position within dated architectural units. Although in a number of cases a burial could not be assigned to a specific phase, the following associations were determined: Buena Fé (53, or 11.9%), Buena Fé or Paquimé (5, or 1.1%), Paquimé (8, or 1.8%), Paquimé or Diablo (199, or 44.5%), Diablo (52, or 11.6%), and phase unidentified in the Medio period (130, or 29.1%). These totals did not include the 125 Type 2 bodies that were associated with the Diablo phase or Types 9 and 13.

The crude death rate calculated for the Casas Grandes population suggested that the excavated portions of the domestic structures (that is, ground floor levels) should have resulted in the recovery of 1,452 burials rather than the 366 associated with those contexts (Vol. 8: 325, 355). This expected total was calculated by using a death rate of 2.3 persons per hundred per year. Assuming that such gross calculations are at least partially accurate, Di Peso, Rinaldo, and Fenner suggested that approximately 75 percent of the dead may have been buried in locations other than near habitation structures. In all probability, then, the burials recovered from Casas Grandes exhibit only a partial picture of mortuary ritual treatment during the Medio period and perhaps represent individuals who belonged only to the high status families (Vol. 8: 325).

The age and gender distribution of individuals in burials recovered from Medio period contexts is presented in Table 4.2. The categories used by Di Peso were those employed by Butler (1971) in her study of the cranial and dental morphology of the Casas Grandes burials.

Table 4.2. Distribution by Age and Gender of Individuals in Medio Period Burials (After Di Peso, Rinaldo, and Fenner 1974, Vol. 8: 357)

Individuals	AGE	Number
Infant	0–2 years	74 (12.9%)
Child	3–5 years	71 (12.3%)
Juvenile	6–12 years	31 (5.3%)
Adolescent	13–17 years	39 (6.8%)
? Subadult	0–18 years	10 (1.8%)
Young adult	19–35 years	141 (24.5%)
Middle-aged adult	36–50 years	77 (13.4%)
Old adult	50+ years	31 (5.3%)
? Adult	18+ years	102 (17.7%)
	Total	576

	GENDER	
Male		104 (18.0%)
Female		171 (29.7%)
Indeterminate		301 (52.3%)
	Total	576

ARCHITECTURAL UNITS

The 576 Medio period burials were recovered from 18 of the 26 excavated architectural units (Table 4.3; *see* Fig.

Table 4.3. Intrasite Distribution of Medio Period Burials by Architectural Unit

Architectural Unit	Number
Unit 1, The House of the Ovens	49 (8.5%)
Unit 4, The Mound of the Offerings	5 (0.9%)
Unit 6, Buena Fé Phase Ranch Style Compound	68 (11.8%)
Unit 8, The House of the Well	57 (9.9%)
Unit 11, The House of the Serpent	66 (11.4%)
Unit 12, The House of the Macaws	49 (8.5%)
Unit 13, The House of the Dead	117 (20.3%)
Unit 14, The House of the Pillars	66 (11.4%)
Unit 15	13 (2.3%)
Unit 16, The House of the Skulls	19 (3.3%)
Unit 18	1 (0.2%)
Unit 19	9 (1.6%)
Unit 20	8 (1.4%)
Unit 21	5 (0.9%)
Unit 22	6 (1.0%)
Unit 23	9 (1.6%)
Central Plaza	28 (4.8%)
East Plaza	1 (0.2%)
Total	576

1.2). Several of these units contained burials that were categorized as unique or high-status (that is, burial types 4, 5, and 8), because the individuals apparently received preferential burial treatment. The excavated architectural units that contained burials and the contexts in which different kinds of burials were found are described briefly to provide a better understanding of the Casas Grandes burial population, specifically elaborate mortuary treatments, on which Di Peso partially based his interpretation of the organizational complexity of Casas Grandes.

The distribution of ritual paraphernalia such as stone stools, stone effigies, bone wands and rasps, and shell trumpets recovered from nonburial contexts is summarized to distinguish between architectural units and rooms in which rituals of sanctification occurred and those in which paraphernalia was produced, ritually disposed of, or stored. Flannery (1976) has shown that a contextual analysis of ritual paraphernalia can be used to help determine whether an artifact functioned in public ritual, at the level of the household or sodality, in personal ritual, or was used to communicate elite status. A detailed description of the distribution and frequency of ritual paraphernalia found within burial contexts is provided in Chapter 5 in order to define grave accompaniments that may have served as symbols or badges of distinct offices of power and authority. Only the ground floor rooms and plazas that produced burials are considered here. A more detailed description of each architectural unit, including two and three story structures, is provided in Volumes 4 and 5 by Di Peso and others (1974).

Unit 1. The House of the Ovens (Figure 4.1)

Unit 1 consisted of a large circular mound that was encircled by two house clusters containing ten one-story rooms, two

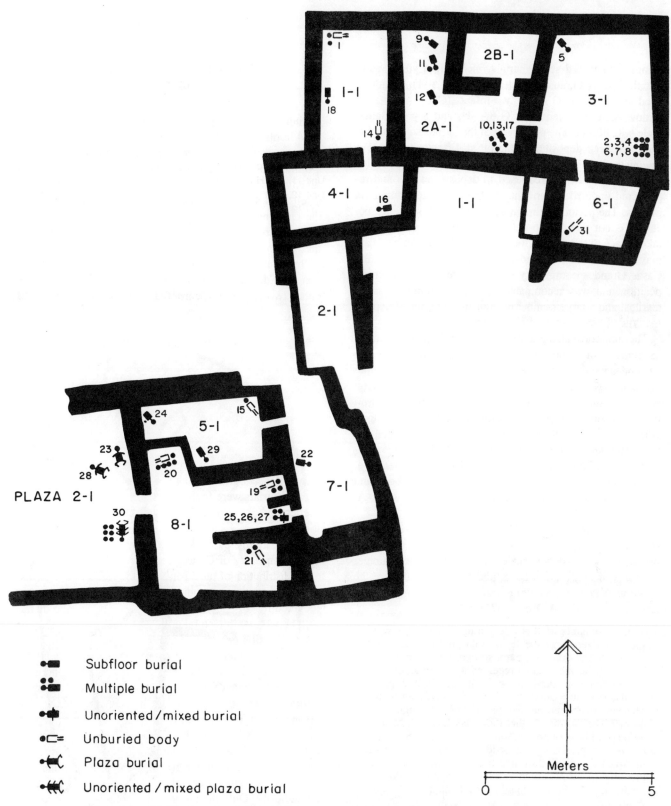

Meters

0   5

Figure 4.1. Distribution of burials in Unit 1, The House of the Ovens. Burial 32–1 is located north of Unit 1. (Adapted from Vol. 4, Figs. 203, 204–4, and from Amerind Foundation field maps.)

plazas, and four pit ovens. In Unit 1 were 33 deliberate burials, including Types 1A, 1B, 3A, and 3D, and 16 Type 2 unburied bodies.

Approximately half of the Casas Grandians buried within the House of the Ovens apparently were not given special treatment upon death, as suggested by the absence of non-perishable grave accompaniments and the simple earthen pits in which they were interred (Vol. 8: 369–371). Two multiple subfloor graves exposed in Rooms 3 and 8 and one of the burials in Plaza 2–1 were exceptions. The grave in

Room 3 contained seven burials, including a young adult female (CG 2–1), an old adult female (CG 3–1), a middle-aged adult male (CG 4–1), two infants (CG 6–1, 7–1), a middle-aged adult female (CG 8A–1), and a young adult male (CG 8B–1). The placement of the burials suggests that each had been deposited in the pit at different times. Following the interment of the first burial (CG 8B–1), the sealed subfloor pit had been reopened to deposit remains and re-plastered upon the interment of each of the remaining six burials. The period of time during which this sequence occurred is not possible to determine, although it may have taken place over a generation or more. The old adult female may have been an individual of some importance in the Casas Grandes community. She was interred in a sitting position and was accompanied by eight ceramic vessels, textiles, and a large number of pigments and mined deposit materials (Appendix A; Vol. 8: 369).

The subfloor sealed grave pit located in Room 8 contained the remains of a child (CG 25–1), an adolescent (CG 26–1), and an old adult male (CG 27–1). Like the multiple grave in Room 3, this pit also apparently was reused on separate occasions. The adolescent and adult male had been interred in sitting positions, possibly at the same time, along with 28 objects, including beads and pendants, mined deposit materials, hammerstones, chipped stone debitage, pigment, and a Ramos Polychrome jar. The child, interred at a later date, was buried with a Ramos Polychrome bowl and jar, a Ramos Black jar, and a hammerstone (Appendix A; Vol. 8: 370–371).

An adult male (CG 28–1) buried in Plaza 2–1 was accompanied by a Ramos Polychrome jar, a Plain bowl, shell ornaments, mined deposit materials, chipped stone debitage, offerings of food, and a bone tube manufactured from the humerus of a lesser sandhill crane (*Grus canadensis canadensis;* Appendix A; Vol.8: 371).

That the tenants of this five-family cluster unit were special citizens was attested to not only by the location of their living quarters, but also by evidence retrieved from their burials, which received a certain amount of uncommon consideration in terms of allotted grave goods. It is suggested that they were involved in the Mesoamerican ceremonial production of maguey liquor.[18] The surmise is that they may have conformed to the rigid laws of production and consumption spelled out by the priests of the goddess Mayahuel,[19] which involved the distillation and use of various other fermenting plants,[20] which were sold in the market as medicines (Di Peso, Rinaldo, and Fenner 1974, Vol. 2: 405).

The relative lack of ritual paraphernalia from the House of the Ovens suggests that the majority of activities that occurred in this architectural unit were domestic ones. Artifacts that may have been used in a ritual context included a shell trumpet from the floor of Plaza 1–1, a stone ceremonial vessel and a ceremonial axe from the floor of Room 2A, and a Ramos Polychrome effigy jar recovered from the floor of Room 8.

Unit 4. The Mound of the Offerings (Figure 4.2)

The Mound of the Offerings had an irregular shape with a retaining wall that had the appearance of a parrot or macaw head in plan view (Vol. 4: 305). A circular platform rested on the summit; it was reached from the central plaza through a number of ramps and steps (*see* Fig. 1.2). A cluster of seven rooms located south of the summit was interpreted as a religious sanctuary. The unit was named the Mound of the Offerings because of the elaborate mortuary complex, stone altars, and statues that were found associated with these rooms.

Room 1–4 was interpreted as an unroofed antechamber that provided access to the sanctuary, and Room 2A contained two contiguous, unroofed, puddled adobe rooms (2B,

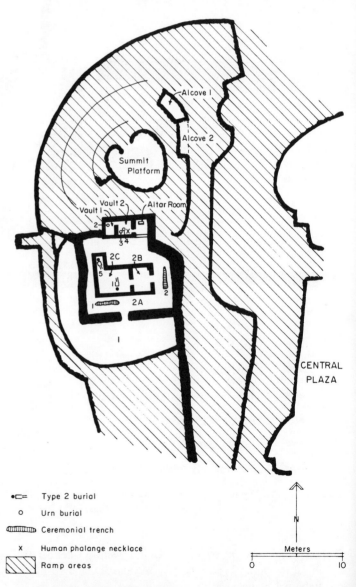

Figure 4.2.   Unit 4, The Mound of the Offerings. (Adapted from Vol. 4, Figs. 218, 221, 222–4, and from Amerind Foundation field maps.)

2C) of unknown function. Two subfloor trenches within Room 2A contained exotic and rare artifacts, including stone and shell ornaments, wooden arrows, worked wood fragments, and textiles (Vol. 4: 308).

Three contiguous, roofed, puddled adobe rooms were located on the north side of Room 2A. Two of these rooms, described as chambers or vaults, housed the secondary post-cranial remains of three individuals that had been interred in unusually large Ramos Polychrome jars. The Ramos Polychrome jar (Fig. 4.3) sitting on the floor in the northwest corner of Vault 1 (CG Burial 2–4) contained the remains of an old adult male (50 plus years). The postcranial remains were very fragmentary and incomplete, consisting primarily of vertebrae, foot, and hand fragments (analysis forms by R. A. Benfer, Jr. on file at the Amerind Foundation). The other two burials were found on the floor of Vault 2 in the southwest corner (Fig. 4.4). The secondary remains recovered from these two jars (Fig. 4.5) were identified as a male (CG Burial 4–4) and a female (CG Burial 3–4), both 36 to 50 years of age. The remains of these two individuals were also fragmentary and incomplete. A Ramos Polychrome miniature bowl, a musical rasp manufactured from a human long bone, two unworked human long bones, and a necklace fashioned from human phalanges (Fig. 4.6) were with the middle-aged adult couple. Entry to the two burial vaults (1–4, 2–4) was gained through Altar Room 1–4.

These three burials, classified as Type 5, were considered to be the remains of the highest ranking Casas Grandians, possibly the members of the original puchteca patriarchal family (Vol. 8: 372).

The original principal merchant 'in foreign parts' who settled in the Casas Grandes Valley with his retinue of traveling merchants (oztomecatl),[59] must have been a very good man, mayhap a humpback who was revered in the eyes of his people. Perhaps so much so that they built the Mound of the Offerings as his private tomb, and later also interred an adult couple, who may have been his successors.[61] Leastwise, the post-cranial remains of three such individuals, interred in jars, were reverently placed in two special adobe burial vaults, secreted in the base of the solid-core portion of this mound.[62] This spectacular construct may well have been a frontier version of a Mesoamerican god house (tecocalli),[63] as it included not only the three enclosed crypts, but also a large walled but roofless temple area (Di Peso 1974, Vol. 2: 419).

Room 2C contained the remains of two Type 2 unburied bodies. The bones of one of these unburied bodies (CG 1–4) were found disarticulated lying on the floor, while the other body (CG 5–4) was fully articulated in floor fill. Di Peso (Vol. 2: 419) interpreted these two adult males as guards of the sanctuary who were killed on the last day of the Diablo phase. Additional evidence offered by the excavators for the destruction of the sanctuary was the scattered and fragmented condition of ritual paraphernalia (for example, fragmented altars and statues) found throughout the complex and what appeared to be the deliberate breakage of two of the large ceramic mortuary urns.

Unit 6. Buena Fé Phase Ranch Style Compound (Figure 4.7)

Unit 6 contained two plazas, 21 ground floor rooms, and numerous jacal structures. Second-story rooms were built over six of the ground floor rooms. This architectural unit, like Unit 14 (The House of the Pillars), possessed a colonnade. In this case, the colonnade, with seven wooden pillars, was remodeled into four domestic rooms (5, 6, 7, 9) during the Paquimé phase, extending the length of Plaza 2–6. Seven pit houses that were constructed during the Viejo period were discovered beneath Plaza 2.

In Unit 6, 58 deliberate burials were found, including Types 1A, 1B, 1H, 3A, 3B, and 3H, along with the remains of 10 Type 2 unburied bodies. Subfloor room burials accounted for 39 of the 58 deliberate burials, and 19 individuals were interred in 13 subfloor grave pits. The majority of the individuals buried in Unit 6 were not accompanied by grave goods (Vol. 8: 373–376). When present, accompaniments consisted of a ceramic vessel or two and utilitarian objects. Two multiple subfloor burials (CG 22–6, 23A–B–6; CG 25–6, 26A–B–6, 27A–B–6, 28A–C–6) in Room 20–6 and a single burial (CG 34–6) interred in Plaza 2 were exceptions to the norm. One of these subfloor graves (CG 22, 23A–B–6) contained the remains of two infants and a child that were interred with shell and stone jewelry and a single Ramos Polychrome jar. The other grave contained the remains of eight individuals, including one child, one juvenile, two young adult males and one female, one middle-aged adult male, one subadult, and one adult of indeterminate age. The age and gender profile of the individuals interred in this grave suggests that it probably represents a family tomb. It is not possible to determine the precise sequence in which the burials were placed in the grave, except to note that three of the individuals in CG 28A–C were clearly interred first.

Unit 8. The House of the Well (Figure 4.8)

Unit 8 was named the House of the Well because of the subterranean walk-in well that was found beneath Plaza 3. In this unit, 8 plazas, 21 single-story rooms, 16 two-story rooms, 7 three-story rooms and 1 subterranean room were excavated (Vol. 4: 363). The 43 deliberate burials found included Types 1A, 1C, 1D, 1F, 3A, 3B, 3E, 7A, and 8A, and 14 Type 2 unburied bodies were recovered. Of the 43 burials, 25 were interred in 20 subfloor room graves, and the remainder were buried in 11 plaza graves. Only 11 burials were interred with grave accompaniments (Appendix A; Vol. 8: 376–379).

Most of the single-story and second-story rooms in the House of the Well were considered by the excavators to have been used for domestic activities, as indicated by internal features and artifacts (Vol. 4: 396). Rooms 11B, 15, 18, 21, 25, 28, 30, 32, 34, 35, 43B, 44, and 46 were classified as public or ceremonial, and six of them (rooms 11B, 28, 30, 32, 34, 43B) were believed to have functioned

Figure 4.3.   Ramos Polychrome jar, Burial CG 2–4. (Photo courtesy of the Amerind Foundation, Inc., Dragoon, Arizona; Negative No. CG 25L–14.)

Figure 4.4.   Burial vault 2–4. (Photo courtesy of the Amerind Foundation, Inc., Dragoon, Arizona; Negative No. CG–263.)

Figure 4.5. Ramos Polychrome jars: *a*, from Burial CG 4–4; *b*, from Burial CG 3–4. (Photos courtesy of the Amerind Foundation, Inc., Dragoon, Arizona; *a*, Negative No. CG 25L–15; *b*, CG 25L–16.)

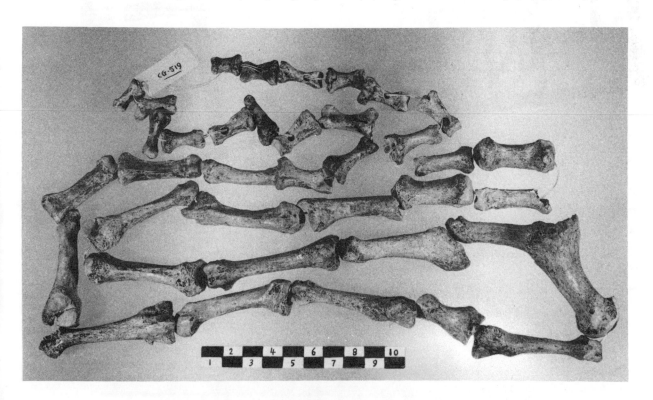

Figure 4.6. Human phalange necklace from burial vault 2–4. (Photo courtesy of the Amerind Foundation, Inc., Dragoon, Arizona; Negative No. CG 25L–31.)

[27]

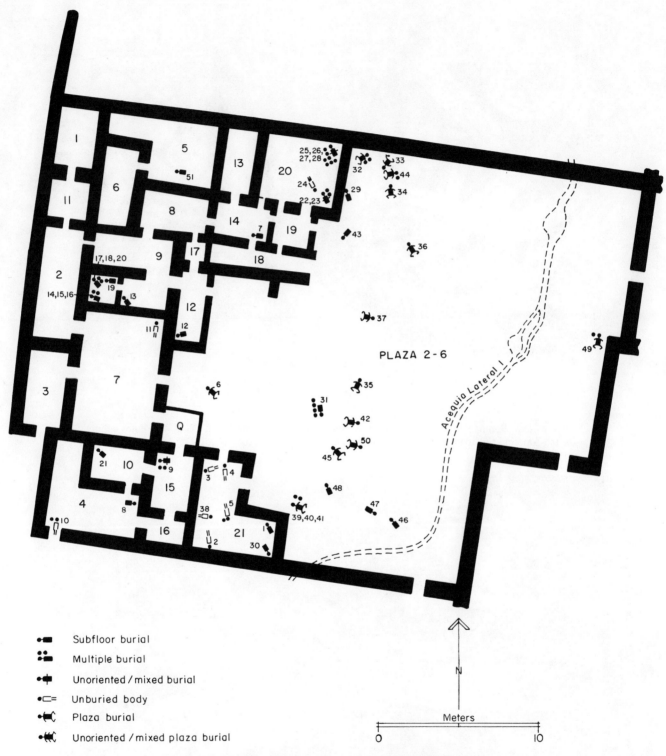

⦁▪	Subfloor burial
⦁⦁▪	Multiple burial
⦁▪	Unoriented / mixed burial
⦁⊏=	Unburied body
⦁⋐	Plaza burial
⦁⋐⋐	Unoriented / mixed plaza burial

Figure 4.7. Distribution of burials in Unit 6, Buena Fé Phase Ranch Style Compound. (Adapted from Vol. 4, Figs. 231, 238, 241–4.)

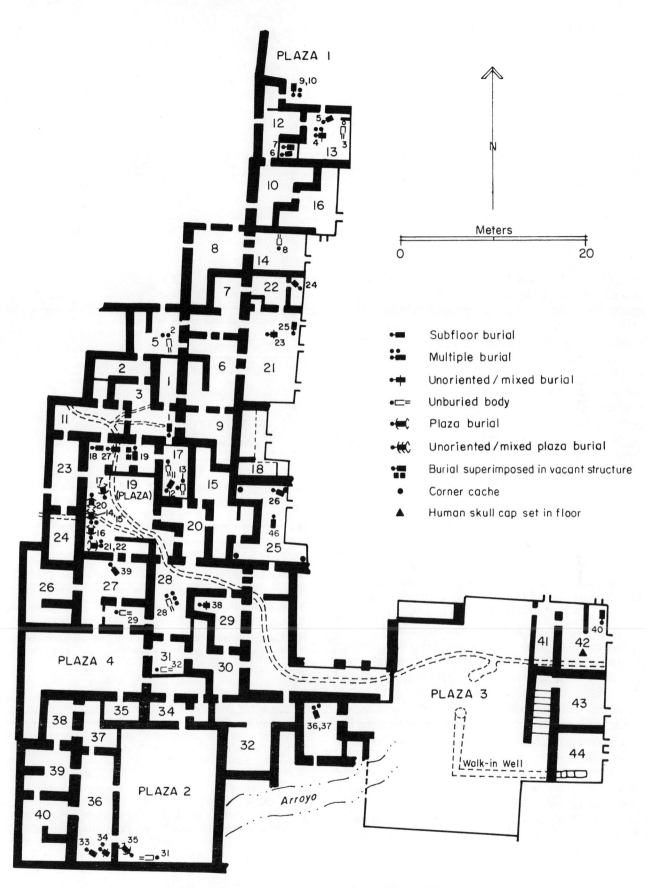

Figure 4.8. Distribution of burials in Unit 8, The House of the Well.
Plan view does not include burials CG 41–8 through 45–8. (Adapted
from Vol. 4, Fig. 264–4 and from Amerind Foundation field maps.)

originally as part of the public transportation system. Three clustered rooms (15, 18, 25) were utilized as storage and manufacturing areas, as indicated by large quantities of finished and unfinished ornaments and socioreligious artifacts fashioned from stone, shell, and copper (Vol. 4: 424–430, 437–439). For example, Di Peso (Vol. 2: 675) reported that 74.2 percent of the raw shell recovered from Casas Grandes was found in rooms 15 and 18. Room 15 also contained 43 of the 71 whole and fragmentary shell trumpets found in the House of the Well. The fill of Room 18 also yielded 49 Gila Polychrome bowls, a Tonto Polychrome bowl, and a Springerville Polychrome bowl.

Four subfloor corner caches containing 990 ornaments were recovered from Room 25, presumably representing ceremonial or dedicatory offerings. Similar caches have been encountered archaeologically in prehistoric pueblos and have been known to occur as part of the ritual dedication of buildings among Pueblo Indians in the American Southwest (Schiffer 1987: 79–80). The Casas Grandes ornaments were manufactured from copper, turquoise, gray slate, ricolite, felsite, red slate, fluorite, apophylite, olivine, and nine identifiable shell species (Vol. 4: 260–261). No ritual paraphernalia was found on the floor of this room, although its fill contained four shell trumpets, a ceremonial axe, a wood paho, and a stone stool. One subfloor grave (CG 26–8), containing the remains of a child without nonperishable accompaniments, was also located in this room.

Room 21 was considered by the excavators to have served primarily a public or ceremonial function when originally constructed because of its size, a turquoise offering in one of its postholes, and a child burial (CG 23–8) that was found in the posthole of one of the central roof supports. The skull had a hole in its left occipital bone and consequently the child was interpreted as representing a sacrifice. An infant (CG 25) also had been buried in this room under a stepped ramp. Neither had been interred with any grave goods.

Entrance to the walk-in well located in Plaza 3 was gained by a stairway in Room 44. A portion of a human skull cap was found set in the adobe floor of Room 44 just south of the unsealed door in the east wall (Vol. 4: 462), and a niche in the east wall contained a stone effigy of a mountain lion. Other ritual paraphernalia found on the floor included two copper crotals and a bone rasp fashioned from a bovine rib (Bovinae).

The stairway of the walk-in well produced a trove of ritual paraphernalia (Fig. 4.9) that the excavators suggested may have been gathered up and thrown into the well on the last day of the Diablo phase. A more plausible explanation for this assemblage of artifacts is that it represents an offertory cache similar to that contained in the Cenote of Sacrifice at the Mayan site of Chichen Itza. Some of the artifacts found on the stairway included two mountain lion effigies, a humpback effigy, two painted pebbles, three ceremonial stone vessels, three shell trumpets, a shell container and altar piece also made from *Strombus galeatus* and decorated with a mosaic of turquoise tesserae, an axe, two copper crotals and

Figure 4.9.   Artifacts on the stairway in the walk-in well. (Photo courtesy of the Amerind Foundation, Inc., Dragoon, Arizona; Negative No. CG 602–37.)

a portion of reworked plaque made from copper, fragments of Ramos Polychrome and Villa Ahumada Polychrome effigy jars, a bone rasp fashioned from a bovine rib (Bovinae), a bone anthropomorphic effigy fashioned from a black bear femur (*Ursus americanus*), a bone skewer made from an unidentified mammal (Mammalia), shell armlets, and stone and shell ornaments that may represent portions of composite necklaces. A more exhaustive listing of the artifacts found on the floor of the stairway is provided by Di Peso, Rinaldo, and Fenner (Vol. 4: 377–379).

The clues that were left in these remnant apartments suggested that the occupants were specialists of one sort or another who were given preferential treatment. For example, the sweat bath[40] and the subterranean well were located within this particular area and their apartments received the best acequia and sewage services.[41] These affluent ones, who were honored by the sacrifice of a young child during the consecrating ceremonies of one of their public rooms,[42] possessed more specialized material goods than any of the other townsmen. Their warehouse area[43] contained millions of marine shell involving 60 species,[44] the bulk of the raw ricolite, turquoise, salt, selenite, and copper ore, as well as a stack of 50 or more Gila Polychrome bowls.[45]

Unit 11. The House of the Serpent (Figure 4.10)

Unit 11 was named the House of the Serpent because of its close proximity to a serpent-shaped mound that was located

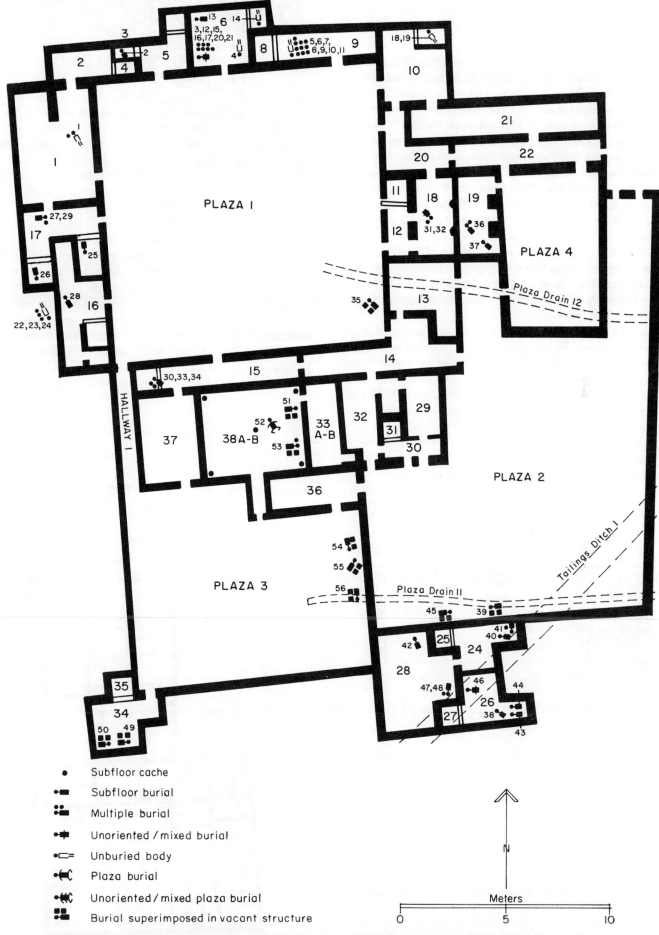

Figure 4.10. Distribution of burials in Unit 11, The House of the Serpent. (Adapted from Vol. 5, Fig. 1–5.)

to the west (Fig. 1.2). This unit, which was constructed and primarily occupied during the Buena Fé phase, contained 4 plazas, 2 multistoried rooms, and 36 single-story rooms (Vol. 5: 475). Of the 66 Casas Grandians interred in the House of the Serpent, 44 were deliberate burials (Types 1A, 1B, 1E, 7A, 7B, 9), 21 were Type 2 unburied bodies, and 1 was Type 9, accidental death. Nine of the deliberate burials were interred with nonperishable grave accompaniments (Vol. 8: 381–383). One subfloor sealed grave found in Room 6 contained the articulated and disarticulated remains of 8 individuals (CG 3, 12, 15, 16, 17A–B, 20, 21), and not one of these burials was accompanied by grave offerings. The age and gender profile of this grave and the way burials were interred suggest that it represents a family tomb that was opened and resealed upon the death of a family member.

The ground floors of the two multistoried rooms (33 and 38), both of which were subterranean, may have been constructed originally to be used for ceremonial activities (Vol. 5: 475). Room 38 had subfloor center and corner caches, the contents of which had been removed. A Ramos Polychrome miniature bird effigy vessel and a ceremonial stone vessel were the only artifacts of a socioreligious nature found on the floor. The floor of Room 32 yielded the only other object of ritual paraphernalia recovered from this unit, a bone wand fashioned from the tibia of a pronghorn antelope (*Antilocapra americana*).

Unit 12. The House of the Macaws (Figure 4.11)

The discovery of puddled adobe nesting boxes, egg shells, and the remains of 234 macaws buried below the surface of Plaza 3 provided the name for Unit 12. On the basis of this abundant evidence for macaw aviculture it was suggested that: "The House of the Macaws was the probable home of a class of people described by Father Sahagún as 'feather merchants', who at Paquimé specialized in the raising of macaws" (Vol. 2: 424).

Unit 12 consisted of four excavated plazas, several adobe and jacal rooms that had been razed, and 31 standing single-story rooms (Vol. 5: 523). Excavation produced 38 deliberate burials, including Types 1A, 1B, 1E, 3A, 3D, 7A, 7B, 11B, 11E, and 12A, and 11 Type 2 unburied bodies. Relatively few of these individuals were interred with grave goods (Appendix A; Vol. 8: 385–387).

Ritual paraphernalia was exceedingly sparse. Shell trumpets were found on the floors of Plaza 6 and rooms 17 and 25, and a single stone stool came from the fill of Plaza 6.

Figure 4.11.   Distribution of burials in Unit 12, The House of the Macaws. (Adapted from Vol. 5, Fig. 36–5.)

Unit 13. The House of the Dead (Figure 4.12)

Unit 13 possessed a relatively high number of burials (117) for its size and, therefore, was named the House of the Dead. This unit contained 3 plazas and 19 single-story rooms. Of the burials recovered from this architectural unit, 104 were classified as deliberate interments (Types 1A, 1B, 1E, 1G, 3A, 3B, 4A, 4E, 11A, 11B, 11D) and the remaining 13 were Type 2 unburied bodies. The majority (72, or 69.2%) of the burials were placed below the floors of rooms.

The House of the Dead is unique when compared with other units investigated at Casas Grandes, because it contained two elaborate subfloor tombs (Type 4 burials) with which a large number of ceramic handdrums were associated (Fig. 4.13). These two subfloor tombs (CG 13–13, 44–13), located in rooms 3 and 9, were covered with board planking and sealed with a layer of adobe that was level with the floor surface of each room. Both of these graves contained a large quantity and diversity of artifact accompaniments compared with burials recovered from other architectural units, and 13 individuals were recovered from the two graves.

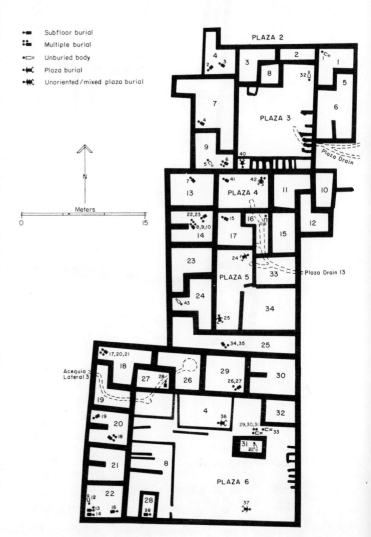

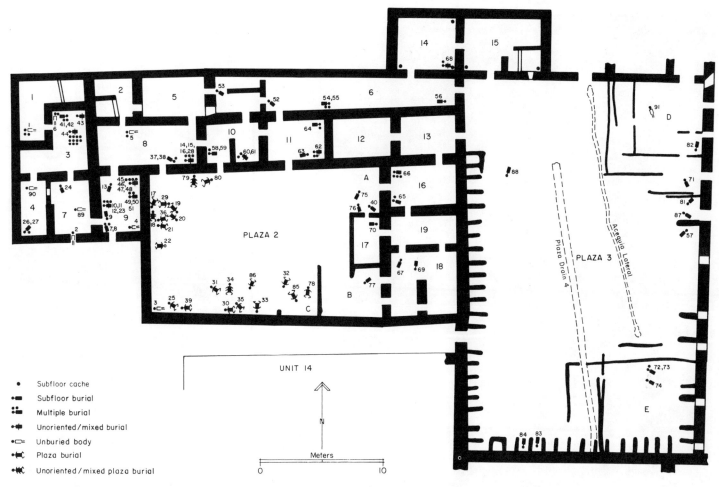

Figure 4.12. Distribution of burials in Unit 13, The House of the Dead. (Adapted from Vol. 5, Figs. 65, 66–5.)

Legend for Figure 4.12:
- Subfloor cache
- Subfloor burial
- Multiple burial
- Unoriented/mixed burial
- Unburied body
- Plaza burial
- Unoriented/mixed plaza burial

PLAZA 2

UNIT 14

N

Meters

0   10

PLAZA 3

Plaza Drain 4

Acequia Lateral

Figure 4.13. Ceramic handdrums on the floor in the southeast corner of Room 9–13. (Photo courtesy of the Amerind Foundation, Inc., Dragoon, Arizona; Negative No. CG 330–36.)

Figure 4.14. Burial CG 44–13 before excavation. (Photo courtesy of the Amerind Foundation, Inc., Dragoon, Arizona; Negative No. CG 340–8.)

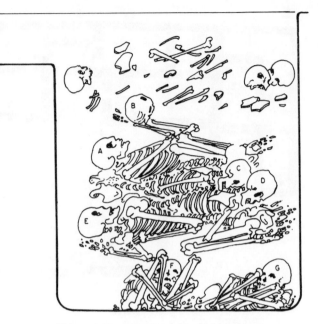

Figure 4.15. Profile of Burial CG 44–13. (Adapted from Vol. 8, Fig. 383–8.)

A single adult male (18 to 35 years) was interred in grave 13–13 in Room 9. Grave accompaniments included a Ramos Polychrome jar, rubbing stones, concretions, stone and shell beads, copper pendants, and lithic artifacts (Appendix A; Vol. 8: 390). The tomb (CG 44 A–L–13) in Room 3 contained 12 individuals ranging in age from 13 to 50 plus years (8 adults and 4 adolescents), representing both males and females (Vol. 8: 387). The individuals buried within this tomb had been placed in the grave in levels rather than side by side (Figs. 4.14, 4.15). Burials A through G were primary (articulated) inhumations and the remains of the others (H–L) were disarticulated, fragmentary, and found mixed in Level 1 of the tomb (Fig. 4.14). A middle-aged adult male (36 to 50 years old; CG 44E) appeared to be the most important individual buried in the tomb. According to the excavators, "Considering the extraordinary nature of this burial, it is possible to speculate that these incomplete upper level remains represented some sort of secondary offering to honor those below" (Vol. 8: 387). Rather than offerings, however, it is possible these remains may represent burials disturbed by generational or long term use of the tomb.

Another unusual aspect of the House of the Dead was the discovery of 175 turkeys, the majority of which were headless, recovered from below the floor of Plaza 3. The plaza may have functioned as a turkey breeding area, and the turkeys, specifically the headless ones, may have been sacrificed during mortuary rites, assuming that such rites were similar to those recorded in various codices for Mesoamerican societies (Vol. 2: 393).

Because of the large number of headless turkeys, ceramic handdrums, and the unusually elaborate burials found in the House of the Dead, Di Peso suggested that the occupants, possibly priests, may have been involved in a complex death cult. The almost total absence of Type 2 unburied bodies is further offered as evidence for the sacred nature of the architectural unit (Vol. 8: 387).

Subfloor corner caches containing gray slate, Conus beads, and turquoise bead pendants were found in rooms 14 and 15 (Vol. 4: 260–261). The fill of Room 14 yielded a bone skewer made from a Mammalia shaft that was decorated with pseudocloisonne and specular iron tesserae, a worked copper sheet, and a copper bead. Two infants (CG 68A–B) had been interred below the floor of this room in the southeast corner. Nonperishable accompaniments placed with these infants consisted of a Carretas Polychrome jar, pigment, and food offerings.

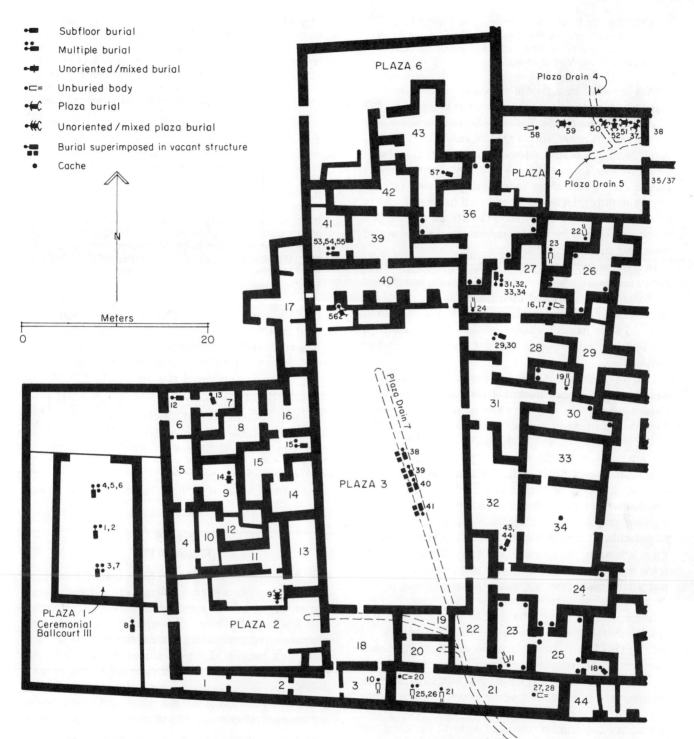

Figure 4.16. Distribution of burials in Unit 14, The House of the Pillars. Additional burials in rooms 38, 45, and Plaza 5 are not illustrated. (Adapted from Vol. 5, Fig. 87–5 and from Amerind Foundation field maps.)

Unit 14. The House of the Pillars (Figure 4.16)

Unit 14 was named the House of the Pillars because of the colonnade of puddled adobe pillars located on the north end of Plaza 3. Six plazas, a ballcourt, and 48 ground-floor rooms were defined within this architectural unit. Recovered from it were 48 deliberate burials and 18 Type 2 unburied

bodies. One of the most unusual architectural features of this unit was the construction of butterfly-shaped rooms (rooms 8, 14, 15, 26, 36).

It was in this complex that the city planners utilized the unique 'butterfly' module in preplanning some of the rooms,[85] in which it is thought that priests and other public figures lived who were involved with the ceremonial enactment of the Quetzalcoatl ball game[86] and with religious rites related to the Mound of the Heroes (Di Peso 1974, Vol. 2: 394).

Only one of the butterfly-shaped rooms contained a subfloor grave pit. A multiple burial consisting of two infants (CG 15 A–B–14) was found in Room 15. Seven ceramic vessels, a wood paho fragment, copper tinklers, stone (jet, turquoise, ricolite) and shell beads, and other artifacts were placed with these two burials (Appendix A; Vol. 8: 399). Subfloor corner caches were in two of the butterfly-shaped rooms (26 and 36). With the exception of several shell trumpets found in rooms 26 (1 Floor, 2 Fill) and 36 (1 Fill), no artifacts that may have represented ritual paraphernalia were recovered from the butterfly-shaped rooms.

In addition to the two butterfly-shaped rooms, subfloor corner caches were found in rooms 23, 24, 25, and 30, and in Room 34 offerings had been placed on the top of the stone seating disk in the central posthole (Vol. 4: 262–263). None of these rooms contained subfloor burials, although one Type 2 unburied body was found in Room 23 and another in Room 30.

Unit 14 contained the second largest concentration of whole and fragmentary shell trumpets (58) recovered from Casas Grandes. The majority came from the fill of Room 34, although trumpets were also found in plazas 3, 4, and 6, and in rooms 26, 28, 32, 33, 36, 38, 40, and 42. Other artifacts may have functioned as ritual paraphernalia. A bone rasp made from a Bovinae rib was found on the floor of Plaza 4. The floor of Plaza 6 contained 13 specimens of pseudocloisonne and a bone rasp made from the scapula of a pronghorn antelope (*Antilocapra americana*). Three bone rasps fashioned from Bovinae ribs were recovered from the fill of Room 33. The floor of Room 45 yielded a bone wand made from the tibia of a mule deer (*Odocoileus hemionus*) and a tube made from a common turkey (*Meleagris gallopavo*) bone.

Three multiple burials classified as Type 8 human sacrifices were found beneath the playing surface of the enclosed ballcourt in Plaza 1. These graves, located along the central axis of the field, contained the remains of seven individuals (CG 1–7–14). The burials (Vol. 8: 398) were interred within the three graves as follows: center grave, two males (one aged 18 to 35 years and one 36 to 50 years); south grave, a fetus and two females (one aged 30 to 32 years and one 18 to 35 years); north grave, two females (one aged 18 to 35 years and one 50 plus years) and an adult male (aged 36 to 50 years). Di Peso (Vol. 2: 414–415) provides the following description and interpretation of these graves.

The center marker, an unshaped stone, was found embedded in the paved playing floor[49] and covered a 'spirit hole,' or symbolic entrance to the underworld.[50] This, in turn, led down to the head of an adult male who was seated upon a flexed male, after the fashion of the Veracruz palma design, wherein Death sits on his victim while cornstalks issue upward from the scene,

supporting the theory that fertility was a considerable measure of the game's religious symbolism.[51] The Tenocha King, Tezozomoc, referred to a similar center hole as a 'place of the skull' (itzompan), and told of the Coatopec gaming arena where waters once gushed from its centrally-located 'well of water,' the symbolic location of the spot where Huitzilopochtli beheaded his sister, Coyolxauhqui.[52]

The south end, which lacked a surface marker, involved another subfloor burial cache, that of a pregnant adult female overlying another woman, whose severed right arm was draped over her shoulders. The north goal, marked by an upright wooden standard, had a third burial group, which consisted of a disjointed adult female, whose severed feet were articulated, and an odd adult male skull complete with mandible scattered above an articulated adult female. These implied that ceremonial dismemberment of humans was associated with this northern ceremonial ball court cult, even as it was in Mesoamerica.[53]

One subfloor tomb (Type 4 burial) similar to tombs described for Unit 13 was found in Room 7 (later determined to be part of Unit 14 rather than Unit 16). The pit had shelves at each end on which board planks were placed to cover the grave. This grave contained two males (CG 2, 3–16), an old adult (50 plus years) and a middle-aged adult (36 to 50 years), who had been interred facing each other in a sitting position. Grave goods placed with these two males included a Ramos Polychrome effigy jar, a Ramos Black miniature bowl, a Ramos Polychrome jar, an Escondida Polychrome bowl, turquoise and shell jewelry, and a bone wand fashioned from an Artiodactyla tibia(?) shaft (Appendix A; Vol. 8: 401).

Unit 15
(Figure 4.17)

Unit 15 consisted of a single-story house cluster. Two rooms and a plaza were excavated, yielding seven deliberate burials (Types 1B, 1D, 3A, 6) and six Type 2 unburied bodies (Vol. 8: 401–402). Three of the burials (CG 1, 6A–B) were interred with nonperishable grave accompaniments. The secondary urn burial (CG 6A–B) contained the fragmentary and charred remains of an adult male and female of questionable age. The excavators suggested that this burial represented the remnants of two individuals that were exhumed and reburied rather than a formal interment (Vol. 8: 401).

Unit 16. The House of the Skulls
(Figure 4.18)

Unit 16 was named the House of the Skulls because of the six human trophy skulls that were found in the fill of Room 23, which was cross-shaped in plan (Figs. 4.18, 4.19). All of the crania lacked mandibles and four possessed one to four drill holes, suggesting that they may have been suspended from the ceiling of the room. Three of the worked skulls and one of the unworked skulls were adult males, and the age and gender of the remaining two are unknown.

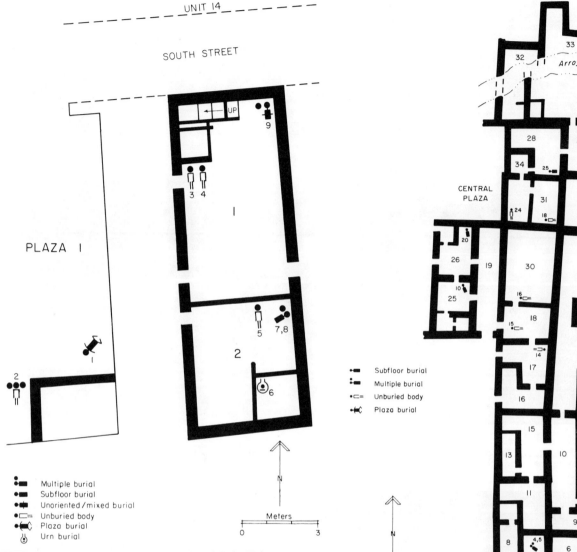

Figure 4.17. Distribution of burials in Unit 15. (Adapted from Vol. 5, Fig. 137–5.)

Figure 4.18. Distribution of burials in Unit 16, The House of the Skulls. (Adapted from Vol. 5, Figs. 139, 141, 147, 161–5, and from Amerind Foundation field maps.)

Turquoise ear pendants were found in association with one of the skulls, suggesting that it had not been defleshed. Animal long bones as well as other human skeletal parts were found accompanying these skulls, causing Di Peso to describe the contents as a ceremonial trove (Fig. 4.20). Some of this material was found in the fill of Room 22. The bone recovered from Room 22, however, is believed to have originated from Room 23 when its second story collapsed. The bone assemblage is distinctive, including 109 long bones and 43 bone wands. Most of the long bones were identified as black bear (81, *Ursus americanus*), representing 27 different individuals. The remainder of the long bone assemblage was identified (Vol. 8: 59) as mountain lion (17, *Felis concolor*), grizzly bear (5, *Ursus nelsoni*), human (2, *Homo sapiens*), pronghorn antelope (1, *Antilocapra americana*), mule deer (1, *Odocoileus*), lesser sandhill crane (1, *Grus canadensis canadensis*) and one unidentified artiodactyl (Vol.

8: 59–63). One of the human bones, probably of an adult male, was the right humerus that had been sawed and exhibited butchering scars, and the other was an unworked femur of an adult of unknown gender. The bone wands were made from the bones of black bear, pronghorn antelope, mule deer, grizzly bear, Bovinae, white-tailed deer, and human (one specimen made from the left tibia of an adult male). Other artifacts of a socioreligious nature found in the fill of rooms 22 and 23 included several bone skewers, one of which was decorated with pseudocloisonne, a bone rasp made from a mule deer, four ceremonial stone axes, two shell trumpets, a carved bone effigy made from a black bear bone, a miscellaneous bone object that was identified as a

Figure 4.19.   Room 23–16. (Photo courtesy of the Amerind Foundation, Inc., Dragoon, Arizona; Negative No. CG 482–11.)

Figure 4.20.   Ceremonial long bone trove found in the fill of Room 23. (Photo courtesy of the Amerind Foundation, Inc., Dragoon, Arizona; Negative No. CG 469–33.)

split and channeled right femur of an adult male, and the mandible of an adult male(?) that had been drilled and decorated with turquoise mosaic and red pigment.

Comparatively few burials were recovered from the House of the Skulls. Of the 23 burials recovered, only 13 were classified as deliberate interments; nine Type 2 unburied bodies and one Type 9 accidental death account for the remainder of the total. Three burials (CG 10–16, CG 22–23–16) in two different grave pits were classified as Type 4. One of these tombs contained the remains of a young adult male and a child, and a young adult male was interred in the other (CG 10). A large diversity of artifacts was found associated with these burials (Appendix A; Vol. 8: 403–404). Two additional burials, a child (CG 21–16) and a young adult female (CG 25–16) interred in simple subfloor sealed grave pits, were found associated with numerous nonperishable grave goods.

Units 18, 19, 20, 21, 22, 23, and East Plaza (Figures 4.21–4.25)

Wall trenching and the excavation of four rooms resulted in the recovery of 37 deliberate burials (Types 1A, 1B, 1C, 1E, 3A, 3B, 3D, 11A) and one Type 2 unburied body. Most of these burials lacked grave associations (Vol. 8: 405–408).

Central Plaza (Figure 4.26)

In the Central Plaza, 24 deliberate burials were found, including Types 3A, 3B, and 3D, along with four Type 2 unburied bodies (Vol 8: 409–410). The majority (18) of the burials had been placed in separate graves beneath Platform 2 in the northeast coner of the plaza. Four (CG 1, 2, 3, 10–CP) of the burials located beneath Platform 2 had been interred with grave goods (Appendix A; Vol. 8: 409).

Figure 4.21. Distribution of burials in Unit 19. (Adapted from Vol. 5, Fig. 187–5.)

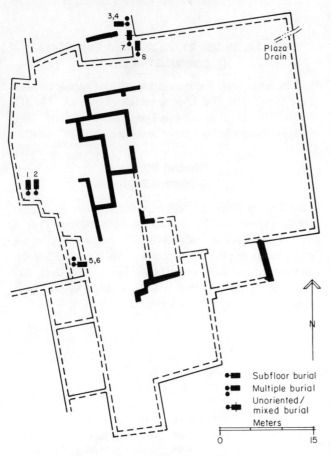

Figure 4.22. Distribution of burials in Unit 20. (Adapted from Vol. 5, Fig. 190–5.)

Plaza Drain

Subfloor burial
Multiple burial
Unoriented / mixed burial
Meters
0   15

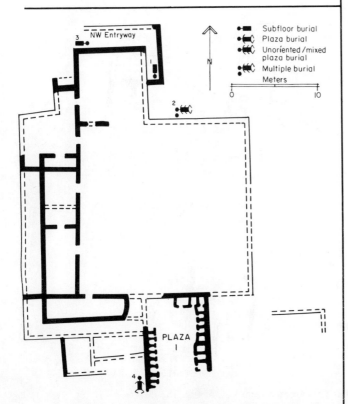

NW Entryway
N

Subfloor burial
Plaza burial
Unoriented / mixed plaza burial
Multiple burial
Meters
0   10

PLAZA

Figure 4.23. Distribution of burials in Unit 21. (Adapted from Vol. 5, Fig. 192–5.)

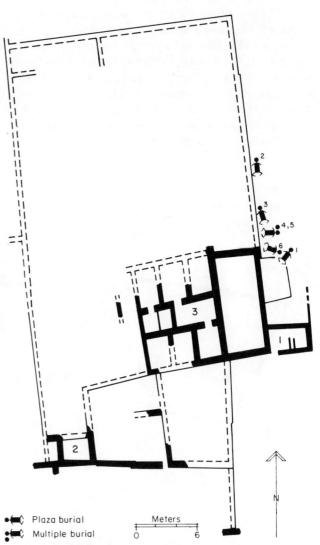

N

Plaza burial
Multiple burial
Meters
0   6

Figure 4.24. Distribution of burials in Unit 22. (Adapted from Vol. 5, Fig. 194–5.)

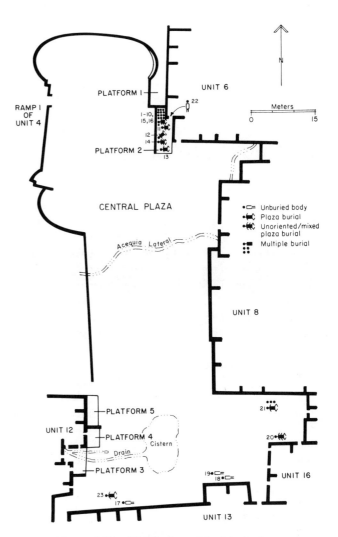

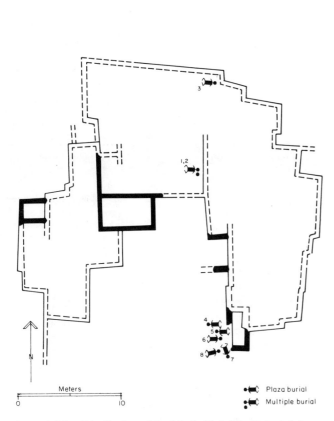

Figure 4.25. Distribution of burials in Unit 23. (Adapted from Vol. 5, Fig. 196–5; Burial CG 9–23 provenience unknown.)

Figure 4.26. Distribution of burials in the Central Plaza. (Adapted from Vol. 5, Fig. 198–5.)

MORTUARY TREATMENT

The burial practices described above exemplify the variability in mortuary treatment at Casas Grandes. Furthermore, they suggest that a small minority of Casas Grandians had access to elaborate burial treatment, including the construction of complex grave facilities, postmortem handling, and high cost or rare accompaniments. This small segment of the population apparently was interred in relatively few of the architectural units investigated, suggesting that certain locales within the community were set aside for high ranking individuals. As previously noted, it has been suggested by Di Peso that this diversity in burial treatments, particularly the specialized treatment (that is, high status tombs) of a few individuals, is evidence for the reorganization of the indigenous population by the Mesoamerican pochteca from an egalitarian to a stratified level of complexity (Vol. 2: 637, Vol. 8: 372).

CHAPTER FIVE

A Univariate Description of the Casas Grandes Burials

To investigate the dimensional structure of Casas Grandes mortuary practices it was necessary to define the variability in burial treatment among the 576 burials recovered during the excavation of the site. My review of the Casas Grandes burials resulted in the delineation of 280 attributes of mortuary treatment (Table 5.1, omitting attributes 1–4). Most of these attributes (248, or 87%) were grave goods that accompanied an individual or were associated with a particular grave facility. The published descriptions of the Casas Grandes burials listed the quantity and type of accompaniments recovered according to gross material classes (that is, ceramic, bone, stone, shell, and metal) but did not include the specific raw material used. Numerous individuals were interred with jewelry composed of ornaments fashioned from stone and shell. Consequently it was necessary to refer to the Casas Grandes volumes pertaining to stone and shell jewelry in order to determine the type of stone material and the species of shell from which the ornament was manufactured (Appendix A).

ATTRIBUTES OF CASAS GRANDES BURIAL TREATMENT

To facilitate analysis, specifically to alleviate the problem of small sample sizes, the diverse types of accompaniments listed in Table 5.1 were combined into a smaller number of analytically more appropriate groups. A procedure was needed to differentiate groups of artifacts that might represent symbols or badges of power and authority associated with certain rank social positions from those that functioned in other capacities, such as ornamental and utilitarian. The typological system devised to isolate potential symbols of rank or authority is based on the arguments of Braun (1977, 1979), Peebles (1974), and Peebles and Kus (1977); it is summarized in Chapter 3 concerning access to "high cost" or rare burial accompaniments.

Ceramic Vessels

Ceramic vessels were the most common kind of accompaniment placed with the dead at Casas Grandes, and 13 of the 25 indigenous ceramic types defined for the Medio period were represented in mortuary contexts (Table 5.2). Vessels of Ramos Polychrome, Casas Grandes Plain, and Ramos Black were the most commonly used and they were found within grave contexts in a variety of shapes (jars, bowls, effigy jars, ladles, bottles, handdrums, and, in miniature form, jars, bowls, and dippers).

Table 5.1. Attribute List for Casas Grandes Burials and Accompaniments (with Frequency) Grouped by Artifact Categories

No.	Attribute	No.	Attribute
1.	Phase association	20.	Room subfloor unsealed grave pit
2.	Unit association	21.	Room fill
3.	Age	22.	Plaza subfloor sealed grave pit
4.	Sex		
5.	Extended interment	23.	Plaza subfloor unsealed grave pit
6.	Semiflexed interment		
7.	Flexed interment	24.	Plaza fill
8.	Legs frogged out	25.	Plaza drain
9.	Interred on back	26.	Single interment
10.	Interred on face	27.	Multiple interment
11.	Interred on right side	28.	Orientation 1–45°
12.	Interred on left side	29.	Orientation 46–90°
13.	Interred sitting	30.	Orientation 91–135°
14.	Primary inhumation	31.	Orientation 136–180°
15.	Secondary burial	32.	Orientation 181–225°
16.	Secondary urn burial	33.	Orientation 226–270°
17.	Burial vault	34.	Orientation 271–315°
18.	Room subfloor tomb	35.	Orientation 316–360°
19.	Room subfloor sealed grave pit	36.	No accompaniments

CERAMIC HANDDRUMS ASSOCIATED WITH GRAVE FACILITY (Variable No. 35)
  Plain ware handdrum (3)
  Plain ware scored handdrum (1)
  Playas Red handdrum (2)

POLYCHROME POTTERY (Variable No. 38)
  Babicora Polychrome bowl (1)
  Babicora Polychrome miniature bowl (1)
  Carretas Polychrome jar (1)
  Corralitos Polychrome jar (5)
  Corralitos Polychrome double jar (3)
  Corralitos Polychrome effigy jar (3)
  Escondida Polychrome jar (2)
  Escondida Polychrome bowl (9)
  Ramos Polychrome jar (34)
  Ramos Polychrome bowl (11)
  Ramos Polychrome miniature jar (1)
  Ramos Polychrome miniature bowl (8)
  Ramos Polychrome miniature dipper (1)
  Ramos Polychrome effigy jar (4)
  Ramos Polychrome bottle (1)
  Ramos Polychrome bowl fragment (1)
  Villa Ahumada Polychrome eccentric jar (1)
  Villa Ahumada Polychrome jar (3)
  Jornada Polychrome jar (1)

NONPOLYCHROME POTTERY (Variable No. 39)
  Plain ware jar (26)
  Plain ware bowl (14)
  Plain ware miniature jar (3)

Table 5.1.
(continued)

Plain ware miniature bowl (7)
Plain ware miniature ladle (1)
Plain ware effigy jar (2)
Plain ware eccentric jar (1)
Plain ware incised jar (1)
Tool punched jar (1)
Tool punched effigy jar (1)
Playas Red bowl (3)
Playas Red jar (7)
Playas Red miniature jar (2)
Unidentified red jar (2)
Ramos Black jar (21)
Ramos Black bowl (12)
Ramos Black miniature bowl (5)
Madera Black-on-red jar (1)
Madera Black-on-red bowl (4)

JEWELRY OF NONLOCAL MATERIAL (Variable No. 36)
Vermetid tubular bead (26)
Conus regularis, truncated bead (5)
Conus regularis, tinkler (22)
Conus ximenes, whole pendant (1)
Conus ximenes, tinkler (3)
Conus perplexus, tinkler (37)
Conus princeps, tinkler (2)
Conus sp., truncated bead (1)
Conus sp., tinkler (8)
Glycymeris maculata, whole bead (15)
Glycymeris gigantea, whole pendant (1)
Glycymeris gigantea, centrally perforated pendant (5)
Glycymeris gigantea, armlet (1)
Olivella dama, whole bead (92)
Oliva incrassata, tinkler (7)
Oliva undatella, whole bead (1)
Persicula bandera, whole bead (289)
Nassarius sp., whole bead (3,536)
Laevicardium elatum, disk bead (15)
Laevicardium elatum, bracelet (1)
Laevicardium elatum, armlet fragment (1)
Chama echinata, disk bead (1)
Spondylus princeps, disk bead (1)
Cerithidea albonodosa, whole bead pendant (8)
Turritella leucostoma, whole bead pendant (1)
Natica chemnitzii, whole pendant (1)
Aequipecten circularis, pendant slightly modified (3)
Aequipecten circularis, pendant centrally perforated (1)
Freshwater mussel, pendant (1)
Dosinia ponderosa, tabular pendant (1)
Dosinia ponderosa, fragmentary pendant (1)
Dosinia pondersa, armlet (1)
Pinctada mazatlanica, fragmentary pendant (1)
Pinctada mazatlanica, discoidal spangle (1)
Unidentified shell, disk bead (4,259)
Unidentified shell, stemmed ovoid bead pendant (1)
Unidentified dentate bead pendant (1)
Unidentified shell, tapered pendant (2)
Unidentified freshwater shell, unworked (1)
Unidentified shell tessera (1)
Conus regularis, unworked (1)
Turquoise flat disk bead (180)
Turquoise multifaceted bead (1)
Turquoise triangular bead (1)
Turquoise tabular bead pendant (36)
Turquoise ovoid pendant (2)
Turquoise miscellaneous dentate pendant (1)
Turquoise pendant fragment (2)
Turquoise tesserae (92)
Ricolite flat disk bead (62)
Ricolite cylindrical bead (2)
Ricolite effigy pendant (1)

Table 5.1.
(continued)

Sepiolite eccentric bead pendant (1)
Sepiolite ovoid pendant (1)
Jet flat disk bead (54)

JEWELRY OF LOCAL MATERIAL (Variable No. 37)
Apophylite flat disk bead (3)
Red slate flat disk bead (201)
Red slate incised finger ring (1)
Gray slate flat disk bead (1,562)
Gray slate subrectangular pendant (1)
Felsite flat disk bead (22)
Felsite discoidal pendant (1)
Felsite trianguloid pendant (1)
Siltstone flat disk bead (34)
Siltstone square pendant (1)
Granite flat disk bead (1)
Flourite flat disk bead (1)
Flourite tabular bead pendant (1)
Flourite ovoid pendant (1)
Silicate flat disk bead (13)
Pyrite flat disk bead (1)
Malachite tabular bead pendant (1)
Malachite tabular pendant (1)
Malachite unidentified stone ornament blank (1)
Selenite ovoid pendant (1)
Selenite pendant fragment (1)
Selenite eccentric pendant (1)
Selenite unidentified stone ornament (8)
Selenite unidentified stone ornament blank (2)
Feldspar trianguloid pendant (1)
Dacite unidentified stone ornament blank (2)
Calcite unidentified stone ornament blank (1)
Calcite ovoid pendant (1)
Limestone eccentric pendant (1)
Mica eccentric pendant (1)
Specular hematite unidentified stone ornament (1)
Unidentified material, flat disk bead (8)
Unidentified material, discoidal pendant (1)
Unidentified ovoid pendant (1)

UTILITARIAN ACCOMPANIMENTS (Variable No. 40)
Plain ware eccentric worked sherd (1)
Ramos Polychrome sherd scoop fragment (1)
Villa Ahumada Polychrome eccentric worked sherd (1)
Playas Red sherd disk (1)
Artiodactyl bone, worked (1)
Hair ornament, Artiodactyl (1)
Hair ornament, Mammalia (1)
Unclassified bone awl, Desert bighorn sheep (1)
Unclassified bone awl, White-tailed deer (1)
Unclassified bone artifact (1)
Coil bone awl, Mule deer (2)
Bone plaiting tool, Antelope (1)
Rodent bone (1)
Unclassified worked wood fragment (1)
Chert projectile point (1)
Obsidian projectile point (2)
Chert knife (5)
Rhyolite knife (1)
Obsidian knife (1)
Chert drill (1)
Chert chipped scraper (1)
Quartz crystal chipped scraper (1)
Chalcedony chipped scraper (1)
Dacite polishing stone (5)
Vesicular basalt rubbing stone (4)
Rhyolite rubbing stone (1)
Andesite rubbing stone (1)
Sandstone rubbing stone (1)
Dacite hammerstone (7)

Table 5.1.
(continued)

Chert hammerstone (1)
Tuff hammerstone (1)
Dacite full axe (1)
Dacite flat blade axe (2)
Marl abrading stone (1)
Felsite maul (1)
Obsidian chipped preform (1)
Chert core (1)
Agate stone ball (1)
Chalcedony stone flake (7)
Chert stone flake (21)
Felsite stone flake (3)
Obsidian stone flake (7)
Basalt stone flake (3)
Rhyolite stone flake (5)
Jasper stone flake (1)
Quartz stone flake (13)

SOCIORELIGIOUS ACCOMPANIMENTS (Variable No. 41)
Agate concretion (2)
Chalcedony concretion (4)
Chert concretion (6)
Quartz concretion (2)
Jasper concretion (2)
Ash, clay(?), reed-formed (crayon-shaped) pigment (6)
Ash(?), black-gray faceted lump pigment (1)
Limonite, clay (?), reed-formed pigment (7)
Limonite, yellow, raw pigment (13)
Limonite, clay(?), cake pigment (5)
Kaolin, white faceted lump pigment (5)
Kaolin, white powder pigment (1)
Kaolin, reed-formed pigment (8)
Hematite, red, raw pigment (3)
Hematite, clay, faceted lump pigment (1)
Hematite, kaolin, cake pigment (1)
Azurite, blue, faceted lump pigment (3)
Azurite, clay(?), blue, unclassified pigment (1)
Malachite, green, raw pigment (1)
Aluminum silicate(?), green, unclassified pigment (1)
Aluminum, green, cake pigment (4)
Celadonite(?), green cake pigment (10)
Unknown green unclassified pigment (1)
Cal(?), raw pigment (1)
Limonite(?), unclassified pigment (1)
Unknown material, reed-formed pigment (1)
Cordage (5)
Matting (13)

Table 5.1.
(continued)

Textile (6)
Petate (3)
Unworked gryphaea fossil (1)
Pitchstone mined deposit material (1)
Turquoise mined deposit material (16)
Sulfur crystal mined deposit material (3)
Specular hematite mined deposit material (2)
Quartz crystal mined deposit material (8)
Gypsum-selenite mined deposit material (10)
Calcite mined deposit material (45)
Mica mined deposit material (1)
Fluorite mined deposit material (8)
Copper ore mined deposit material (3)
Malachite mined deposit material (21)
Molybdenite mined deposit material (2)
Azurite mined deposit material (23)
Felsite raw material (2)
Flourite raw material (1)

VEGETAL ACCOMPANIMENTS (Variable No. 42)
Unidentified plant material (16)
Unidentified seed cotyledon (1)
Unidentified food material (38)
Unidentified organic material (1)
Cucurbit rind fragment (1)
Angiosperm fragment (1)
Corncob (19)
Cotton seed (4)
Gymosperm (1)

RARE ACCOMPANIMENTS (Variable No. 43)
Pronghorn antelope fawn (1)
Lilac-crowned parrot (3)
Scarlet macaw (7)
Military macaw (2)
Common turkey (7)
Canada goose (1)
Bone rasp I, antelope (1)
Bone rasp III, human (1)
Bone tube, Lesser Sandhill Crane (1)
Bone wand, Artiodactyla (2)
Long bone trove, human (1)
Bone necklace, human (1)
Copper stain on chest (1)
Copper tubular bead (3)
Copper disk bead (234)
Copper pendant (2)
Copper tinkler (2)

A Jornada Polychrome jar and two unidentified red ware jars were the only nonlocally manufactured ceramics identified from burial contexts (Vol. 8: 364). The almost complete absence of trade ceramics in burials is interesting; of the 36 ceramic types identified at Casas Grandes, two, Gila Polychrome and El Paso Polychrome, were found in larger quantities throughout the site than some of the indigenous types. The total absence of Gila Polychrome from burial contexts does little to support Di Peso's contention that this ceramic type might have been indigenous, unless it was being manufactured primarily for export.

For analytical purposes, the ceramic artifact class was condensed into two categories, polychrome and nonpolychrome, to determine if polychrome pottery, which presumably required a larger input of energy in manufacturing than

nonpolychrome, was restricted in access to any segment of the Casas Grandes burial population. In addition, several archaeologists have suggested that polychrome ceramics, turquoise ornaments, shell, and certain minerals were "status markers" among Southwestern groups (Lightfoot and Feinman 1982; Upham, Lightfoot, and Feinman 1981). They used the presence of these goods in burials to define status levels within prehistoric Southwestern societies. Unfortunately, these studies did not initially evaluate the distribution of these goods within the overall cultural system or examine their distribution within the burial sample before using them as correlates of social differentiation (Whittlesey 1984).

Ceramic handdrums were not included within the nonpolychrome ceramic category because in all but one instance (Burial 44–13) this artifact was identified as a feature in-

Table 5.2. Casas Grandes Indigenous Ceramic Types Identified from Burial Contexts

Ceramic Type	Restorable Vessels	
	Site Total	Burial Total
Casas Grandes Plain	199	53
Ramos Plain	1	1
Casas Grandes Scored	20	
Casas Grandes Rubbed Scored	13	
Casas Grandes Pattern Scored	5	
Casas Grandes Corrugated	3	
Casas Grandes Rubbed Corrugated	2	
Casas Grades Incised Corrugated	1	
Casas Grandes Incised	4	1
Casas Grandes Tool Punched	4	2
Casas Grandes Broad Coil	4	
Casas Grandes Armadillo	1	
Playas Red	59	12
Ramos Black	56	38
Madera Black-on-red	32	4
Ramos Black-on-red	1	
Babicora Polychrome	30	2
Carretas Polychrome	45	1
Corralitos Polychrome	19	11
Dublan Polychrome	1	
Escondida Polychrome	43	11
Huerigos Polychrome	25	
Ramos Polychrome	238	60
Villa Ahumada Polychrome	29	4
Total	835	200

Table 5.3. Architectural Distribution of Medio Period Ceramic Handdrums* (after Di Peso and others 1974, Vol. 6: 356–365)

Ceramic Type	Site Total	Architectural Unit		
		8	13	14
Casas Grandes Plain	63		56	7
Casas Grandes Scored	15	1	14	
Casas Grandes Rubbed Scored	7		7	
Casas Grandes Incised	1		1	
Playas Red	15		13	2
Ramos Black	3		2	1
Madera Black-on-red	2		2	
Babicora Polychrome	1			1
Ramos Polychrome	2		2	
Total	109	1	97	11

*Restorable and fragmentary drums.
An additional 7,662 drum sherds were recovered from the site.

clusion rather than as an accompaniment associated with any specific individual. Consequently, handdrums (Table 5.3) were recorded as a separate variable (*see* Table 5.8). Over 96 percent of the ceramic handdrums found at Casas Grandes were recovered from Unit 13, specifically rooms 1, 4, and 9.

Jewelry

Following pottery in frequency of burial occurrence were jewelry and other items of personal adornment (such as pendants, necklaces, and hair ornaments). Jewelry was categorized according to the origin of the raw material from which individual elements were manufactured, that is local versus nonlocal material. This distinction was made in order to determine whether some individuals were unable to obtain ornaments made from expensive or high cost materials in terms of the energy or labor expended in procurement. Jewelry was made from a number of different material classes: shell, stone, bone, and metal.

Shell Ornaments

The shell assemblage recovered from Casas Grandes for the Medio period consisted of 3,906,154 individual items, representing aproximately 70 different species (Vol. 6: 401–525, Vol. 8: 162–182). The vast majority of this shell originated from the Panamic Province, specifically the

Guaymas area or the deltas of the Yaqui and Matape rivers. Fifty of the species identified were used to fashion various ornaments such as beads, bead pendants, pendants, tinklers, bracelets, armlets, spangles, and tesserae.

Nearly all of the shell (96%) was recovered from two adjoining rooms in Unit 8 (*see* Chapter 4). Di Peso and others (Vol. 6: 405–406) interpreted this concentration of shell as representing a major storage and production center for this commodity. Unit 8 was identified as a major storage center not only for raw and finished shell artifacts, but also for numerous other objects such as pottery and raw minerals, including copper. The remainder of the shell was located in Unit 14 (10,848 pieces, or 0.3%), Unit 16 (110,051 pieces, or 2.9%), and the Central Plaza (8,213 pieces, or 0.2%).

Table 5.4 lists in order of overall abundance the shell species identified from architectural and mortuary contexts and their corresponding frequencies. The bulk of the shell identified from burial contexts was concentrated in Units 13 and 14, and relatively few of the burials in Unit 8 had shell jewelry (Appendix A; Ravesloot 1984). The relative absence of shell jewelry from burial contexts was noted by Di Peso, Rinaldo, and Fenner (Vol. 6: 385).

> . . . the Casas Grandes studies revealed that prior to A.D. 1060 the local people valued shell as personal ornaments, as many went to their final resting place wearing these items for which they bartered. After this date, at least in the city of Paquimé, there was a change in community attitude toward the material, for it became a commercial commodity and people were rarely buried with shell jewelry. Whether it became a mundane product because of overfamiliarity with the raw material or because of its commercial value is unknown.

The rarity of shell in mortuary contexts indicates the material may have been imported and worked primarily for export rather than for local consumption. It is conceivable that individuals interred with this commodity may have occupied a higher social position in the community than those

Table 5.4. Shell Species from Medio Period Burial Contexts

Shell Species	Site Total	Burial Total
Nassarius sp.	3,725,570	3,536
Conus perplexus	53,004	37
Conus regularis	49,962	28
Olivella dama	13,835	92
Vermetid	10,804	26
Chama echinata	4,765	1
Cerithidea albonodosa	2,534	8
Laevicardium elatum	1,973	17
Conus sp.	1,478	10
Conus ximenes	1,443	4
Glycymeris gigantea	1,425	7
Persicula bandera	1,122	289
Oliva incrassata	758	7
Turritella leucostoma	347	1
Aequipecten circularis	310	5
Conus princeps	213	2
Oliva undatella	184	1
Glycymeris maculata	82	15
Dosinia ponderosa	69	3
Pinctada mazatlanica	48	2
Freshwater mussel	43	1
Natica chemnitzii	1	1
Unidentified	36,184	4,265
Total	3,906,154	8,358

Table 5.5. Stone Material of Ornaments from Medio Period Burial Contexts

Stone Material	Site Total	Burial Frequency
Gray slate	8,386	1,563
Turquoise	4,824	315
Red slate	4,498	202
Ricolite	1,701	65
Siltstone	603	35
Felsite	498	24
Specular hematite	148	1
Malachite	91	3
Jet	54	54
Fluorite	52	3
Apophylite	35	3
Mica	28	1
Selenite	24	13
Silicate	20	13
Calcite	17	2
Dacite	8	2
Feldspar	5	1
Limestone	5	1
Sepiolite	2	2
Pyrite	1	1
Granite	1	1
Total	21,001	2,305

Table 5.6. Intrasite Distribution of Medio Period Turquoise and Serpentine-ricolite

Location	Turquoise		Serpentine-ricolite	
	Site Total	Burial Total	Site Total	Burial Total
Unit 1			1	
Unit 3 (Ballcourt)	21		1	
Unit 4	54		8	
Unit 6	16	1	13	
Unit 8	3,003		2,018	
Unit 11	15		3	
Unit 12	7	2	7	
Unit 13	435	156	79	59
Unit 14	373	143	35	1
Unit 16	1,122	6	137	5
Unit 19	66		2	
East Plaza	8			
Central Plaza	94	7	3	
Reservoir	633		3	
Surface	2			
Unknown provenience	46		1	
Total	5,895	315	2,311	65

who were not. This assumption is based on the fact that a considerable investment of time and energy was necessary to acquire shell and to make the various ornamental forms recovered from mortuary contexts. All of the shell accompaniments listed in Table 5.1, with the exception of a freshwater mussel pendant, were placed within the artifact category encompassing jewelry fashioned from nonlocal raw material.

Stone Ornaments

From Medio period contexts, 21,001 stone ornaments were recovered made from 43 different minerals. These ornaments were used as elements in necklaces, bracelets, and other forms of jewelry, and as ceremonial offerings (Vol. 7: 238–282). Over half of the stone ornaments were made of slate, and relatively few of them, like ornaments of shell, were recovered from burial contexts. All of the stone material listed in Table 5.5 was available within a short distance of Casas Grandes with the exception of turquoise, ricolite, and sepiolite (Vol. 8: 187–192).

The turquoise at Casas Grandes may have been imported from the Cerrillos and Burros mountain region of southwestern New Mexico (Vol. 8: 186). There were 5,895 objects of turquoise recovered. Most of the pieces were associated with architectural contexts, specifically corner subfloor room caches (Vol. 8: 187; *see* Chapter 4 for location of caches), and 70 percent of them came from units 8 and 16 (Table 5.6). Of the total amount, 4,824 individual elements were fashioned into jewelry. Only 315 of them were used as burial accompaniments and 95 percent of these items

were recovered from units 13 and 14 (Table 5.6).

The closest known source of serpentine-ricolite is the Red Rock area of southwestern New Mexico, 265 km north of Casas Grandes. This material was apparently a valued commodity during the Medio period; objects made from it included effigies, ceremonial axeheads, ceremonial stone vessels, ceremonial stools, and numerous pieces of jewelry.

Of the 2,311 objects of serpentine-ricolite, 2,018 pieces (87%) were recovered from Unit 8 (Table 5.6), and 1,701 (74%) of the nonutilitarian objects fashioned from it were classified as elements of jewelry. Only 65 (3.8%) of these ornaments were found in burial contexts, and 59 of them were associated with burials interred in Unit 13.

A relatively small amount of sepiolite (merschaum) was recovered from Casas Grandes. The material probably was imported from the north, specifically the Sapillo Creek district of Grant County, New Mexico. Fifteen items of this material were classified as enigmatic objects, although sepiolite was also fashioned into pendants and a single pipe. Ten objects were recovered from Unit 8, but only two, an ovoid pendant from Unit 11 and an eccentric bead pendant from Unit 13, were identified as burial accompaniments.

All stone ornaments, with the exception of those made from turquoise, ricolite, and sepiolite, were classified as jewelry manufactured from local material. Two hair ornaments fashioned from bone were the only other objects placed within the local material category.

Copper Ornaments

The 684 copper objects recovered from Medio period contexts at Casas Grandes (Vol. 7: 500–532) included workshop material (5), worked sheets (18), needles (2), an awl, beads (494), tinklers (15), pendants (10), a button, tesserae (8), back shield plaques (7), a skewer, an armlet, a bezel, wires (4), an axehead, and crotals or bells (115). Ninety percent of these copper artifacts were found in Unit 14 (241), Unit 8 (228), and Unit 16 (141). Chemical analyses of several of these items and selected samples of copper ore indicate that Casas Grandes was a copper-producing center during the Medio period (Vol. 7: 501). Although 241 (35.5%) of the copper items were found in burial contexts, a finger ring consisting of 234 copper disk beads found on one young adult female (CG 55–14) represented the majority of them.

Copper ornaments or jewelry were placed within the rare artifact category because of their scarcity not only in burial contexts but throughout the site in general. In addition, objects manufactured from this material, even though it was locally available, nevertheless required a considerable amount of energy expenditure.

The absence of crotals or bells from burial contexts was an interesting and unexpected pattern, suggesting that these objects may have been manufactured for export rather than local consumption. One hundred (87%) of these items were recovered from Unit 8.

Utilitarian, Socioreligious, and Vegetal Accompaniments

The rest of the items listed in Table 5.1, except for those classified as rare, were regrouped within the general categories of utilitarian, socioreligious, and vegetal accompaniments. The objects or tools that functioned in a technological capacity were listed as utilitarian and they were found in architectural contexts throughout the site. The socioreligious artifact category was defined primarily on the basis of an assemblage, interpreted as a medicine man's kit, that consisted of a Casas Grandes Plain jar containing 298 items, including concretions, pigments, fossils, mined deposit materials, and raw materials (Vol. 2: 587–588, Vol. 8: 240). These accompaniments presumably had a function within the social subsystem of Casas Grandes society in the area of magic and curing. All plant remains observed in burial contexts were placed within the vegetal category.

Rare Accompaniments

Other than copper ornaments, artifact accompaniments placed within the rare category consisted of parrots and macaws or objects made from bone, including bone wands, rasps, a necklace, a bone tube, and a long bone trove. These artifacts were not only rare in terms of their occurrence within burials, but also in their distribution in other contexts within the site. For example, only 57 bone wands were recovered from Casas Grandes and 48 (over 80%) of them were found in Unit 16 associated with the human trophy skulls and the long bone assemblage previously described in Chapter 4. This association clearly suggests that these artifacts represent ritual paraphernalia that was used primarily in a ceremonial context. Bone rasps, which presumably also had a function in religious ceremonies, were observed even less frequently than bone wands; only 15 were recovered (Vol. 8: 51–52).

Three of the artifacts categorized as rare (a rasp, a necklace, and a long bone trove) that were associated with burials were manufactured from human bone. Table 5.7 presents the intrasite distribution of items made from human bone by architectural unit, showing that 15 of the 20 objects were recovered from Unit 16, The House of the Skulls.

Table 5.7. Intrasite Distribution of Objects Manufactured from Human Bone

Frequency	Object	Architectural Association
1	Coarse coil basketry awl	Unit 8
1	Human hand effigy pendant	Unit 16
1	Rasp	Unit 4, Burial Vault
6	Trophy skulls	Unit 16
2	Wands	Unit 16
4	Long bone troves	Unit 16 (3); Unit 4 Burial Vault (1)
1	Dish	Unit 8
1	Mandible with turquoise mosaic	Unit 16
1	Human phalange necklace	Unit 4, Burial Vault
1	Miscellaneous object	Unit 16
1	Miscellaneous worked bone	Unit 6

REGROUPED BURIAL ATTRIBUTES

The regrouping of artifact types into the eight categories listed in Table 5.1 reduced the 280 attributes of Casas Grandes burial treatment to 39 variables. A 43 variable data set (Table

Table 5.8. Condensed Attribute List for the 43 Variable Data Set

No.	Variable	No.	Variable
1.	Phase association	23.	Plaza fill
2.	Unit association	24.	Single interment
3.	Age	25.	Multiple interment
4.	Sex	26.	Orientation 1–45°
5.	Extended interment	27.	Orientation 46–90°
6.	Semiflexed interment	28.	Orientation 91–135°
7.	Flexed interment	29.	Orientation 136–180°
8.	Legs frogged out	30.	Orientation 181–225°
9.	Interred on back	31.	Orientation 226–270°
10.	Interred on face	32.	Orientation 271–315°
11.	Interred on right side	33.	Orientation 316–360°
12.	Interred on left side	34.	No accompaniments
13.	Interred sitting	35.	Ceramic handdrums associated with grave facility
14.	Primary inhumation	36.	Jewelry of nonlocal material
15.	Secondary burial	37.	Jewelry of local material
16.	Burial vault	38.	Ceramic vessel, polychrome pottery
17.	Room subfloor tomb	39.	Ceramic vessel, nonpolychrome pottery
18.	Room subfloor sealed grave pit	40.	Utilitarian accompaniments
19.	Room subfloor unsealed grave pit	41.	Socioreligious accompaniments
20.	Room fill	42.	Vegetal accompaniments
21.	Plaza subfloor sealed grave pit	43.	Rare accompaniments
22.	Plaza subfloor unsealed grave pit		

Table 5.9. Coding for Phase Association, Location Association, Age, and Gender

Code	Variables 1–4	
	1. PHASE ASSOCIATION	
01	Buena Fé Phase	
02	Buena Fé or Paquimé Phase	
03	Paquimé Phase	
04	Paquimé or Diablo Phase	
05	Diablo Phase	
06	Medio Period	
	2. LOCATION ASSOCIATION	
01	Unit 1, The House of the Ovens	
02	Unit 4, The Mound of the Offerings	
03	Unit 6, Buena Fé Phase Ranch Style Compound	
04	Unit 8, The House of the Well	
05	Unit 11, The House of the Serpent	
06	Unit 12, The House of the Macaws	
07	Unit 13, The House of the Dead	
08	Unit 14, The House of the Pillars	
09	Unit 15	
10	Unit 16, The House of the Skulls	
11	Unit 18	
12	Unit 19	
13	Unit 20	
14	Unit 21	
15	Unit 22	
16	Unit 23	
17	Central Plaza	
18	East Plaza	
	3. AGE	
01	Infant	0–2 years
02	Child	3–5 years
03	Juvenile	6–12 years
04	Adolescent	13–17 years
05	?Subadult	less than 18 years
06	Young adult	19–35 years
07	Middle-aged adult	36–50 years
08	Old Adult	50 + years
09	?Adult	18 + years
	4. GENDER	
01	Male	
02	Female	
03	Subadult (Infant, child, juvenile, adolescent)	
04	?Adult	

5.8) was then used to evaluate the hypothesis of ascriptive ranking as symbolized in mortuary treatment and to describe the Casas Grandes mortuary program.

Initially each burial was assigned an analysis identification number (Appendix B). The published Casas Grandes numbering system ordered burials by excavation unit and, consequently, did not provide a continuous enumeration. Of the 576 burials recovered, 4 were not included in the analysis because information concerning them was incomplete (Casas Grandes 38–8, 89–13, 14–14, 52–14).

To delineate qualitative differences in mortuary ritual treatment among Casas Grandians, variables 5 through 43 (Table 5.8) were coded present (1) or absent (0), and variables 1 through 4 were coded according to the categories presented in Table 5.9 (*see* Ravesloot 1984 for a listing of the 43-variable data set).

Many of the variables listed in Table 5.8 are logically redundant or autoassociated. For example, extended, semiflexed, and flexed interments are alternative states of the same variable. There is some disagreement among archaeologists who have investigated social variation through multivariate analyses of mortuary data with regard to the most appropriate procedure for coding burial attributes (Braun 1981; Tainter 1981). In this study, alternative states of variables are coded as separate attributes in order to identify dimensions of social variability in the mortuary program. Although this approach introduces logical redundancies within

the analysis, it is necessary because the possibility exists that alternative states of treatment may symbolize mutually exclusive social identities.

The coding of the defined artifact categories posed a significant problem when dealing with multiple burials. In many instances, it was not possible to determine with which burial the observed grave goods were associated. Multiple burials where associations could not be made with certainty were coded "absent" for variables 36 through 43 (Table 5.8, *see* Appendix A).

The archaeological study of mortuary practices to infer

social complexity is dependent to a large degree on the length of time during which the burial collection in question accumulated (Peebles 1971; O'Shea 1981, 1984). A consideration of the stability of the society's social system during this period is of utmost importance. Variation in burial treatments, often interpreted as indicating social distinctions, in some instances may represent merely temporally related diversity that occurred as a result of organizational changes. Studies of mortuary practices require adequate dating of the burial collection or other evidence that indicates that the organizational structure of the society's social system remained relatively stable.

The Casas Grandes burial collection was recovered from selected portions of the site, and it represents a time interval of roughly 300 years. In contrast to most southwestern sites, ceramic vessel accompaniments were not useful for providing relative dates of burials. Interments were assigned to phases on the basis of stratigraphic relationships within minimally dated architectural units. For approximately 29 percent of the burials it was not possible to even assign the remains to a phase; these burials were recorded as Medio period (Vol. 8: 355).

Regrettably, a reevaluation of the Casas Grandes tree-ring dates (Ravesloot and others 1986) provides some inferences about the internal chronology of the site but too few dates to clarify the temporal relationships of burials. Thirty-one rooms from five architectural units (8, 12, 13, 14, and 16) yielded tree-ring dates, only nine of which had burials. In addition, these nine rooms contained less than 3 percent of the total number of burials recovered.

For this reason, it was necessary to assume that the organizational structure of Casas Grandes society remained relatively stable throughout the Medio period. The diversity or variation observed in burial treatment was assumed for the most part to symbolize distinctions in status and prestige among Casas Grandians rather than differences reflecting temporal variability or change in the society's mortuary program. However, some of the described diversity in burial treatments may have been temporally related. Those individuals classified as Type 2 or unburied bodies (N 125) by the excavators were considered to represent the remains of Casas Grandians killed on the last day of the Diablo phase (Chapter 4). Many of these individuals did consist of disarticulated and fragmentary remains identified in the laboratory; however, numerous others were fully articulated and were recovered from contexts such as room fill or plaza drains. Some of the articulated ones were originally classified in the field as deliberate interments and subsequently reclassified as Type 2 during report preparation. Two additional interpretations for the Type 2 unburied bodies need to be evaluated: (1) they represent the remains of individuals who occupied Casas Grandes during its period of decay (about A.D. 1400 to 1500), and (2) the mortuary treatment observed among them represents another component of the society's mortuary program that has not been identified previously.

The dimensional structure of the Casas Grandes burial program was initially examined by computing frequencies for variables 5 through 43 (Table 5.8). This frequency description was followed by the cross-tabulation of these variables with the biological (that is, age and gender) and locational variables to become familiar with the data set and to determine which variables, if any, were associated. The chi-square test was used to determine if any significant correlations exist in the data set. The null hypothesis in this case predicts that no statistically significant relationships exist between the biological, locational, and other variables of mortuary treatment. The analysis examined separately those individuals that were classified as Type 2 (cases 448–572) unburied bodies and those burials (cases 1–447) that were defined as deliberate interments by the excavators.

FREQUENCIES OF BURIAL VARIABLES

For cases 1 through 447, 130 burials (29.1%) were found in contexts where it was impossible to assign the remains to a specific temporal phase; these burials were recorded as Medio period by Di Peso, Rinaldo, and Fenner (Vol. 8: 355). The remaining 317 burials were assigned to the following phases on the basis of dated architectural associations: Paquimé-Diablo (198, or 44.3%), Buena Fé (53, or 11.9%), Diablo (53, or 11.9%), Paquimé (8, or 1.8%), and Buena Fé-Paquimé (5, or 1.1%).

The frequencies of burials by architectural unit are illustrated in Figure 5.1. Compared to the other excavated architectural units, a relatively large portion of the burial collection was recovered from Unit 13 (104, or 23.3%).

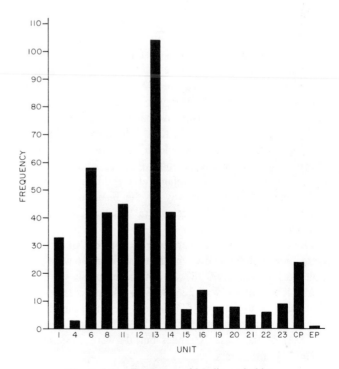

Figure 5.1. Frequency of Medio period burials by architectural unit.

Studies of social organization through analyses of mortuary data are based on the assumption that the recovered burials are a representative sample of those who died in the society (Ubelaker 1984). Anthropologists working in the Greater Southwest (Palkovich 1980; Berry 1985; Cordell and others 1987) and other areas of North America have increasingly used the life tables of Weiss (1973) derived from preindustrial societies to assess the representativeness of prehistoric burial collections. The use of these life tables may not be appropriate models for assessing the representativeness of prehistoric populations (Berry 1985: 43). In addition, Berry (1985: 43) argued that their use with archaeological collections is compromised because it is impossible to determine if the collections represent an accurate cross-section of the prehistoric society.

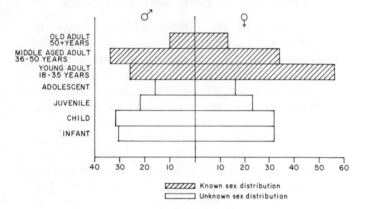

Figure 5.2.   Mortality pyramid for Medio period burials.

Age distribution of the Casas Grandes interments is listed under Burial Frequency in Tables 5.15 and 5.16. A mortality pyramid is presented in Figure 5.2. A demographic evaluation of the burial collection was considered not feasible because the data base was recovered from selected portions of the site and it represented a time span of over 300 years. Consequently, it is not possible to say with certainty that the collection reflects a representative sample of the society's age distribution. Clearly, infants and children are underrepresented. This pattern may be the result of one or a number of factors, including cultural practices, excavation procedures, or preservation.

Of the 447 deliberate interments excavated, 201 (45.0%) were interred individually, and the remaining 246 were multiple burials. Also 390 (87.2%) of these burials were primarily inhumations, with 326 (83.6%) fully articulated. The remaining inhumations (16.4%) were disturbed burials and fragmentary remains identified in the laboratory. Only 57 (12.8%) of the Casas Grandes burials were classified as secondary interments.

Fully flexed individuals numbered 265 (67.9%) of the primary inhumations for which body position was determined. A few individuals were in a semiflexed (28) or extended (16) position, and some were placed with legs frogged (3), on the back (96), on the face or prone (6), on right (71) or left (66) side, and sitting (75).

Of the deceased, 260 (58.2%) were interred in simple earthen pits located beneath the floors of rooms and 141 (31.5%) were beneath plazas. Over 90 percent of these subfloor pits had been filled with dirt and sealed over with adobe. A few (30), however, had been left unsealed, and in some instances accompanying grave goods protruded above the top of the grave facility. Occasionally, burials were placed within the fill of abandoned rooms (13, or 2.9%) and plazas (9, or 2.0%). One individual was interred within a plaza drain. Relatively few of the burials were placed in elaborate grave facilities (described in Chapter 4) such as the room subfloor tombs (18, or 4.0%) and the two puddled adobe burial vaults (3, or 0.7%).

Data on orientation were available for 313 burials (70%). The orientation of a burial was obtained by " . . . noting the direction of the vertebral column from the point of the pelvis to that of the cranium" (Vol. 8: 328). Oriented to the west were 85 burials (19%), followed in frequency by southwest (43, or 9.6%), northeast (42, or 9.4%), northwest (40, or 8.9%), south (34, or 7.6%), southeast (28, or 6.3%), east (28, or 6.3%), and north (13, or 2.9%).

There were 195 burials (43.6%) interred in grave facilities that contained accompaniments, but specific grave goods could be directly associated with only 143 individuals (73.3%). As indicated in Table 5.10, only a few burials were accompanied by a vast quantity of grave goods; 80 percent of the burials were interred with 10 or fewer items and only 30 burials possessed more than 9 artifacts. Of these 30 burials, 11 were associated with more than 150 items. In most instances, these large numbers of objects reflected the separate recording of individual shell and stone items that presumably were parts of larger composite necklaces and other jewelry. For example, Burial CG 35–12 was accompanied by a shell necklace composed of 638 unidentified disk beads and 76 whole *Nassarius* beads.

Frequencies computed for the artifact categories indicated that 26 percent of the burials contained polychrome (46, or 10.3%) and nonpolychrome (71, or 15.9%) ceramic vessels. Jewelry fashioned from nonlocal raw material was in 40 burials, whereas only 23 had jewelry made from local material. Utilitarian accompaniments were placed in 37 (8.3%) graves, and socioreligious items occurred in 21 (4.7%) separate instances. Vegetal material accompanied 31 burials (6.9%). Only 12 burials (2.7%) were interred with rare accompaniments.

The attributes of burial treatment defined for the interments symbolize the different social identities that Casas Grandians maintained in life and that were recognized by

Table 5.10. Quantity of Burial Accompaniments

Number of Artifacts	Casas Grandes Burial Number	Burial Frequency	Percent
1		48	33.5
2		31	21.6
3		12	8.3
4		7	4.9
5		5	3.5
6		3	2.1
7		4	2.8
8		1	0.7
9		2	1.3
10	43–13; 33, 34–11	2	1.3
11	2–1; 44E–13	2	1.3
12	28–1	1	0.7
19	1–CP	1	0.7
21	36–14	1	0.7
30	34–6	1	0.7
39	44B–13; 55–11	2	1.3
43	25–16	1	0.7
48	38–11; 10–16	2	1.3
50	38–13	1	0.7
56	13–13	1	0.7
58	3–1	1	0.7
64	63–13	1	0.7
66	21–16	1	0.7
84	7–16	1	0.7
158	40–13	1	0.7
184	24–13	1	0.7
204	23–16	1	0.7
306	55–14	1	0.7
323	26A–6	1	0.7
341	58–13	1	0.7
386	23A–6	1	0.7
391	5–23	1	0.7
638	7–12	1	0.7
1122	8–16	1	0.7
1246	35–12	1	0.7

Table 5.11. Modal Characteristics of Casas Grandes Mortuary Treatment

Burial Variable	Frequency	Percent
Flexed interment	265	59.3
Interred on back	96	21.5
Primary inhumation	390	87.2
Room subfloor sealed pit	230	51.5
Multiple interment	246	55.0
Oriented to the west	85	19.0
Absence of accompaniments	253	56.6
Nonpolychrome pottery	71	15.9

Table 5.12. Suggested Symbols of Rank and Authority

Body Preparation	Grave Facilities	Artifact Accompaniments
Secondary burial	Burial vault	Ceramic handdrums with grave facility
Legs frogged out	Room subfloor tomb	Polychrome pottery
		Jewelry manufactured from nonlocal material
		Rare artifacts

these units and on the assumption that differential access to space is an important indicator of social status differences, as are body preparation, grave facilities, and grave accompaniments.

CROSS-TABULATIONS OF BURIAL VARIABLES

Analysis of the dimensional structure of the Casas Grandes burial population consisted of cross-tabulating all other variables of burial treatment with the variables of location, age, and gender. The strength of the relationship, or lack of it, between these variables on the one hand and the variables of mortuary ritual treatment that have been suggested as symbols of rank on the other, is of particular interest. The overall summary statistics calculated for these cross-tabulations are presented in Table 5.13.

As expected, there is a significant relationship between burial location (that is architectural unit) and several of the burial variables suggested as symbols and privileges of rank and authority. Room subfloor tombs were found only in Unit 13 (The House of the Dead) and Unit 16 (The House of the Skulls), and Unit 4 (The Mound of the Offerings) was the only locale where burial vaults were constructed.

Significant relationships also exist between the location of burial facilities and the type of grave goods placed with the deceased. The cross-tabulation of defined artifact categories by architectural association are presented in Table 5.14. Tables generated by these cross-tabulations indicate that a significant relationship exists at the 0.05 level between burial location and the presence of certain items (jewelry

the society at death. Table 5.11 indicates that these forms of burial treatment did not occur with equal frequencies within the mortuary program. More specifically, it is evident that only a small portion of the burial population had access to the most elaborate and specialized forms of burial treatment. Table 5.12 lists those variables that may have functioned as status-specific symbols of rank and authority as defined on the basis of the mortuary theory presented in Chapter 3.

In addition, four locations within the site are isolated as possible formal disposal areas maintained for certain "high ranking" segments of the Casas Grandes population: Unit 4 (The Mound of the Offerings), Unit 13 (The House of the Dead), Unit 14 (The House of the Pillars), and Unit 16 (The House of Skulls). This proposition is based on the elaborate and specialized forms of burial treatment observed within

Table 5.13. Chi-square Statistics for Burial Variables Cross-tabulated by Location, Age, and Gender
(Summary statistics)

Burial Variables	Frequency	Location df = 16	Age df = 8	Gender df = 1
Extended interment	16	13.64636	14.50656	0.17613
Semiflexed interment	28	31.04077*	13.44699	0.29415
Flexed interment	265	23.38811	28.70424*	0.01684
Legs frogged out	3	6.32079	7.77466	0.06542
Interred on back	96	14.93058	9.41476	0.20218
Interred on face	6	8.46747	7.85370	0.70256
Interred on right side	71	14.75134	11.96970	0.01077
Interred on left side	66	14.67127	12.31813	0.37265
Interred sitting	75	20.50774	11.65856	2.06754
Primary inhumation	390	54.13385*	17.46083	1.68073
Secondary burial	57	54.13387*	17.46083	1.68073
Burial vault	3	446.99536*	10.78819	0.87897
Room subfloor tomb	18	69.49779*	20.08360*	1.55313
Room subfloor sealed pit	230	84.74158*	31.87375*	1.82961
Room subfloor unsealed pit	30	47.94531*	4.38436	1.39313
Room fill	13	65.60231*	14.52080	0.37697
Plaza subfloor sealed pit	136	126.87685*	25.50615*	0.79175
Plaza subfloor unsealed pit	5	23.83414	18.43419*	4.37852*
Plaza fill	9	25.08911	4.41370	0.57701
Single interment	201	23.71927	5.30024	1.35176
Multiple interment	246	23.71927	5.30024	1.35176
Orientation 1–45°	13	13.19373	4.55171	0.46229
46–90°	42	22.79675	2.35262	0.02896
91–135°	28	34.17427*	5.14792	0.00873
136–180°	28	19.05919	4.18838	0.30608
181–225°	34	27.74104	18.15446*	0.00811
226–270°	43	27.20866	13.42513	0.01614
271–315°	85	22.08139	3.42513	0.00741
316–360°	40	20.00252	4.63522	0.23277
No accompaniments	253	41.45880*	14.29682	1.50192
Ceramic handdrums with grave facility	20	69.05093*	28.30356*	1.86397
Jewelry, nonlocal material	40	38.41460*	11.47194	4.09091*
Jewelry, local material	23	12.59618	8.06239	2.52234
Polychrome pottery	46	46.30881*	14.41086	5.09093*
Nonpolychrome pottery	71	23.11948	6.15965	0.02046
Utilitarian accompaniments	37	21.32184	5.33575	0.00947
Socioreligious accompaniments	21	13.44278	5.49663	0.14772
Vegetal accompaniments	31	22.58865	8.93683	0.33536
Rare accompaniments	12	59.72067*	22.54335*	1.58423

Note: The chi-square approximations are generally thought to be suspect or invalid if expected frequencies are less than 5.
*Significant at the 0.05 level
Location: x^2 = 26.30
Age: x^2 = 15.51
Gender: x^2 = 3.84

manufactured from nonlocal raw material, polychrome ceramics, and rare accompaniments). Individuals interred wearing jewelry made of shell, turquoise, ricolite, and sepiolite were observed in all architectural units except units 15, 19, 20, 21, and the East Plaza. About 30 percent of the burials possessing jewelry made from those materials were recovered from Unit 13.

Composite necklaces composed of ornaments made from local and nonlocal material were identified in 22 separate graves (Vol. 8: 235–239), and 59 percent of these necklaces accompanied burials interred within Unit 13 (The House of the Dead) and Unit 16 (The House of the Skulls).

Burials that were accompanied with polychrome pottery occurred in the majority of the excavated architectural units.

Table 5.14. Cross-tabulation of Artifact Categories by Architectural Unit
(Summary statistics provided in Table 5.13)

Architectural Unit	Burial Frequency (%)	Artifact Category Frequency (and Percent)							
		Jewelry, nonlocal material	Jewelry, local material	Polychrome ceramics	Nonpolychrome ceramics	Utilitarian objects	Socio-religious objects	Vegetal objects	Rare objects
1	33 (7.4)	2 (5.0)	2 (8.7)	8 (17.4)	5 (7.1)	5 (13.5)	4 (19.0)	3 (9.7)	2 (16.7)
4	3 (0.7)	2 (5.0)		3 (6.5)					2 (16.7)
6	58 (13.0)	3 (7.5)	3 (13.1)	9 (19.6)	12 (16.9)	4 (10.8)	1 (4.8)		
8	42 (9.4)	1 (2.5)		2 (4.3)	7 (9.9)	1 (2.7)	1 (4.8)		1 (8.3)
11	45 (10.0)	2 (5.0)	3 (13.1)	1 (2.2)	4 (5.6)	3 (8.1)	2 (9.5)	4 (12.9)	1 (8.3)
12	38 (8.5)	5 (12.5)	2 (8.7)	5 (10.9)	7 (9.9)	1 (2.7)	1 (4.8)	1 (3.2)	
13	104 (23.3)	12 (30.0)	8 (34.8)	10 (21.7)	16 (22.6)	9 (24.4)	7 (33.3)	10 (32.3)	3 (25.0)
14	42 (9.4)	3 (7.5)	1 (4.3)	3 (6.5)	4 (5.6)	7 (18.9)	1 (4.8)	6 (19.4)	1 (8.3)
15	7 (1.6)				1 (1.4)	1 (2.7)			
16	14 (3.1)	5 (12.5)	2 (8.7)	2 (4.3)	4 (5.6)	4 (10.8)	2 (9.5)	3 (9.7)	1 (8.3)
19	8 (1.8)		1 (4.3)	1 (2.2)	4 (5.6)		1 (4.8)	1 (3.2)	
20	8 (1.8)							1 (3.2)	
21	5 (1.1)			1 (2.2)	1 (1.4)			1 (3.2)	1 (8.3)
22	6 (1.3)	2 (5.0)	1 (4.3)		1 (1.4)				
23	9 (2.0)	1 (2.5)		1 (2.2)	4 (5.6)				
Central Plaza	24 (5.4)	2 (5.0)			1 (1.4)	2 (5.4)	1 (4.8)	1 (3.2)	
East Plaza	1 (0.2)								
Total	447	40	23	46	71	37	21	31	12

For this variable, however, Unit 1 (8 burials, or 17.4%), Unit 6 (9, or 19.6%), and Unit 13 (10, or 21.7%) represented approximately 60 percent of such burials. More specifically, the distribution of Ramos and Escondida polychrome vessels as grave accompaniments was significantly associated with this variable (Table 5.14). Unit 13 was the only architectural unit within the site where ceramic handdrums were associated with grave facilities.

Grave goods categorized as rare (for example, copper ornaments, macaws, bone rasps, wands) were associated with burials recovered from 8 of the 17 excavated architectural units. The frequency distributions by unit for those rare accompaniments that could be associated with a specific burial are listed in Table 5.14. It was not possible to examine statistically the distribution of specific artifact types included within the rare artifact category. In many cases rare artifacts were observed only as an accompaniment in a single burial or were placed within graves containing multiple burials. The intrasite distribution of rare artifacts is as follows: bone tube (male 36–50 years, Unit 1); Canada goose (female 36–50 years, Unit 1); long bone trove, bone necklace, and bone rasp III (male and female 36–50 years, Unit 4); scarlet and military macaw (male 36–50 years, Unit 8); common turkey (male 36–50 years, Unit 11), copper pendants (male 18–35 years, Unit 13); pronghorn antelope fawn (female 36–50 years, Unit 13); common turkey (male 50+ years, Unit 13); lilac-crowned parrots (juvenile and child, Unit 13); bone rasp I (adolescent and child, Unit 13); bone wand (juvenile, adolescent female 18–35 years, Unit 14); copper beads (female 18–35 years, Unit 14); copper tinklers (two infants, Unit 14); bone wand (male 50+ years, Unit 16); and common turkey and scarlet macaw (female 18–35 years, Unit 21). This listing indicates that most of the rare accompaniments were recovered from burials interred in Unit 4 (The

Table 5.15. Cross-tabulation of Elaborate Grave Facilities by Age and Gender (Summary statistics provided in Table 5.13)

Variable	Burial Frequency (%)	Elaborate Grave Facility	
		Burial Vault	Room Subfloor Tombs
AGE			
Infant	63 (14.1)		
Child	64 (14.3)		1 (5.6)
Juvenile	25 (5.6)		
Adolescent	32 (7.2)		4 (22.2)
?Subadult	7 (1.6)		
Young Adult	105 (23.4)		4 (22.2)
Middle-aged Adult	71 (15.9)	2 (66.7)	7 (38.9)
Old Adult	28 (6.3)	1 (33.3)	2 (11.1)
?Adult	52 (11.6)	—	—
Total	447	3	18
GENDER			
Male	93 (41.2)	2 (66.7)	7 (58.3)
Female	133 (58.8)	1 (33.3)	5 (41.7)
Total	226	3	12*

*Gender could not be determined for 6 of the 18 bodies.

Mound of the Offerings), Unit 13 (The House of the Dead), and Unit 14 (The House of the Pillars).

The cross-tabulation of age and gender with the suggested symbolic indicators of social rank also revealed some interesting patterns (Tables 5.15, 5.16). In general, burials recovered from room subfloor tombs crosscut both age and gender categories. Adults recovered from room subfloor tombs were fairly evenly distributed among males and females. The age range and frequency distribution for room subfloor tombs includes one child, four adolescents, four young adults, seven middle-aged adults, and two old adults (Table 5.15), a pattern that contrasts significantly with the one observed for the burial vault from Unit 4. Vaults were evidently restricted to mature adults (that is, 36–50 + years).

Relatively few significant relationships occur between the age and gender of burials and the occurrence of artifactual accompaniments (Table 5.16). Only the rare artifact category has a significant chi-square value when compared with age; most of these individuals were 36 years of age or older. The other statistically significant pattern that emerges from these comparisons is the distribution of burial gender with jewelry manufactured from nonlocal raw material and with polychrome ceramics. Males were more frequently interred with these two kinds of accompaniments than were females.

The cross-tabulation of the presence versus absence of accompaniments within grave facilities with the variables of location, age, and gender (Table 5.17) reveals patterns similar to those summarized above. The chi-square statistics calculated for these cross-tabulations indicate that burial location was the only variable that yielded a significant association with accompaniment presence and absence.

TYPE 2: UNBURIED BODIES

As previously discussed, burial cases 448 through 572 were classified as Type 2, or unburied bodies (Vol. 8: 337), and they were analyzed separately from cases 1 through 447. The majority of the Type 2 cases consisted of fragmentary remains that were identified in the laboratory. Consequently, many of the defined variables of Casas Grandes mortuary treatment (Table 5.8) were simply coded absent for these individuals; those coded present are discussed here.

Over 30 percent (43) of the individuals could be assigned only to the broad grouping of adult. This age group was followed in frequency by young adults (36, or 28.8%), infants (11, or 8.8%), children (8, or 6.4%), juveniles (7, or 5.6%), adolescents (7, or 5.6%), old adults (3, or 2.4%), and subadults (3, or 2.4%). Of the 92 classified as adults, 36 (39.1%) were females, 17 (18.5%) were males, and 39 adults could not be assigned to a specific gender.

The intrasite distribution of Type 2 individuals was: Unit 11, 21 (16.8%); Unit 14, 18 (14.4%); Unit 1, 16 (12.8%); Unit 8, 14 (11.2%); Unit 13, 12 (9.6%); Unit 12, 11 (8.8%); Unit 6, 10 (8.0%); Unit 16, 9 (7.2%); Unit 15, 6 (4.8%); Central Plaza, 4 (3.2%); Unit 4, 2 (1.6%); and 1 (0.8%) each from units 18 and 19. Most of these individuals (116, or 93%) were in too fragmentary a condition to determine whether they represented primary inhumations or secondary burials. The following body positions were observed for the primary inhumations: flexed (3), semiflexed (3), extended (3), right side (5), back (3), and left side (1). As to location, 123 were within the fill or on the occupation surface of abandoned rooms (108) and plazas (15), and 2 were placed within the city-wide plaza drain system. Only one individual (CG 27–14) was associated with grave accompaniments.

BURIAL RITUAL PROGRAM OF THE MEDIO PERIOD

A model for the Medio period mortuary ritual program was constructed from the univariate description of Casas Grandes burials, incorporating all the physical evidence of burial treatment recovered from the excavations. Analysis of the burials in terms of postmortem processing, grave facility construction, grave accompaniments, and demographic profiles resulted in the delineation of at least four distinct burial types. The standard treatment of a Casas Grandian involved placement of the corpse in an extended, flexed, or semiflexed position within a simple earthen grave that was located

Table 5.16. Cross-tabulation of Artifact Categories by Age and Gender
(Summary statistics provided in Table 5.13)

Variable	Burial Frequency (%)	Artifact Category Frequency (and Percent)							
		Jewelry, nonlocal material	Jewelry, local material	Poly-chrome ceramics	Nonpoly-chrome ceramics	Utili-tarian objects	Socio-religious objects	Vegetal objects	Rare objects
AGE									
Infant	63 (14.1)	4 (10.0)	6 (26.1)	7 (15.2)	15 (21.1)	6 (16.2)	2 (9.5)	2 (6.4)	
Child	64 (14.3)	8 (20.0)	4 (17.4)	6 (13.0)	12 (16.9)	7 (18.9)	3 (14.3)	6 (19.4)	
Juvenile	25 (5.6)	1 (2.5)			4 (5.6)	1 (2.7)	1 (4.8)	2 (6.4)	1 (8.3)
Adolescent	32 (7.2)			1 (2.2)	4 (5.6)			2 (6.4)	
Subadult	7 (1.6)			1 (2.2)	1 (1.4)				
Young adult	105 (23.4)	9 (22.5)	7 (30.4)	13 (28.3)	14 (19.7)	9 (24.4)	5 (23.8)	9 (29.0)	2 (16.7)
Middle-aged adult	71 (15.9)	11 (27.5)	3 (13.1)	12 (26.0)	8 (11.3)	7 (18.9)	5 (23.8)	8 (26.0)	7 (58.3)
Old adult	28 (6.3)	4 (10.0)	2 (8.7)	5 (10.9)	6 (8.5)	3 (8.1)	3 (14.3)	2 (6.4)	2 (16.7)
?Adult	52 (11.6)	3 (7.5)	1 (4.3)	1 (2.2)	7 (9.9)	4 (10.8)	2 (9.5)		
Total	447	40	23	46	71	37	21	31	12
GENDER									
Male	93 (41.2)	14 (60.9)	2 (18.2)	18 (60.0)	13 (43.3)	8 (42.1)	6 (46.2)	9 (47.4)	7 (58.3)
Female	133 (58.8)	9 (39.1)	9 (81.8)	12 (40.0)	17 (56.7)	11 (57.9)	7 (53.8)	10 (52.6)	5 (41.7)
Total	226	23	11	30	30	19	13	19	12

Table 5.17. Cross-tabulation of Burials With and Without Accompaniments by Location, Age, and Gender

Table 5.17. *(continued)*

Variable	With Accompaniments No.	%	Without Accompaniments No.	%	Total No. of Burials	Variable	With Accompaniments No.	%	Without Accompaniments No.	%	Total No. of Burials
LOCATION						**AGE**					
Unit 1	15	7.7	18	7.1	33	Infant	33	17.0	30	11.9	63
Unit 4	3	1.5	0	0	3	Child	27	13.9	37	14.6	64
Unit 6	24	12.4	34	13.4	58	Juvenile	11	5.7	14	5.5	25
Unit 8	17	8.8	25	9.9	42	Adolescent	11	5.7	21	8.3	32
Unit 11	9	4.7	36	14.2	45	?Subadult	2	1.0	5	2.0	7
Unit 12	14	7.2	24	9.5	38	Young Adult	37	19.1	68	26.9	105
Unit 13	58	29.9	46	18.2	104	Middle-aged Adult	40	20.6	31	12.3	71
Unit 14	22	11.4	20	7.9	42	Old Adult	15	7.7	13	5.1	28
Unit 15	3	1.5	4	1.6	7	?Adult	18	9.3	34	13.4	52
Unit 16	11	5.7	3	1.2	14	Total	194		253		447
Unit 19	3	1.5	5	2.0	8						
Unit 20	1	0.5	7	2.7	8						
Unit 21	3	1.5	2	0.8	5						
Unit 22	3	1.5	3	1.2	6						
Unit 23	4	2.1	5	2.0	9	**GENDER**					
Central Plaza	4	2.1	20	7.9	24	Male	45	46.4	48	37.2	93
East Plaza	0	0	1	0.4	1	Female	52	53.6	81	62.8	133
Total	194		253		447	Total	97		129		226

$x^2 = 14.29682$, df = 8, $\alpha = 0.05$, $x^2 = 15.51$ not significant

$x^2 = 41.45880$, df = 16, $\alpha = 0.05$, $x^2 = 26.30$ significant

$x^2 = 1,9362$, df = 1, $\alpha = 0.05$, $x^2 = 3.84$ not significant

beneath the floor of residential quarters or plazas. Frequently, more than one individual was interred within a single grave facility. Some of these graves were sealed with adobe following the interment of a corpse, and others were simply filled with dirt. Grave goods associated with burials of this type consisted of jewelry fashioned from local material, utilitarian items, and pottery. No indicators of power and authority, as defined in the analysis, were associated with these burials. Furthermore, there was no evidence to suggest any additional postmortem processing of these dead. Occasionally, burials processed in this manner were interred within the fill of abandoned structures without grave goods of any kind.

In contrast, a few of the deceased were interred with a large diversity and quantity of grave accompaniments that included composite necklaces of turquoise, shell, ricolite, and slate ornaments; utilitarian items; socioreligious objects such as minerals and pigments; and numerous different types of ceramic vessels. Some of these burials were housed in subfloor tomblike graves that had been covered with board planks or cribbed log roofs. These specially prepared facilities also contained single and multiple burials. Decorated and undecorated ceramic handdrums were frequently found lying on top of these tombs, suggesting their use in the ritual burial of the deceased. Occasionally, disarticulated skeletons, interpreted by the excavators to represent secondary burials, were interred within these tombs in association with primary inhumations. The association of elaborate grave furnishings and specially prepared tombs suggests that these people may have belonged to a higher status group than those previously described.

Throughout the city, the disarticulated remains of single and multiple individuals were interred in simple earthen graves located beneath the floors of rooms and within the fill of abandoned rooms and plazas. Generally, these individuals were not associated with grave goods. However, many of the interments did exhibit evidence of postmortem handling, suggesting that they may have been secondary burials. The placement of these individuals within the society's status hierarchy is unclear. This mortuary patterning may represent temporally related diversity that occurred as a result of organizational changes within Casas Grandes society near the end of the Medio period.

The highest ranking individuals identified at Casas Grandes were interred within two specially prepared burial vaults that were housed within an elaborate mortuary-religious complex. The bodies of these deceased were initially left to decay, after which the disarticulated bones, minus skulls, were placed inside large Ramos Polychrome ceramic vessels. Indicators of power and authority among these individuals, in addition to the postmortem processing of their corpses, included the association of numerous rare accompaniments: a bone rasp fashioned from a human femur, a bone necklace composed of human phalange bones, and a trove of human long bones. These kinds of objects were not associated with any other burials.

In summary, this descriptive model of the Casas Grandes mortuary ritual program indicates that there was considerable variability with regard to certain treatments such as postmortem handling, grave associations with possible symbols of rank and authority, and grave facility preparation, which represent distinct categories of social status among the deceased. In the following chapter the hypothesis of the existence of ascriptive ranking at Casas Grandes during the Medio period is further evaluated through multivariate analyses of the defined variables of burial treatment.

CHAPTER SIX

A Multivariate Analysis of the Casas Grandes Burials

An initial description of the Casas Grandes mortuary program, presented in Chapter 5, indicated that several attributes of burial treatment crosscut demographic profiles and were restricted to burials interred at a few specific locales within the site. These attributes were identified as potential symbols of distinct offices of power and authority, suggesting that recruitment to positions within the decision-making hierarchy was based on principles of ascription. The hypothesis of ascriptive ranking is further evaluated through principal components analyses of the variables of Casas Grandes mortuary treatment.

The principal components factoring technique was selected as the most appropriate procedure with which to identify statistically significant dimensions of variability in the Casas Grandes mortuary program as indicated by the covariation of burial attributes. This multivariate technique reduces the correlation coefficients for a set of variables into a smaller number of factors or components. These factors are interpreted as source variables and describe the observed interrelationships in the data (Rummel 1967; Doran and Hodson 1975; Nie and others 1975).

The initial step in a factor analysis consists of preparing the correlation matrix. Most investigations of mortuary patterning that have used this technique rely on the Q-mode procedure of factor analysis to delineate subsets of a mortuary program that represent different social personae, while relatively few studies have utilized the R-mode procedure. The Q-mode procedure of factor analysis isolates clusters of units, whereas the R-mode technique generates clusters of redundant variables or properties. The R-mode technique has been selected for this analysis because this study attempts to isolate sets of covarying attributes that presumably define dimensions of differentiation in mortuary ritual treatment.

Principal components analysis reduces the correlation matrix into a set of components or factors that account for the variability present in the Casas Grandes data set. This technique has been adopted because it makes relatively few assumptions concerning the underlying structure of the variables. It transforms the original set of variables into a new set of composite variables, or principal components, that are uncorrelated or orthogonal (Nie and others 1975: 470). These components, termed eigenvectors, represent the correlations or associations that are present between the input variables. The resulting analysis defines as many components as there are variables in the data set. The first component is interpreted as the best summary of linear relationships among variables revealed in the data. The second component defines the combination of variables that account for the most variability remaining after the first component is removed, and so forth (Nie and others 1975: 470). Each of these components is associated with an "eigenvalue" that summarizes the total amount of variability that each factor or component accounts for within the data set.

Principal components analysis usually relies on the Pearson's "r" or product moment correlation coefficient to calculate the degree of relationship between two variables. The value of Pearson's "r" can range from $+1.0$, indicating a perfect association between two variables, to -1.0, which represents a perfect negative relationship. This correlation coefficient is known as phi (ϕ) when it is applied to dichotomous data, that is, presence or absence (Rummel 1967: 299; Doran and Hodson 1975: 147). The phi (ϕ) coefficient as a measure of association when applied to dichotomous data is affected by the marginal frequency distributions of individual attribute occurrence (Braun 1977, 1979; Cole 1949; Speth and Johnson 1976).

Braun (1977, 1979, 1981) suggested, on the basis of the arguments of Cole (1949) and Speth and Johnson (1976), that the correlation coefficient known as Cole's C_7 should be used rather than Pearson's "r" in a principal component analysis of mortuary treatment. This coefficient, which is algebraically equivalent to the ϕ/ϕ maximum equation, corrects the problem inherent when applying the phi (ϕ) coefficient to dichotomous variables. The ϕ/ϕ maximum equation divides observed phi (ϕ) by the largest positive or negative value possible for each pair of variables. Speth and Johnson (1976) provide a formula to calculate ϕ maximum ($+$) and ϕ maximum ($-$) that may be used to obtain the maximum phi value for any pairwise comparison.

The use of this coefficient ensures that all variables of mortuary treatment are weighted equally regardless of their relative frequencies of occurrence (that is, whether they are rare or common). The replacement of phi (ϕ) with ϕ/ϕ maximum or Cole's C_7 coefficient with the use of mortuary data permits the extraction of eigenvectors representing dimensions of covariation of burial variables that are related to frequency of individual occurrence. This approach may introduce logical redundancies within the analysis but was required since the possibility existed that alternative states

Table 6.1. Principal Components Output Matrix (not rotated)

	FACTOR 1	FACTOR 2	FACTOR 3	FACTOR 4	FACTOR 5	FACTOR 6	FACTOR 7	FACTOR 8	FACTOR 9	FACTOR 10
VAR05	0.00966	0.00713	0.17330	−0.60927	0.28939	0.27274	−0.02880	0.04229	0.19070	−0.15673
VAR06	0.02920	0.07486	0.17699	−0.49597	0.10817	0.25200	0.21564	−0.17190	−0.32172	0.36655
VAR07	−0.68101	0.64135	−0.32745	0.88452	−0.13058	−0.18089	0.02349	0.04925	0.15703	−0.06996
VAR08	0.62800	0.36994	0.24652	−0.26498	0.62277	−0.33147	−0.27178	−0.07457	0.00450	−0.15147
VAR09	−0.21723	0.28268	0.32093	−0.26622	0.40161	−0.19076	−0.30933	−0.09598	0.53399	0.06075
VAR10	0.05334	−0.10710	0.32177	−0.15302	0.30096	0.37964	0.26375	0.03823	−0.12234	−0.50363
VAR11	−0.17001	0.29191	−0.25119	0.11999	−0.15550	−0.13665	0.17251	0.56416	−0.02939	−0.09528
VAR12	−0.27726	0.15297	0.21364	0.10572	−0.21034	0.18461	−0.02072	0.05923	−0.23127	0.45795
VAR13	0.04408	0.20442	−0.43164	0.39403	0.02606	0.03443	0.20245	−0.51670	−0.16267	−0.14007
VAR14	−0.56652	0.66564	−0.00560	0.14017	0.36618	0.20402	0.01449	−0.12383	−0.08325	−0.12629
VAR15	0.56650	−0.66562	0.00563	−0.14020	−0.36611	−0.20406	−0.01457	0.12380	0.08341	0.12631
VAR16	0.75411	−0.15536	0.44317	−0.16717	−0.79563	−0.23230	0.10118	−0.12885	0.08748	−0.17125
VAR17	0.66093	0.11740	0.18299	0.44345	0.36970	0.00156	−0.01304	0.07938	−0.08325	−0.15468
VAR18	−0.25256	0.17126	−1.13983	−0.70198	0.00452	−0.12628	0.18180	0.07694	0.01318	−0.02309
VAR19	0.36151	−0.12648	0.00625	0.50751	0.18508	0.08508	0.12980	−0.11924	0.02818	0.33231
VAR20	0.04754	−0.19189	0.49118	−0.09437	0.14282	0.08980	0.13413	−0.07380	−0.43612	0.08353
VAR21	−0.34133	−0.12071	0.16060	0.09914	−0.27093	0.57174	−0.72187	0.01164	0.16069	−0.14087
VAR22	−0.49445	0.09245	0.66097	0.26123	0.00293	−0.51925	0.09501	0.30881	−0.23625	−0.03157
VAR23	−0.29319	0.00473	0.60659	0.06083	0.11059	−0.17585	0.42205	−0.26414	0.43642	0.21852
VAR24	−0.72515	0.53608	0.48146	−0.30822	−0.19547	−0.06781	0.00855	−0.08254	−0.09342	−0.05596
VAR25	0.72516	−0.53608	−0.48148	0.30822	0.19547	0.06784	−0.00855	0.08252	0.09343	0.05596
VAR26	0.04290	0.06903	0.00403	0.43345	0.02523	0.39670	0.17949	−0.16168	−0.10903	−0.15001
VAR27	−0.06454	0.09588	0.26542	0.04679	0.26414	−0.18347	−0.00232	0.44959	−0.16582	−0.17400
VAR28	−0.14381	0.13141	0.02027	0.03754	0.00972	0.13957	−0.05187	−0.03670	0.28028	0.26703
VAR29	−0.13958	0.17626	−0.04722	−0.20526	−0.06658	0.03177	0.35654	−0.18972	−0.23185	−0.20224
VAR30	−0.23055	0.08961	−0.09146	0.11224	−0.09065	0.00549	0.10152	0.02760	0.15377	−0.34514
VAR31	−0.04585	0.24895	−0.05296	−0.00755	0.01008	0.06127	−0.12129	−0.21471	0.19523	−0.06214
VAR32	−0.14767	0.27934	−0.11170	0.06581	−0.00334	−0.27514	−0.55236	−0.05151	−0.28538	0.13500
VAR33	−0.10775	0.18668	0.10096	0.08773	0.06861	−0.01216	0.49702	−0.11773	0.33919	0.17535
VAR34	−0.93062	−0.99436	0.07867	−0.01322	0.09550	−0.14126	0.04421	0.06178	0.01982	0.04265
VAR35	0.75542	−0.11352	0.11740	0.28980	0.47497	−0.06550	0.04879	0.11919	0.04050	0.06072
VAR36	0.36477	0.57037	0.27162	−0.02927	−0.25696	0.18547	0.08912	0.20793	0.24196	−0.06735
VAR37	0.30058	0.54447	−0.03698	−0.10082	−0.01051	0.23351	0.20465	0.41530	0.15607	−0.04087
VAR38	0.42645	0.53530	−0.03067	−0.16351	−0.36102	−0.37716	0.05868	−0.27566	0.00271	−0.26167
VAR39	0.24384	0.67852	−0.25264	−0.12948	0.08967	−0.19910	−0.09329	−0.09493	−0.07883	0.21205
VAR40	0.20182	0.59880	0.09418	−0.12121	−0.04906	0.30072	−0.09147	0.07060	−0.08871	0.15911
VAR41	0.19926	0.58233	−0.04347	−0.08957	−0.12129	0.23009	0.18914	0.40152	0.02842	0.32296
VAR42	0.28321	0.62156	−0.05175	−0.04803	0.11985	−0.21955	−0.11614	−0.12243	−0.12919	0.15246
VAR43	0.42571	0.35176	0.34280	0.26783	−0.44901	0.16351	−0.14534	−0.10451	−0.06686	−0.03394

of burial treatment could symbolize mutually exclusive social identities. The introduction of logical redundancies among
variables will result in the generation of correlation matrices
that contain some imaginary variance (Rummel 1970: 260).
This variance is acceptable and will not statistically inval-
idate the results of the analysis. Davis (1973: 127–168,
473–500) provides additional rationale and validity for the
use of the φ/φ maximum association matrix.

PRINCIPAL COMPONENTS ANALYSIS

The hypothesized existence of ascriptive ranking at Casas

Grandes was evaluated through a principal component analysis using the SPSS Factor Program (Nie and others 1975:
468–514) on variables 5 through 43 (Table 5.8) for burial
cases 1 through 447. Principal components were generated
separately using the φ/φ maximum correlation coefficient
as input data (Ravesloot 1987). The factor matrix output
generated for the first ten components is presented in Table
6.1. The eigenvalues for these components are illustrated
in a histogram (Fig. 6.1), and an examination of them suggests that eigenvectors 1 and 2 appear to be relatively more
significant than the other eigenvectors. The first ten eigenvectors generated represent over 80 percent of the observed
variability.

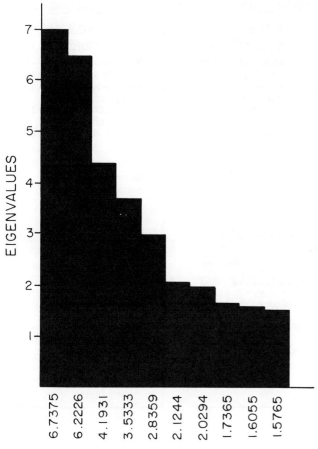

Figure 6.1. Histograms of eigenvalues.

The principal components analysis utilizing the ϕ/ϕ maximum correlation coefficient isolated three significant dimensions of covariation among the variables in the mortuary program (Table 6.2, Fig. 6.2). The positive loadings within the eigenvector represent significant covariation in associations among variables of burial treatment, whereas the negative loadings indicate disassociation with the positively loaded variables that comprise this dimension.

Crossplots of variables generated for the three dimensions are presented in Figure 6.3. These crossplots of variables may be used to describe the degree of correlation among components, to illustrate the positive and negative loadings of variables as indicated by the factor matrix output, and to define clusters of covarying variables (Nie and others 1975: 486–487). In addition, it should be noted that variables that cluster near the intersect of the two axes possess small loadings on both dimensions. The crossplots identified several clusters of covarying variables. The crossplot of dimensions I and II indicates a positive association among all eight of the artifact categories (Table 5.8, variables 36–43). In addition, flexed interments, single burials, and primary inhumations also form a definite cluster (Fig. 6.3*a*).

Component Scores

Dimensions I, II, and III were further examined by generating component scores for each burial (Appendix C) and comparing these scores with the variables of unit association, age, and gender. Component scores were computed for each dimension on the basis of the factor score coefficient matrix (Appendix D) that was produced during the principal components analysis of attributes 5 through 43 (see SPSS Factor programs, Nie and others 1975: 487–789, for a summary of the procedure for calculating component scores). Figure 6.4 displays in histogram form the distribution of these scores for each dimension. These histograms indicate that relatively few burials possess a high positive score (greater than +1.0) for any of the dimensions. A high positive score for a burial would mean that the individual possessed "full inclusion" with the variables of the mortuary program that loaded positively for the eigenvector in question. For example, the dimension I positive variables include burial vault, room subfloor tomb, secondary burial, multiple burial, legs frogged, ceramic handdrums, and, to a lesser extent, polychrome ceramics and rare accompaniments (Table 6.2). A high negative score for dimension I would mean that the individual was disassociated with these positive loaded variables (Braun 1977: 300; Orser 1980: 236–237).

The component scores for each dimension were subdivided into negative, neutral, and positive groupings in order to compute frequencies of similar scoring burials that could be compared to the variables of unit, age, and gender. This subdivision was performed on the basis of apparent modalities in the histograms of scores for each dimension (Fig. 6.4). The component score ranges for dimensions I through III are listed in Table 6.3, and Table 6.4 presents the frequencies of positive, neutral, and negative scoring burials by each dimension. Positive scoring burials represent approximately three percent of the total population for dimension I and three percent for dimension II. The low percentage of burials occurring in the positively loaded segments for these two dimensions corresponds well with the proposition that individuals receiving preferred burial treatment should comprise a small portion of the population.

Component score segments for each dimension were cross-tabulated with the variables of unit association, age, and gender and chi-square values were computed (Tables 6.5–6.11). The cross-tabulation of the component scores by gender did not include the categories of subadult and indeterminate; their inclusion would have resulted in testing for age as well as gender associations. Chi-square tests revealed a number of significant associations for each of the defined dimensions and these variables.

For the variable of unit association for dimension I, all burials possessing a positive score were interred in either Unit 4 (The Mound of the Offerings) or Unit 13 (The House

Table 6.2. Positive and Negative Variable Loadings for Dimensions I, II, and III from the Principal Components Analysis

Dimension	Casas Grandes Burial Numbers*	◊◊ Maximum Positive Loadings	◊◊ Maximum Negative Loadings
I	CG 2–4, 3–4, 4–4, 28–13, 44A–13, 44B–13, 44D–13, 44E–13, 44H–13, 44I–13, 44J–13, 44K–13, 44L–13	Ceramic handdrums with grave facility Burial vault Multiple burial Room subfloor tomb Legs frogged Secondary burial Polychrome ceramics Rare accompaniments	No accompaniments Single burial Flexed interment Primary inhumation Plaza subfloor unsealed grave pits
II	CG 3–1, 24–1, 28–1, 34–6, 13–13, 24–13, 40–13, 44A–13, 44E–13, 66–13, 13–14, 10–16, 21–16, 25–16	Nonpolychrome ceramics Primary inhumation Flexed interment Vegetal accompaniments Utilitarian accompaniments Socioreligious accompaniments Jewelry of local material Jewelry of nonlocal material Single burial Polychrome ceramics	No accompaniments Secondary burial Multiple burial
III	CG 28–1, 34–6, 36–6, 37–6, 42–6, 19–8, 35–11, 45–11, 49–11, 50–11, 51–11, 52–11, 54–11, 55–11, 56–11, 10A–11, 14–12, 24–12, 25–12, 36–12, 37–12, 17–13, 21–13, 44D–13, 57–13, 84–13, 8–14, 9–14, 37–14, 38–14, 39–14, 40–14, 41–14, 50–14, 51–14, 8–16, 4–21, 1–22, 3–23, 10–CP	Plaza subfloor unsealed grave pits Plaza fill Room fill Single burial	Room subfloor sealed grave pits Multiple burial Interred in sitting position Flexed interment

*CG burial numbers are for Positive Loadings only

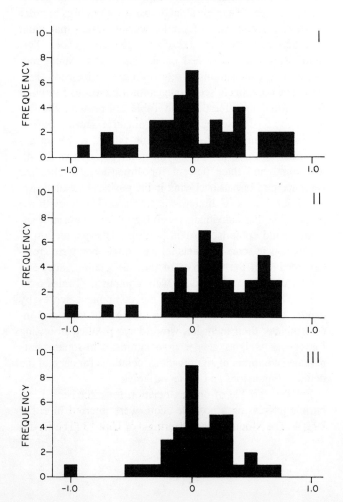

Table 6.3. Component Score Ranges for Dimensions I, II, and III

Dimension	Range		
	Positive	Neutral	Negative
I	3.335 to 1.600	1.600 to −0.200	−0.200 to −1.391
II	2.921 to 1.400	1.400 to −0.400	−0.400 to −1.507
III	2.263 to 0.800	0.800 to −0.400	−0.400 to −1.198

Table 6.4. Frequencies of Component Scores for Dimensions I, II, and III

Loadings	Frequency	Percent
Dimension I		
Negative	197	44.1
Neutral	237	53.0
Positive	13	2.9
Dimension II		
Negative	109	24.4
Neutral	324	72.5
Positive	14	3.1
Dimension III		
Negative	152	34.0
Neutral	255	57.1
Positive	40	8.9

Figure 6.2. Histograms of eigenvector loadings for dimensions I, II, and III.

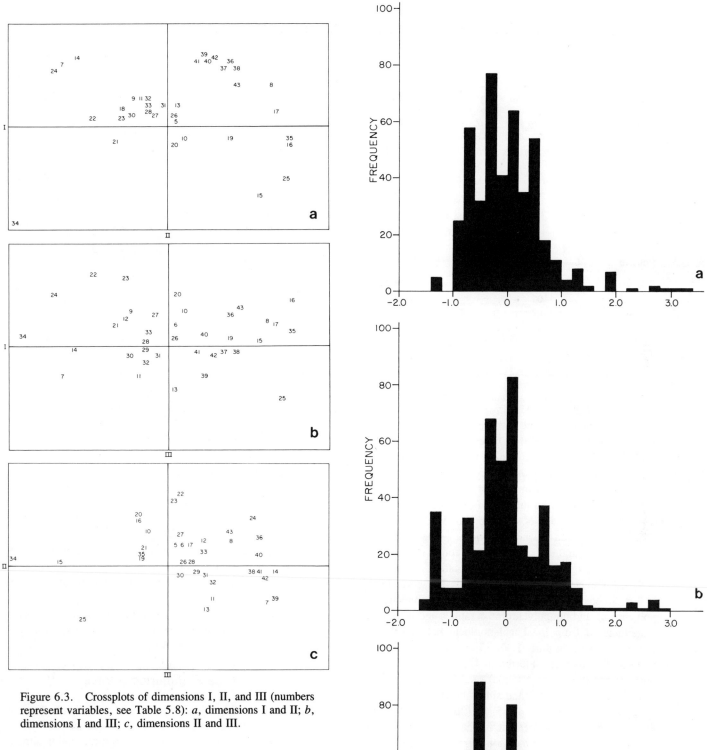

Figure 6.3.   Crossplots of dimensions I, II, and III (numbers represent variables, see Table 5.8): *a*, dimensions I and II; *b*, dimensions I and III; *c*, dimensions II and III.

Figure 6.4.   Histograms of component scores: *a*, dimension I; *b*, dimension II; *c*, dimension III.

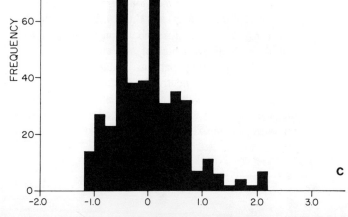

Table 6.5. Component Scores by Architectural Unit Association for Dimension I

Loadings	Architectural Unit															Central Plaza	East Plaza	Total	%
	1	4	6	8	11	12	13	14	15	16	19	20	21	22	23	Central Plaza	East Plaza	Total	%
Negative	8	0	24	23	25	13	45	17	2	5	2	4	1	4	7	16	1	197	44.1
Row %	4.1		12.2	11.7	12.7	6.6	22.9	8.6	1.0	2.5	1.0	2.0	0.5	2.0	3.6	8.1	0.5		
Column %	24.2		41.4	54.8	55.6	34.2	43.3	40.5	28.6	35.7	25.0	50.0	20.0	66.7	77.8	66.7	100		
Total %	1.8		5.3	5.1	5.5	2.9	10.0	3.8	0.4	1.1	0.4	0.9	0.2	0.9	1.6	3.6	0.2		
Neutral	25	0	34	19	20	25	49	25	5	9	6	4	4	2	2	8	0	237	53.0
Row %	10.5		14.4	8.0	8.4	10.6	20.7	10.6	2.1	3.8	2.5	1.7	1.7	0.8	0.8	3.4			
Column %	75.8		58.6	45.2	44.4	65.8	47.1	59.5	71.4	64.3	75.0	50.0	80.0	33.3	22.2	33.3			
Total %	5.6		7.6	4.3	4.5	5.6	10.9	5.6	1.1	2.0	1.3	0.9	0.9	0.9	0.4	1.8			
Positive	0	3	0	0	0	0	10	0	0	0	0	0	0	0	0	0	0	13	2.9
Row %		23.1					76.9												
Column %		100					9.6												
Total %		0.7					2.2												
Total	33	3	58	42	45	38	104	42	7	14	8	8	5	6	9	24	1	447	

$x^2 = 154.46790$, df = 32, $\alpha = 0.05$, $x^2 = 46.19$, significant

of the Dead; Table 6.5). This distribution of positively scoring burials for dimension I was expected, because it was proposed on the basis of the Di Peso, Rinaldo, and Fenner (Vol. 8: 325–412) description of the Casas Grandes mortuary program that individuals accorded the most elaborate burial treatment (for example, burial vault, room subfloor tomb, and secondary burial) would be associated with these two units. The remainder of the burials were fairly evenly distributed between the neutral and negative score ranges for all architectural units, with the exception of Unit 4. The cross-tabulation of dimension II with location was significant at the 0.05 level (Table 6.6). Individuals that scored positive in this dimension (that is, single, flexed, accompanied with polychrome and nonpolychrome ceramics and with jewelry manufactured from local and nonlocal raw material; *see* Table 6.2) were in units 1, 6, 13, 14, and 16. Six (43%) of these burials were interred in Unit 13. Burials scoring positive for dimension III (plaza subfloor unsealed grave pit, plaza fill, room fill, and single burial) were found interred in all units except 4, 15, 19, 20, and the East Plaza (Table 6.7). Over 40 percent of the burials possessing a positive score for this dimension were associated with Unit 11 (House of the Serpent) and Unit 14 (House of the Pillars).

The results of the cross-tabulation of dimensions I, II, and III with the variables of age and gender revealed a number of interesting patterns (Tables 6.8, 6.9). Burials scoring negative and neutral for dimension I crosscut all age categories, whereas the opposite occurred for positive scoring ones (Table 6.8). Middle-aged adults (36 to 50 years) represented approximately 46 percent of positive scoring

burials, whereas adolescents (4, or 31%), young adults (1, or 8%), and old adults (2, or 15%) made up the balance. Infants, children, and juveniles were absent from this score range. The age distribution for dimension I is statistically significant at the 0.05 level (Table 6.9).

In dimension II, children (4, or 28%), young adults (4, or 28%), old adults (3, or 21%), middle-aged adults (2, or 14%), and questionable adults (1, or 7%) were represented within the positive score range, whereas infants, juveniles, and adolescents were absent (Table 6.8). Five of these burials were identified as adult males; three were females. In contrast, the negative and neutral segments for this dimension crosscut both age and gender lines.

In general, the positive, neutral, and negative scoring burials defined for dimension III crosscut both age and gender categories (Tables 6.8, 6.9).

Type 2: Unburied Bodies

Prior to discussing additional implications of this study, it is necessary to review those burials classified as Type 2 (cases 448–572) in relationship to the three major dimensions of status differentiation isolated through the principal components analysis of burial cases 1 through 447. The Type 2 unburied bodies were investigated by computing component scores for each individual for dimensions I, II, and III. Component scores were generated using the factor score coefficient matrix that was produced through the principal components analysis of attributes 5 through 43 (Table 5.8).

Table 6.6. Component Scores by Architectural Unit Association for Dimension II

Loadings								Architectural Unit									Central Plaza	East Plaza	Total	%
	1	4	6	8	11	12	13	14	15	16	19	20	21	22	23				
Negative	12	2	14	14	13	12	17	7	4	1	2	3	2	0	0	6	0	109	24.4
Row %	11.0	1.8	12.9	12.9	11.9	11.0	15.6	6.4	3.7	0.9	1.8	2.8	1.8			5.5			
Column %	36.4	66.7	24.1	33.3	28.9	31.6	16.3	16.7	57.1	7.2	25.0	37.5	40.0			25.0			
Total %	2.7	0.4	3.1	3.1	2.9	2.7	3.8	1.6	0.9	0.2	0.4	0.7	0.4			1.3			
Neutral	18	1	43	28	32	26	81	34	3	10	6	5	3	6	9	18	1	324	72.5
Row %	5.6	0.3	13.2	8.6	9.9	8.0	25.0	10.5	0.9	3.1	1.9	1.5	0.9	1.9	2.8	5.6	0.3		
Column %	54.5	33.3	74.1	66.7	71.1	68.4	77.9	80.9	42.9	71.4	75.0	62.5	60.0	100	100	75.0	100		
Total %	4.1	0.2	9.7	6.3	7.2	5.8	18.2	7.6	0.7	2.2	1.3	1.1	0.7	1.3	2.0	4.1	0.2		
Positive	3	0	1	0	0	0	6	1	0	3	0	0	0	0	0	0	0	14	3.1
Row %	21.4		7.1				42.9	7.1		21.4									
Column %	9.1		1.7				5.8	2.4		21.4									
Total %	0.7		0.2				1.3	0.2		0.7									
Total	33	3	58	42	45	38	104	42	7	14	8	8	5	6	9	24	1	447	

$x^2 = 53.85518$, df = 32, $\alpha = 0.05$, $x^2 = 46.19$, significant

Table 6.7. Component Scores by Architectural Unit Association for Dimension III

Loadings								Architectural Unit									Central Plaza	East Plaza	Total	%
	1	4	6	8	11	12	13	14	15	16	19	20	21	22	23				
Negative	17	0	26	12	18	9	37	12	3	4	5	6	3	0	0	0	0	152	34.0
Row %	11.2		17.1	7.9	11.9	5.9	24.3	7.9	2.0	2.6	3.3	3.9	2.0						
Column %	51.5		44.8	28.6	40.0	23.7	35.6	28.6	42.9	28.6	62.5	75.0	60.0						
Total %	3.8		5.8	2.7	4.0	2.0	8.3	2.7	0.7	0.9	1.1	1.4	0.7						
Neutral	15	3	28	29	18	24	61	21	4	9	3	2	1	5	8	23	1	255	57.1
Row %	5.9	1.2	11.0	11.4	7.1	9.4	23.9	8.1	1.6	3.5	1.2	0.8	0.4	2.0	3.1	9.0	0.4		
Column %	45.5	100	48.3	69.0	40.0	63.1	58.6	50.0	57.1	64.3	37.5	25.0	20.0	83.3	88.9	95.8	100		
Total %	3.4	0.7	6.3	6.5	4.0	5.4	13.7	4.7	0.9	2.0	0.7	0.4	0.2	1.1	1.8	5.1	0.2		
Positive	1	0	4	1	9	5	6	9	0	1	0	0	1	1	1	1	0	40	8.9
Row %	2.5		10.0	2.5	22.5	12.5	15.0	22.5		2.5			2.5	2.5	2.5	2.5			
Column %	3.0		6.9	2.4	20.0	13.2	5.8	21.4		7.1			20.0	16.7	11.1	4.2			
Total %	0.2		0.9	0.2	2.0	1.1	1.4	2.0		0.2			0.2	0.2	0.2	0.2			
Total	33	3	58	42	45	38	104	42	7	14	8	8	5	6	9	24	1	447	

$x^2 = 71.21448$, df = 32, $\alpha = 0.05$, $x^2 = 46.19$, significant

Component scores for the three dimensions were subdivided into negative, neutral, and positive segments on the basis of apparent modalities in the histograms for these dimensions and the segment ranges, as for burial cases 1 through 447, are listed in Table 6.3. These segments were used to compute frequencies of like-scoring burials for each dimension and to compare them with the variables of unit, age, and gender. Table 6.10 presents the frequencies of positive, neutral, and negative scoring of Type 2 unburied bodies computed for each dimension.

These frequencies indicate that the Type 2 unburied bodies scored positive only for dimension III (that is, plaza fill,

Table 6.8. Component Scores by Age for Dimensions I, II, and III

Loadings	Infant	Child	Juvenile	Adolescent	?Subadult	Young Adult	Middle-aged Adult	Old Adult	?Adult	Total	%
DIMENSION I											
Negative	18	28	10	15	3	58	27	15	23	197	44.1
Row %	9.1	14.2	5.1	7.6	1.5	29.5	13.7	7.6	11.7		
Column %	28.6	43.8	40.0	46.9	42.9	55.2	38.0	53.6	44.2		
Total %	4.0	6.3	2.2	3.4	0.7	13.0	6.0	3.4	5.1		
Neutral	45	36	15	13	4	46	38	11	29	237	53.0
Row %	19.0	15.2	6.3	5.5	1.7	19.5	16.0	4.6	12.2		
Column %	71.4	56.2	60.0	40.6	57.1	43.8	53.5	39.3	55.8		
Total %	10.1	8.1	3.4	2.9	0.9	10.2	8.5	2.5	6.5		
Positive	0	0	0	4	0	1	6	2	0	13	2.9
Row %				30.8		7.7	46.1	15.4			
Column %				12.5		1.0	8.5	7.1			
Total %				0.9		0.2	1.3	0.4			
Total	63	64	25	32	7	105	71	28	52	447	

($x^2 = 42.67404$, df = 16, $\alpha = 0.05$, $x^2 = 26.30$, significant)

Loadings	Infant	Child	Juvenile	Adolescent	?Subadult	Young Adult	Middle-aged Adult	Old Adult	?Adult	Total	%
DIMENSION II											
Negative	19	18	10	13	2	17	9	3	18	109	24.4
Row %	17.4	16.5	9.2	11.9	1.8	15.6	8.3	2.8	16.5		
Column %	30.2	28.1	40.0	40.6	28.6	16.2	12.7	10.7	34.6		
Total %	4.3	4.1	2.2	2.9	0.4	3.8	2.0	0.7	4.1		
Neutral	44	42	15	19	5	84	60	22	33	324	72.5
Row %	13.6	13.0	4.6	5.9	1.5	25.9	18.5	6.8	10.2		
Column %	69.0	65.6	60.0	59.4	71.4	80.0	84.5	78.6	63.5		
Total %	9.9	9.4	3.4	4.3	1.1	18.8	13.5	4.9	7.4		
Positive	0	4	0	0	0	4	2	3	1	14	3.1
Row %		28.6				28.6	14.3	21.4	7.1		
Column %		6.3				3.8	2.8	10.7	1.9		
Total %		0.9				0.9	0.4	0.4	0.2		
Total	63	64	25	32	7	105	71	28	52	447	

($x^2 = 34.75830$, df = 16, $\alpha = 0.05$, $x^2 = 26.30$, significant)

Loadings	Infant	Child	Juvenile	Adolescent	?Subadult	Young Adult	Middle-aged Adult	Old Adult	?Adult	Total	%
DIMENSION III											
Negative	27	25	8	9	2	34	22	12	13	152	34.0
Row %	17.8	16.5	5.3	5.9	1.3	22.4	14.5	7.9	8.6		
Column %	42.8	39.1	32.0	28.1	28.6	32.4	31.0	42.9	25.0		
Total %	6.0	5.6	1.8	2.0	0.4	7.6	4.9	2.7	2.9		
Neutral	34	37	15	19	4	59	39	12	36	255	57.1
Row %	13.3	14.5	5.9	7.5	1.6	23.1	15.3	4.7	14.1		
Column %	54.0	57.8	60.0	59.4	57.1	56.2	54.9	42.9	69.2		
Total %	7.6	8.3	3.4	4.3	0.9	13.2	8.8	2.7	8.1		
Positive	2	2	2	4	1	12	10	4	3	40	8.9
Row %	5.0	5.0	5.0	10.0	2.5	30.0	25.0	10.0	7.5		
Column %	3.2	3.1	8.0	12.5	14.3	11.4	14.1	14.2	5.8		
Total %	0.4	0.4	0.4	0.9	0.2	2.7	2.2	0.9	0.7		
Total	63	64	25	32	7	105	71	28	52	447	

($x^2 = 16.86136$, df = 16, $\alpha = 0.05$, $x^2 = 26.30$, not significant)

Table 6.9. Component Scores by Gender for Dimensions I, II, and III

Loadings	Gender		Total
	Male	Female	
Dimension I			
Negative	45	67	112
Neutral	44	62	106
Positive	4	4	8
	93	133	226

$x^2 = 0.20304$, df $= 2$, $\alpha = 0.05$, $x^2 = 5.99$

Loadings	Male	Female	Total
Dimension II			
Negative	13	24	37
Neutral	75	106	181
Positive	5	3	8
	93	133	226

$x^2 = 2.0535$, df $= 2$, $\alpha = 0.05$, $x^2 = 5.99$

Loadings	Male	Female	Total
Dimension III			
Negative	29	43	72
Neutral	50	77	127
Positive	14	13	27
	93	133	226

$x^2 = 1.47195$, df $= 2$, $\alpha = 0.05$, $x^2 = 5.99$

Table 6.10. Frequencies of Component Scores by Dimension for Type 2 Unburied Bodies

Dimension		Frequency	%
I	Negative	61	48.8
	Neutral	64	51.2
	Total	125	
II	Negative	125	100.0
III	Neutral	55	44.0
	Positive	70	56.0
	Total	125	

room fill, plaza unsealed grave pit, and single burial). Tables 6.11 through 6.13 present the results of the cross-tabulation of the positive, negative, and neutral scoring segments with the variables of unit, age, and gender. These chi-square tests reveal that significant associations occur only between the cross-tabulation of dimensions I and III and the variable of unit association.

Table 6.11. Component Scores by Architectural Unit Association for Dimensions I and III, Type 2 Unburied Bodies

Loadings	Architectural Unit																Central Plaza	East Plaza	Total	%
	1	4	6	8	11	12	13	14	15	16	18	19	20	21	22	23				
DIMENSION I																				
Negative	12	0	4	8	19	4	7	7	3	0	0	0	0	0	0	0	0	0	64	48.8
Row %	18.7		6.3	12.5	29.7	6.3	10.9	10.9	4.7											
Column %	75.0		40.0	57.1	90.5	36.4	58.3	38.9	50.0											
Total %	9.6		3.2	6.4	15.2	3.2	5.6	5.6	2.4											
Neutral	4	2	6	6	2	7	5	11	3	9	1	1	0	0	0	0	4	0	61	51.2
Row %	6.5	3.3	9.8	9.8	3.3	11.6	8.2	18.1	4.9	14.8	1.6	1.6					6.5			
Column %	25.0	100	60.0	42.9	9.5	63.6	41.7	61.1	50.0	100	100	100					100			
Total %	3.2	1.6	4.8	4.8	1.6	5.6	4.0	8.8	2.4	7.2	0.8	0.8					3.2			
Total	16	2	10	14	21	11	12	18	6	9	1	1	0	0	0	0	4	0	125	

($x^2 = 35.0511$, df $= 17$, $\alpha = 0.05$, $x^2 = 27.59$, significant)

Loadings	1	4	6	8	11	12	13	14	15	16	18	19	20	21	22	23	Central Plaza	East Plaza	Total	%
DIMENSION III																				
Neutral	12	0	5	8	19	0	6	5	0	0	0	0	0	0	0	0	0	0	55	44.0
Row %	21.8		9.1	14.5	34.6		10.9	9.1												
Column %	75.0		50.0	57.1	90.5		50.0	27.8												
Total %	9.6		4.0	6.4	15.2		4.8	4.0												
Positive	4	2	5	6	2	11	6	13	6	9	1	1	0	0	0	0	4	0	70	56.0
Row %	5.7	2.9	7.1	8.6	2.9	15.8	8.6	18.7	8.6	12.6	1.4	1.4					5.7			
Column %	25.0	100	50.0	42.9	9.5	100	50.0	72.2	100	100	100	100					100			
Total %	3.2	1.6	4.0	4.8	1.6	8.8	4.8	10.4	4.8	7.2	0.8	0.8					3.2			
Total	16	2	10	14	21	11	12	18	6	9	1	1	0	0	0	0	4	0	125	

($x^2 = 52.82869$, df $= 17$, $\alpha = 0.05$, $x^2 = 27.59$, significant)

Table 6.12. Component Scores by Age for Dimensions I and III, Type 2 Unburied Bodies

Loadings	Infant	Child	Juvenile	Adolescent	?Subadult	Young Adult	Middle-aged Adult	Old Adult	?Adult	Total	%
DIMENSION I											
Negative	3	2	2	4	1	19	3	1	26	61	48.8
Row %	4.9	3.3	3.3	6.6	1.6	31.1	4.9	1.6	42.7		
Column %	27.3	25.0	28.6	57.1	33.3	52.8	42.9	33.3	60.5		
Total %	2.4	1.6	1.6	3.2	0.8	15.2	2.4	0.8	20.8		
Neutral	8	6	5	3	2	17	4	2	17	64	51.2
Row %	12.4	9.4	7.8	4.7	3.1	26.6	6.3	3.1	26.6		
Column %	72.7	75.0	71.4	42.9	66.7	47.2	57.1	66.7	39.5		
Total %	6.4	4.8	4.0	2.4	1.6	13.6	3.2	1.6	13.6		
Total	11	8	7	7	3	36	7	3	43	125	

($x^2 = 8.41026$, df = 8, $\alpha = 0.05$, $x^2 = 15.51$, not significant)

Loadings	Infant	Child	Juvenile	Adolescent	?Subadult	Young Adult	Middle-aged Adult	Old Adult	?Adult	Total	%
DIMENSION III											
Neutral	6	5	4	3	1	15	4	1	16	55	44.0
Row %	10.9	9.1	7.3	5.3	1.8	27.3	7.3	1.8	29.2		
Column %	54.6	62.5	57.1	42.9	33.3	41.7	57.1	33.3	37.2		
Total %	4.8	4.0	3.2	2.4	0.8	12.0	3.2	0.8	12.8		
Positive	5	3	3	4	2	21	3	2	27	70	56.0
Row %	7.1	4.3	4.3	5.7	2.9	30.0	4.3	2.9	38.5		
Column %	45.4	37.5	42.9	57.1	66.7	58.3	42.9	66.7	62.8		
Total %	4.0	2.4	2.4	3.2	1.6	16.8	2.4	1.6	21.6		
Total	11	8	7	7	3	36	7	3	43	125	

($x^2 = 3.7538$, df = 8, $\alpha = 0.05$, $x^2 = 15.51$, not significant)

Table 6.13. Component Scores by Gender for Dimensions I, II, and III, Type 2 Unburied Bodies

	Gender		
Loadings	Male	Female	Total
DIMENSION I			
Negative	8	20	28
Neutral	9	16	25
Total	17	36	53

$x^2 = 0.34$, df = 1, $\alpha = 0.05$, $x^2 = 3.84$

	Gender		
DIMENSION II			
Negative	17	36	53
DIMENSION III			
Neutral	8	15	23
Positive	9	21	30
Total	17	36	53

$x^2 = 0.13$, df = 1, $\alpha = 0.05$, $x^2 = 0.384$

EVALUATION OF THE HYPOTHESIS OF ASCRIPTIVE RANKING

The results of the principal components analyses of the 39 variables of mortuary treatment suggest that a system of social ranking based on inheritance probably operated at Casas Grandes during the Medio period. An examination of the first eigenvector or dimension generated through the principal components analysis indicates that those variables of burial treatment that were defined as potential status-specific symbols of rank and authority do covary. These burial variables include: secondary burial, legs frogged, burial vault, room subfloor tomb, ceramic handdrums, polychrome ceramics, and rare accompaniments. Relatively few (13, or 2.9%) Casas Grandians in the available sample were accorded such elaborate mortuary treatment. Furthermore, the computation of component burial scores for this dimension indicates that access to this burial treatment was not limited solely to mature adults, specifically males, but equally included females and adolescents.

The second dimension of differentiation isolated covariation among the following variables of Casas Grandes mortuary treatment: primary inhumation, single burial, flexed interment, nonpolychrome and polychrome ceramics, jewelry manufactured from local and nonlocal material and socioreligious, vegetal, and utilitarian accompaniments. This dimension, which included two of the postulated symbols of rank, excluded infants, juveniles, and adolescents. Access to these attributes of mortuary treatment was restricted primarily to adults, but not exclusively to males. The absence of individuals aged 6 to 17 years means that access to this dimension of burial treatment may have been based on achievement rather than ascription.

The third dimension of differentiation isolated positive covariation among the following variables: plaza subfloor unsealed grave pits, plaza and room fill, and single interments. Access to this dimension of differentiation was not restricted to any age category, and adult males and females were equally represented.

Additional implications of these analyses, including consideration of the "deliberate" and "unburied bodies" and alternative explanations for these mortuary patterns are discussed in Chapter 7.

CHAPTER SEVEN

The Social Dimensions of Casas Grandes Mortuary Variability

Through the analysis of mortuary practices, this study has attempted to define dimensions of social differentiation that separated members of Casas Grandes society into different social positions of rank and authority within the decision-making hierarchy. Not all members of Casas Grandes society were treated in the same manner at death, and a major assumption of this study was that social status distinctions would be symbolized by the variability in mortuary treatment. This assumption provided the means with which to link social organization to variability in mortuary treatment. Specifically, the hypothesis that Casas Grandes society was organized hierarchically on the basis of ascriptive social ranking during the Medio period (A.D. 1200 to 1450?; Ravesloot and others 1986) was tested.

The theoretical framework underlying this research was based on theories concerning the functioning of contemporary hierarchically structured organizations and the sociological analysis of mortuary ritual behavior. Casas Grandes society was viewed as a formal organization in order to make use of concepts concerning the general properties of hierarchically structured organizations. These include vertical differentiation and levels of authority, concepts that can be behaviorally defined and inferred with archaeological data. This uniformitarian view of prehistoric social systems provides an approach to the study of social variation that emphasizes the measurement of abstract organizational variables rather than merely the classification of social variability. Unfortunately, in this case, the inability to determine precisely the chronological relationships of Casas Grandes burials made it impossible to fully integrate this theory with the burial analysis. Consequently, the use of the uniformitarian approach was confined to defining general properties of hierarchical organization rather than to describing and explaining the processes responsible for the social variation observed at Casas Grandes.

This investigation of social ranking at Casas Grandes using mortuary data was also based to a large extent on the so-called dimensional approach (Braun 1977, 1979, 1981; Orser 1980; Ravesloot 1984). This perspective views social organization as consisting of multidimensional social spaces (that is, identities or social positions) that are assigned to members based on the criteria a society employs to differentiate them. The dimensional perspective as applied to the study of mortuary data is based on the assumption that the criteria used to differentiate qualitatively different social positions or identities should be symbolized in a society's mortuary program by qualitative distinctions in burial treatments among individuals.

The results of the univariate and multivariate analyses of the Casas Grandes burial collection indicated that a system of social ranking based on inheritance probably integrated Casas Grandes society during the Medio period. Positions of authority and power within Casas Grandes society were most likely based on the control of the distribution of agricultural goods and products obtained through exchange. Vertical social distinctions were marked by qualitative differences in mortuary treatment such as special burial locations, expensive grave facility constructions, variability in postmortem processing of the body, and the relative cost of grave accompaniments as measured in terms of procurement and production. These attributes were redundant or covaried and defined several dimensions of variability within the Casas Grandes mortuary program. The relative cost of these qualitative burial attributes was found in general to increase from the bottom to the top of the social hierarchy. In addition, the number of individuals associated with the exclusive access to symbols of social rank, authority, and power was few as compared to the number of individuals given common burial treatment.

The multivariate analysis of a 43 variable data set isolated three dimensions of covariation among variables of burial treatment defined for the Casas Grandes mortuary program. Dimension I isolated positive loadings among the variables of ceramic handdrums with the grave facility, burial vault interment, multiple burial, room subfloor tomb, legs frogged, secondary burial, and, to a lesser extent, polychrome ceramic vessels and rare accompaniments. The negative loadings for these variables included single burials, flexed burials, primary inhumations, plaza subfloor unsealed grave pits, and the absence of accompaniments. Dimension II indicated that primary inhumations, flexed burials, single burials, polychrome and nonpolychrome ceramic vessels, socioreligious artifacts, utilitarian artifacts, and jewelry ornaments manufactured from local and nonlocal material were positively associated. Negative loadings for dimension II were absence of accompaniments, secondary burials, and multiple burials. Dimension III indicated positive covariation among the variables of plaza subfloor unsealed grave pits, single burials, and plaza and room fill burial locations. The negative loadings were room subfloor sealed grave pits, multiple burials, and burials interred in a flexed and sitting position.

These three dimensions are assumed to indicate different degrees of access to increasingly less common facets of burial treatment that may signify differences in social differentiation. The demographic profiles associated with these dimensions of differentiation generally crosscut not only the categories of age and gender, but also the rites of passage from child to adolescent to adult status.

This chapter reviews the archaeological evidence for social ranking defined from variability in mortuary treatment given to Casas Grandians at death. The evidence is presented in terms of the qualitative attributes of burial treatment identified as symbols of social ranking. Also discussed are the representativeness of the burial collection, temporal considerations, regional organization of settlements and mortuary treatment, ethnohistorical evidence for complex social organization, and the role of organized warfare in Casas Grandes society.

QUALITATIVE ATTRIBUTES

Mortuary Facility and Burial Location

An investigation of the spatial component of the Casas Grandes mortuary program revealed that at least on an intrasite level distinctions of rank, authority, and power were clearly symbolized by special burial locations. The Mound of the Offerings (Unit 4, Fig. 4.2) contained two vaults that housed the secondary postcranial remains of three adults who are interpreted as representing the ruling elite of Casas Grandes. The lack of temporal control made it impossible to determine if these individuals were interred at roughly the same time or if they represented successional leaders. The Mound of the Offerings contained not only the most elaborately constructed mortuary facility at the site, it also was centrally located. It could be reached by steps from the Central Plaza and was constructed, along with other ceremonial structures like platform mounds and ballcourts, to the west of the U-shaped highrise that contained individual house clusters (Fig. 1.2).

The House of the Dead (Unit 3, Fig. 4.12), the House of the Pillars (Unit 14, Fig. 4.16), and the House of the Skulls (Unit 16, Fig. 4.18) also contained special burial locations that were symbolized by exclusive access for a small segment of the population. Each of these architectural units contained at least one room subfloor tomb. These specially prepared tombs often contained multiple burials and they were covered with board planks or cribbed log roofs. In the House of the Dead, particularly on the floors of rooms 1, 3, and 9, reconstructible ceramic handdrums were found near two of these tombs (CG 44 A–L–13, Room 3–13; CG 13–13, Room 9–13), suggesting that they had

been played during mortuary rituals. In terms of energy expenditure, this type of grave facility required the next largest labor output after the vaults in the Mound of the Offerings.

Most Casas Grandians, however, even in architectural units 13, 14, and 16, were buried in simple earthen pits located beneath the floors of habitation rooms and plazas (Chapters 5 and 6). Some of these pits were left unsealed and, in a few instances, grave accompaniments were visible above the top of the facility. As first suggested by Di Peso and others (Vol. 8: 364), it appears that social distinctions among Casas Grandians were also indicated by interment within rooms versus beneath plazas. In general, individuals buried in plazas were not specially prepared for burial and usually were interred without accompaniments. These individuals may have occupied the least important social positions within the community. Some of the spatial differences in mortuary treatment within and among graves in the architectural units may also symbolize horizontal social distinctions in Casas Grandes society. As noted in Chapter 3, ethnographic studies of the spatial components of mortuary practices have shown that corporate group affiliation is often marked by formal disposal areas within cemeteries (Saxe 1970; Goldstein 1980, 1981; Chapman and Randsborg 1981).

A visual inspection of the spatial patterning of graves within architectural units also suggests that rooms that functioned in a public or ceremonial capacity were seldom used as disposal areas. Such space use is best seen by the distribution of graves within Unit 14 and Unit 16. For example, in Unit 14 no burials were recovered from butterfly-shaped rooms except for one subfloor multiple burial removed from Room 15. Interestingly, only Type 2 unburied bodies as defined by the excavators were recovered from those rooms where subfloor caches were found. The context of these bodies suggested that the individuals had been placed in these rooms long after the rooms had served ceremonial or public functions.

Postmortem Processing of the Body

Upon death, Casas Grandians were subjected to different degrees of postmortem processing that ranged from none to total disarticulation of the skeleton. The majority of the burials exhibited no evidence of postmortem processing. Those few individuals that received the most extensive skeletal treatment also were interred in elaborate graves and were associated with expensive or high cost accompaniments. Burials that scored positive for dimension I of the Casas Grandes mortuary program are interpreted as representing the highest-ranking social group. As expected, then, the energy expended in processing the corpse was found to decrease significantly from the top to the bottom of the social hierarchy.

Brown (1981) has indicated that different burial types may represent stages in multiphased disposal programs rather than symbolize social status distinctions. In order to avoid this interpretive error, he (Brown 1981: 31) suggests constructing a model that relates "physical interments and their contexts (tombs, mounds, etc.) to phases of burial programmes, which are treatment sequences of the corpse (and skeleton if secondary burial is involved) particular to specific status categories."

The possibility that some of the burial types identified at Casas Grandes represent stages in a burial program rather than reflect differences in social rank should not be dismissed lightly. If this were true, it would have profound implications for the dimensions of social status defined in this study. For example, are some of the dimension I burials, specifically those interred in the Mound of the Offerings, actually representing recycled dimension II burials? Do the trophy skulls recovered from Unit 16 actually belong to the postcranial remains of the three individuals buried in the Mound of the Offerings? How many of the 109 burials that originally scored negative (that is, no accompaniments, secondary burial, multiple burial) for dimension II were primary inhumations that were disturbed with building activity and subsequently reinterred in mass graves? Questions such as these must be considered lest we interpret phases of a burial program as variations in social rank. All evidence currently available indicates that the variability in mortuary treatment given Casas Grandians does reflect social distinctions, with the exception of burials that scored negatively for dimension II. Unfortunately, it is not possible to determine with certainty the relationship between the trophy skulls and those individuals buried in the Mound of the Offerings.

Artifact Accompaniments

Individuals representing a little over half of the Casas Grandes burials, spanning all age groups, were interred with grave accompaniments. There was considerable variability in the quantity and relative cost (that is, availability of raw materials and energy expended in producing the object) of the items associated with these individuals.

Accompaniments placed with the dead included plain ware, red ware, and polychrome ceramic vessels; jewelry composed of ornaments manufactured from local material (for example, slate, siltstone, felsite) and nonlocal material (for example, turquoise, ricolite, shell); utilitarian objects; socioreligious offerings; vegetal items; and rare objects (Table 5.1). Most of the dead were buried with a single piece such as a ceramic pot, whereas others were interred with many items (Table 5.10).

It has become commonplace in the literature to emphasize the importance of wealth distinctions as indicated by grave associations to infer social differences over other, more significant, symbolic differences such as corpse processing and burial location (Tainter 1978: 119; Brown 1981: 29). This is particularly true of many recent studies of prehistoric Southwestern mortuary patterning where archaeologically visible distinctions between the dead are often limited to the type and quantity of associated grave goods. These differences in burial treatment probably reflect family wealth or statuses acquired by ability, age, and gender rather than hierarchically structured societies where "high status" individuals were given elaborate treatment. Regrettably, in their desire to find evidence for social ranking among prehistoric Southwestern societies, some archaeologists have neglected to consider the total mortuary program in their interpretation and, consequently, have overestimated social complexity.

Wealthy grave assemblages at Casas Grandes are interpreted as representing the economic standing of the deceased family as well as symbolizing discrete rank and authority positions. It is not surprising that individuals buried with rare objects are also associated with a large diversity and quantity of other grave goods. Presumably these individuals had more prestige and greater wealth than other members of Casas Grandes society and consequently there was more community participation in mortuary rituals when they died.

Accompaniments that are suggested to represent symbols or badges of power and authority are some of the rare accompaniments such as copper jewelry, scarlet and military macaws, lilac-crowned parrots, bone rasps made from animal and human bone, the bone necklace made from human phalanges (Fig. 4.6), and the three specially prepared Ramos Polychrome ceramic urns (Figs. 4.3 and 4.5a, b). These artifacts were not only costly in terms of their procurement and production but were also rare with regard to their distribution and availability within other site contexts (see Chapters 4 and 5 for contextual analysis of ritual paraphernalia and artifact accompaniments). More importantly, these objects covaried with other variables of burial treatment interpreted as symbols of authority (Chapter 6).

The three Ramos Polychrome mortuary urns recovered from Unit 4, the Mound of the Offerings, are presumed to have been specially prepared because of their unusual size. The standard Ramos Polychrome jar averaged around 7,500 milliliters in capacity. In contrast, the two mortuary urns for which we have capacity measurements were 30,000 (Fig. 4.3) and 38,000 (Fig. 4.5b) milliliters. Only one other Ramos Polychrome vessel (CG/6137), recovered from the floor of Room 26 in Unit 8, the House of the Well, compares in size, with a capacity of 30,000 milliliters (Fig. 7.1). The discovery of this vessel in a nonburial context suggests either that the urns recovered from the Mound of the Offerings may have been made and used for other purposes prior to the mortuary ritual, or that the vessel recovered from Room 26 may have been manufactured specifically for use as a burial container. The context in which it was found archaeologically may not reflect its intended function. Schiffer (1987: 88) commented that the most direct line of evidence for distinguishing grave goods that may have had prior functions is use-wear analysis. I did not investigate use-wear patterns because the vessels in question are curated in Mexico City.

It is important to recognize that the absence of appropriate symbols such as rare accompaniments cannot always be used to assume the nonexistence of inherited power and authority, because in most cases only the most durable remains of material culture are preserved for study (Brown 1981; O'-Shea 1981, 1984). Many items such as costumes and insignia made from perishable materials that may have accompanied the dead and symbolized badges or privileges of rank and authority have not survived. Some of the Casas Grandians that lacked "high cost" grave accompaniments but were interred in special burial locations and expensive burial facilities may actually belong in dimension I rather than II. Furthermore, in a cross-cultural study of mortuary practices, Tainter (1978: 121) has observed that grave accompaniments are rarely used by themselves to mark social distinctions.

Some of the rare accompaniments made from durable materials such as the phalange necklace (Fig. 4.6), rasps, and human long bones convey important symbolic meaning because of the material from which they were made. The necklace consists of the hand and foot phalanges of at least two different individuals (Vol. 8: 65). The three femurs in the long bone trove, also recovered from the Mound of the Offerings (Unit 4), may be from three different individuals. These artifacts probably represent personal trophies taken in battle and suggest that military force and organized warfare played an important part in the emergence and persistence of a hierarchical social structure at Casas Grandes (Ravesloot and Spoerl 1987).

The taking of human head trophies and other body parts from captured chiefs, priests, and other important personages was a common practice throughout most of Mexico and Central America during prehistoric and historic times (Beals 1932; Moser 1973). Moser has shown that there is considerable evidence in Mesoamerica for human decapitation that indicates the trophy heads taken in battle were used by individuals as symbols or badges of authority and power. As an example of this use he refers to the Huastecans and other peoples of the west coast of Mexico where skulls were carved, painted, and plastered and kept as personal trophies (Moser 1973: 49).

Often they were buried with them as a mark of achieved status and power obtained through outstanding victories over opponents in war or for positions of power and authority within the hierarchy. In this case the head or skull of a predecessor may have symbolized the actual transmission of authority as well as honored the former priest or lord (Moser 1973: 49).

For example, Ekholm (1942: 43, 120) noted that several of the burials recovered from the prehistoric site of Guasave in Sinaloa, Mexico (Fig. 1.1) were buried with extra skulls that may represent trophies. In particular, one adult male burial (No. 29) contained two additional skulls that had been placed beneath the body. Both of these skulls lacked mandibles and had been covered with red ocher. Ekholm suggested that the extra skulls were defleshed prior to burial because they were better preserved than the skull of Burial 29.

No Casas Grandes burials were interred with extra skulls. As noted in Chapter 4, however, the six skulls and other miscellaneous human skeletal parts found as part of a larger ceremonial assemblage in the House of the Skulls (Unit 16) were interpreted by Di Peso and others (Vol. 8: 53–55) as representing trophies. The fact that these skulls were larger

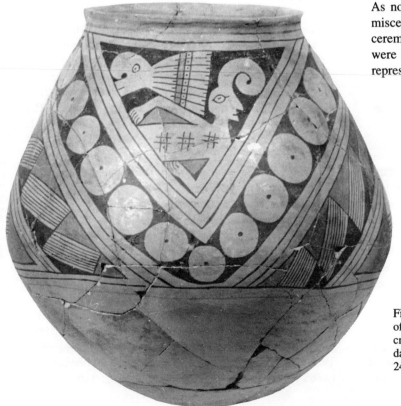

Figure 7.1. Ramos Polychrome jar from the floor of Room 26 in the House of the Well. Vessel is 41.4 cm in height. (Photo courtesy of the Amerind Foundation, Inc., Dragoon, Arizona; Negative No. CG 248L–13.)

and more robust than the other Casas Grandes burial skulls (Benfer 1968: 16) and that the gender of the identifiable ones was male lend some support to this position. The bone assemblage found accompanying these "trophy skulls" also included 109 long bones and 43 bone wands. Although the majority of the bone has been identified as black bear (*Ursus americanus*), several of the objects included in this assemblage were made from human skeletal parts. The trophy skulls and some of the other objects have been interpreted by Di Peso as a bone mobile that was suspended from the ceiling of the room. An assemblage similar to the Casas Grandes one consisting of perforated skulls and human femurs has been reported for the site of Alta Vista located in Zacatecas, Mexico (Kelley 1978; Pickering 1985).

This study of the Casas Grandes burials indicates that grave accompaniments should not be used as symbols of authority without initially evaluating their availability and determining the range of contexts in which the items were produced, stored, ritually disposed of, or used. Rare or costly artifact accompaniments determined to potentially symbolize badges or privileges of authority should covary with other variables of burial treatment (for example, burial facility, corpse processing, spatial structure of mortuary practices) that a society used to symbolize social status distinctions. In their studies of prehistoric social systems, archaeologists who use burial data must examine the total mortuary program rather than limiting analysis to one aspect such as grave accompaniments, because a diversity of symbolic forms may have been used in the mortuary ritual.

Tainter (1978: 121) observed that "mortuary ritual is a process of symbolizing." Consequently, all aspects of the mortuary ritual program potentially convey information about the social standing of the deceased. One feature of mortuary studies of hierarchical organization that has not been developed to the extent of others is the symbolic meaning of decorative abstract motifs on artifacts. Di Peso and others (Vol. 6: 276) observed that "the greatest variety of design elements and motifs for any of the Casas Grandes painted decorated pottery types was found on the Standard variant of Ramos Polychrome." As examples, the Ramos Polychrome jar (Fig. 7.1) recovered from Room 26–8 depicts the upper portion of a man wearing a plumed headdress that was associated with a decorative macaw, and the urn (Fig. 4.5*b*) that contained the bones of one of the burials interred in the Mound of the Offerings was decorated with numerous macaw motifs. Future studies should attempt to develop methods to differentiate those design elements and motifs that are potential symbols of vertical and horizontal social distinctions. The 238 restorable Ramos Polychrome vessels from Casas Grandes, of which 60 were from mortuary contexts (Table 5.2), represent a reasonable sample for this kind of research.

This study of Casas Grandes mortuary variability has provided some preliminary insights to the organization of the regional exchange system in which this community par-

ticipated. Objects made from nonlocal materials such as turquoise, shell, and ricolite rarely occurred within grave contexts, and, with the exception of shell, they were rare throughout the site. Millions of individual items of shell were found within storage and workshop contexts. Less than one percent of this shell came from burials. The multivariate analyses indicated that only those individuals who scored positive for dimensions I and II were interred with composite jewelry fashioned from these nonlocal raw materials. Access to objects manufactured from these raw materials, then, appears to have been limited to those individuals who were members of the Medio period ruling elite.

The analysis of copper ore from local deposits and copper items recovered from the site suggests that Casas Grandes was a copper producing center during the Medio period (Vol. 7: 501). The majority of the items manufactured there appear to have been copper bells. As noted in Chapter 5, the relatively few copper objects found in burial contexts included beads, pendants, and tinklers. The absence of copper bells as grave accompaniments is curious, because archaeologists believe these objects represent luxury goods that have been identified as status markers elsewhere within the regional interaction system in which Casas Grandes participated. Copper bells may have been manufactured at Casas Grandes for export rather than local consumption (Plog, Upham, and Weigand 1982).

TEMPORAL CONSIDERATIONS

O'Shea (1981: 52) has called attention to the importance of understanding the role of time in social reconstructions using mortuary patterning. He states, "If accurate social inferences are to be drawn, mortuary practices must be viewed within their temporal context, and as reflective of adaptive changes occurring within the living society at large." Clearly, a major shortcoming of this study of social ranking was the absence of a technique with which to temporally relate burials. The inability to define the length of time during which the burials accumulated within specific architectural units made it necessary to assume that that organizational structure of Casas Grandes remained relatively stable during the Medio period (Chapter 5). As a consequence, it was not possible to explain some of the variability in mortuary treatment observed. For example, many of the burials classified as Type 2 or unburied bodies by the excavators were processed in a manner similar to the deliberate interments that scored positive for dimension III (that is, plaza subfloor unsealed grave pits, plaza fill, room fill, and single interments). Two explanations for this patterning are offered. It may reflect a digression in the organizational complexity of the community near the time of its decay and abandonment. On the basis of a reanalysis of the Casas Grandes tree-ring samples (Ravesloot and others 1986), it appears that this period may date somewhere between A.D. 1400 and 1470 rather than A.D. 1261 to 1340 as originally suggested. Or, this mortuary treatment may merely represent another dimension of status differentiation operating during the Medio period. An understanding of this patterning, while critical to a more complete description of Casas Grandes social organization, can only be adequately addressed when the developmental sequence of the site is better understood. The method developed by Steponaitis (1983) to seriate grave lots using ceramic vessels at the Mississippian site of Moundville represents an example of how this chronology problem might be approached.

REPRESENTATIVENESS OF THE BURIAL COLLECTION

An important consideration that is often neglected in social reconstructions using mortuary data is the representativeness of the sample. The Casas Grandes burial collection was not recovered through the use of any sampling procedures that ensured that a representative cultural or biological sample was obtained. The excavators focused on the western portion of the site and only approximately 42 percent of the site area was unearthed. The collection of 576 burials recovered from the site is small, considering the length of time the community was occupied, probably some 300 years. It is highly probable, then, as suggested by Di Peso and others (Vol. 8: 325), that the mortuary variability observed at Casas Grandes represents only a partial picture of the society's mortuary program. In addition, the patterns observed in mortuary variability at Casas Grandes may not be typical for the region if this community functioned primarily as a ceremonial and trade center occupied solely by "high status" families and craft specialists as proposed by Di Peso.

Despite the question of the representativeness of the burial collection, the results of the analyses of the Casas Grandes burial data fulfill all of the test implications of the hypothesis that a system of social ranking based on inheritance operated at Casas Grandes during the Medio period, thereby providing empirical support for Di Peso's conclusion that Casas Grandes was organized hierarchically on the basis of hereditary inequality. Nevertheless, the hypothesis that a system of ascriptive ranking existed at Casas Grandes additionally should be supported through other lines of evidence such as the regional organization of settlements and ethnohistorical accounts of mortuary treatment prior to its unequivocal acceptance.

REGIONAL ORGANIZATION

On a regional scale, Casas Grandes presumably represents the focal point or primary center of a complex settlement hierarchy where economic, social, and religious activities were coordinated. Di Peso (1974) believed this settlement hierarchy consisted of Casas Grandes, smaller secondary centers, and associated satellite farming villages.

Reconnaissance by the Amerind Foundation of the Casas Grandes river drainage and adjacent drainages recorded 85 additional sites. Unfortunately, the unsystematic nature of this survey and the lack of specific information such as site type and size make this data set incomplete for examining the organizational characteristics of the Casas Grandes regional settlement system.

Relatively few students of hierarchical social organization include investigations of patterns of mortuary treatment on a regional basis (Chapman and Randsborg 1981: 23). Studies by Peebles (1971, 1974, 1978) and Goldstein (1976, 1980, 1981), who have attempted to demonstrate the presence of social ranking, specifically hereditary inequality, for the eastern United States Mississippian period by utilizing intrasite and intersite variability in mortuary treatment, are exceptions. Variability in mortuary practices observed at different kinds of sites (for example, regional centers, local centers, and local communities within the Mississippian period settlement system) is used to support the hypothesis that Mississippian society was organized hierarchically. Symbolic indicators of high status social positions as defined within the society's mortuary program were restricted solely to individuals interred within the cemeteries of the regional centers. Mortuary practices observed at other kinds of sites within the settlement system appeared to have been organized on the basis of egalitarian principles, where age, gender, and ability were the major determinants of access to prestige or other status positions.

Additional spatial evidence for a pattern of hierarchical organization within the Casas Grandes cultural system may be delineated by examining intersite mortuary patterning. Assuming that Casas Grandes society was organized on the basis of hereditary inequality, we would not expect to observe those attributes of mortuary treatment interpreted as potential symbols of authority and rank among individuals interred in small settlements located on the peripheries of Paquimé. The limited information currently available for burial practices from sites within the Casas Grandes settlement system tentatively supports this hypothesis.

The Amerind Foundation conducted excavations at two small Medio period sites located within the Casas Grandes river valley. One of the sites (Reyes site no. 2, D:9:14) was completely excavated and contained three rectangular surface houses, two plazas, and one pit house, and excavation on the other site (Reyes site no. 1, D:9:13) was limited to one room (Vol. 5: 854–865). The exact size of Reyes site 1 is not known. Fourteen burials were recovered from these two sites (Vol. 8: 410–412). Eight of these burials were interred in simple earthen pits located beneath the floors of rooms. The remainder were recovered from unexcavated plazas and rooms while wall trenching. Five of the burials were interred with grave goods, including stone and shell jewelry, plain ware, and corrugated and polychrome ceramic vessels. Descriptions of these burials indicate that none of the qualitative attributes of mortuary treatment defined as possible symbols of rank and authority for Paquimé were present. These burials compare most closely with those Casas Grandians that scored negative for dimension I and positive for dimension II (Chapter 6). Clearly, a much larger sample of burials from a wider range of site types is needed to compare regional patterning with the mortuary program at the community of Casas Grandes.

ETHNOHISTORIC DATA

An examination of ethnohistoric sources pertinent to northern Mexico, specifically Sonora, suggests that there existed in the 16th century complex political hierarchies that integrated ethnically similar clusters of villages into confederations (Beals 1932; Riley 1982). These ethnic confederations were integrated on the basis of alliance, exchange, and warfare relationships. Di Peso (1968a) and Riley (1979, 1982) have hypothesized that following the collapse of Casas Grandes in the 14th century, remnants of this population spread to the Sonoran valleys. Aboriginal Indian groups in Sonora during the 16th century may have been socially organized on levels similar to, but perhaps more complex than, Casas Grandes. Riley (1979: 32–33) states:

> What seems to have happened is that around A.D. 1300–50, waves of influence produced a series of provinces or statelets, more or less on the Casas Grandes model although somewhat barbarized. These, possibly, included the Civano phase of Classic Hohokam, and such 'Kingdoms' as Marata located somewhat to the north of Casas Grandes (Di Peso 1974, III, 767). It also included the Sonoran statelets of Corazones, Señora, Batuco, Guaraspi, Cumpa, Saguaripa and Oera.

Spanish parties traveling through northwestern Mexico in the 16th century provided descriptions of the aboriginal groups inhabiting the Sonoran region that suggest they were organized differently than in the later 17th and 18th centuries. Documents from the travels of Alvar Nuñez Cabeza de Vaca during 1528 to 1536, Francisco Vazquez de Coronado in 1540, and Francisco de Ibarra in 1565 describe town-dwelling agriculturalists, whereas 17th century accounts by Jesuit priests traveling and working in the same region indicate that the Indians lived in rancheria settlements (Riley 1979, 1982; Spicer 1962). Obviously, many changes occurred in the demographic and cultural aspects of the Sonoran populations between the 16th and 18th centuries as a result of the introduction of new diseases and lifeways by the Spanish (Spicer 1962).

The narratives of these expeditions provide relatively little information concerning the social and political organization of 16th century Sonoran cultures. The data that are available, however, support the description of the organizational structure of Casas Grandes presented herein. Assuming that the organizational characteristics of Sonoran groups remained relatively stable from the 13th through at least the first half of the 16th century, the narratives of the early Spanish explorers may provide testable hypotheses for consideration in future studies of sociopolitical complexity in prehistoric northern Mexico. Riley (1982: 27–53) has presented a comprehensive summary of the social, political, and economic organization of Sonoran groups in the Serrana Province during the 16th century; they are discussed only briefly here.

The diary of Alvar Nuñez Cabeza de Vaca summarizes his journey from a shipwreck off the coast of Florida in 1528 to his arrival in Culiacan, Mexico in 1536 (Vol. 4: 56–60; Riley 1979: 56). This party was the first group of Europeans to travel through the Sonoran region and describe its aboriginal inhabitants. The journal contains relatively limited information regarding the lifeways of the native Indians encountered, but the account does describe an area of "plains that lie between the chains of very great mountains" where Indians were living in permanent houses of earth and cane mats and were growing maize (Hodge 1907: 105–106):

> Some houses are of earth, the rest all of cane mats. From this point we marched through more than a hundred leagues of country, and continually found settled domiciles, with plenty of maize and beans. The people gave us many deer and cotton shawls, better than those of New Spain, many beads and certain corals found on the South Sea, and fine turquoises that come from the north. Indeed, they gave us everything they had. To me they gave five emeralds made into arrowheads, which they use at their singing and dancing. They appeared to be very precious. I asked whence they got these; and they said toward the north, where were populous towns and very large houses, and that they were purchased with plumes and feathers of parrots.

The middle Sonora or the middle and upper Yaqui River valleys are probably the areas where Cabeza de Vaca, and later Spanish explorers, saw large concentrations of Indians living in permanent houses. Numerous large ruins have been located in the Sonora and Yaqui River valleys (Bandelier 1892; Pailes 1971, 1979, 1980; Doolittle 1988).

The next expedition to pass through northwestern Mexico was that of Francisco Vazquez de Coronado in 1540. Pedro de Castañeda de Najera's narrative of the Coronado expedition provides additional descriptions of the Señora region. According to Castañeda (Hammond and Rey 1940: 250):

> Señora is a river and valley thickly settled with comely people. The women wear skirts of dressed deerskins and small tunics reaching to their waists. In the morning the dignitaries of the pueblo stand on some terraces which they have for that purpose and remain there for one hour, calling like a town crier, instructing the people in what they are to do. They have their temples in small houses, into which they drive numerous arrows, making them look like porcupines on the outside. They do this when war is about to break out. Around this province, toward the sierras, there are large settlements forming separate small provinces. They are composed of ten or twelve pueblos. Seven or eight of them whose names I know are Comu, Patrico, Mochil, Agua, Arispa, and Vallecillo. There are others which we did not visit.

Castañeda's narrative, like Cabeza de Vaca's, indicates that the Señoran area was densely populated in the 16th century. A description of provinces composed of several pueblos suggests that pueblos were not autonomous but were integrated or allied economically and politically (Riley 1979, 1982). The reference to dignitaries directing daily activities suggests that political leadership in these towns may have been in the hands of a governing elite. Castañeda also stated that these dignitaries utilized royal eagles as emblems of power and authority (Hammond and Rey 1940: 251).

The narrative of Bartolome de Las Casas entitled "Apologetica Historia Summaria," describing the Señora region during the 16th century, is supposedly based on descriptions of the area by Cabeza de Vaca and Marcos de Niza. Of particular interest are Las Casas's descriptions of the burial treatment given the presumed rulers of these towns.

From there, six leagues further on in the valley was another town larger than Corazones which the Indians in their language called Agastan. It was well arranged and well done like the other. The principal city and government center of this region was comprised of three thousand very good houses and rather large in the majority. Of them, the house of the ruler of the valley was constructed like those previously described while some were built of adobe. This city was named, or they called it, Señora or Sonora. There were many other towns, and in some of them were very tall stone and mud temples for idols and for the entombment of principal personages (Las Casas 1967, Vol. I: 280–281.)

. . . in another town in the valley, six leagues from there toward Cibola, was the main oratory of Chicamastle, the lord and king of the area—the place where he went to offer up his sacrifices. There was found a very tall stone and adobe temple, which we mentioned when we were talking about temples. And in the temple was a stone statue, filled with blood, and around its neck were many animal hearts. Near the statue there were also many dead, dessicated, disembowled human bodies leaning against the walls. They must have been the past lords of the valley, and that was their sepulchre (Las Casas 1967, Vol. II: 182–183).

These ethnohistoric descriptions of the organizational characteristics of populations inhabiting Sonora during the 16th century provide some interesting parallels with organizational characteristics identified for Casas Grandes. The ethnohistoric data corroborate conclusions reached in the Casas Grandes mortuary research that some individuals, specifically those that occupied the highest positions in the social hierarchy, were accorded special burial treatment. Bartolome de Las Casas's description of burial treatment given town rulers suggests that social position was symbolized by differential treatment of the dead. However, his reference indicating that the remains of the highest-ranking individuals were mummified is curious. It is possible that his description of burial treatment may only document one stage in a multicomponent mortuary sequence. The final stage in that interment program may have been similar to the urn burials recovered from the Mound of the Offerings at Casas Grandes.

WARFARE

The above ethnohistoric sources also document endemic warfare for northern Mexico during the 16th century. The role that warfare may have played in the development and persistence of a hierarchically structured society at Casas Grandes during the Medio period has not been seriously considered, despite the ethnohistorical and archaeological evidence. In his interpretation of Casas Grandes, Di Peso emphasized long distance trade as the major factor that contributed to the appearance of public architecture, craft specialization, elaborate religious complexes and variability in mortuary treatment of the dead. Evidence identified for conflict or organized warfare was used in a more traditional manner to explain the presence of unburied bodies, fragmented religious edifices, burned architectural units, destruction of ritual paraphernalia, and subsequent abandonment of the community. Organized militarism was also viewed as necessary to control resources important to the community such as agricultural land and water.

Many anthropologists have considered warfare as an adaptational response that figured prominently in the evolutionary development of complex forms of social organization (for example, Service 1962; Fried 1967; Webster 1975, 1977). Webster (1977: 348) views this choice as self-reinforcing, since "successfully expanding groups are likely to continue this competitive behavior, with concomitant organizational changes, and groups which are competitively disadvantaged are either decimated, subordinated, or forced to make appropriate defensive and organizational adjustments of their own."

Warfare may have been an important variable in the sociopolitical development and adaptation of Casas Grandes society and not merely a cause of its demise (Ravesloot and Spoerl 1987). The eventual abandonment of Casas Grandes occurred long after it functioned as a major ceremonial and trade center and followed decades, and possibly even a century, of social stagnation, disintegration, and decline. Superiority in warfare may have provided an avenue for upward social mobility in Casas Grandes society that eventually resulted in the development and maintenance of a society organized hierarchically on the basis of ranked social positions.

Archaeological Evidence for Warfare

Bandelier's (1892) description of Casas Grandes noted that the terrace on which it was constructed was well selected, because it provided an unobstructed view of the river valley. He suggested that "no enemy could approach Casas Grandes in the daytime without being discovered" (Bandelier 1892: 545). The multistoried and partially enclosed architectural configuration of the community suggests that it may have been constructed with defense in mind. The House of the Serpent (Unit 11; Fig. 4.10) covered nearly an acre, contained a single entry, and was marked by a bastion corner (Vol. 2: 372). Buildings also had angled exterior windows that may have functioned in a defensive capacity. One of these windows located in the House of the Skulls had a direct view to the stone tower located on the top of Cerro de Moctezuma (Vol. 4: 227), hypothesized by Di Peso to have functioned as a signaling tower. The discovery of the walk-in well in the House of the Well (Unit 8; Fig. 4.7) indicates that the town contained at least one permanent and defensible supply of domestic water.

In addition to the trophy skulls and other human skeletal parts discussed previously, several individuals were identified with pathologies that might have represented wounds suffered in battle (Benfer 1968: 14). The face of one male over 50 years of age (CG Burial 20–8) showed evidence of a severe blow that caused extensive damage but had completely healed prior to death. Another male of similar age (CG Burial 2–16) had also suffered a blow to the head that had partially healed, as shown by new bone growth.

One of the unroofed rooms (2C) in the Mound of the Offerings (Unit 4; Fig. 3.2) contained the remains of two unburied bodies. The skeletal remains of one were found disarticulated lying on the floor, and the other was fully articulated. These two adult males have been interpreted as guards of the religious sanctuary who were killed on the last day of the Diablo phase. Additional evidence offered by the excavators for the deliberate destruction of the Mound of the Offerings was the scattered and fragmented condition of ritual paraphernalia and the smashing of two of the ceramic mortuary urns.

Whether the above two individuals as well as the other 124 people identified by Di Peso and others as unburied bodies actually represent persons killed during an attack is impossible to evaluate. Many of these "unburied bodies" were found in the fill of rooms mixed in rooffall and scattered on room floors. Numerous others were fully articulated and were recovered from contexts such as room fill or plaza drains. Some of these burials are believed to represent the remains of people, possibly Casas Grandians, who occupied the community during its period of decay (Ravesloot 1984).

De Soto's descriptions of the southeastern United States indicate that the mortuary complex that housed the remains of past ancestors was viewed as the ideological focal point of the community. Brown (1975: 17) notes that these historic documents reveal that military defeat of an enemy was considered to be ". . . complete once the mortuary was breached, the structure burned, and the bones defiled and scattered." No ethnohistorical sources for northern Mexico describe a similar pattern, but according to Di Peso, the archaeological evidence from Casas Grandes suggests that the Mound of the Offerings was ransacked and destroyed on the last day of the Diablo phase.

Iconographic evidence for warfare in the form of murals or other mediums depicting battle scenes, the taking of captives, or sacrifices was not found at Casas Grandes. Anthropomorphic human effigy vessels did provide some limited depictions of the types of costumes, particularly headdresses, that may have been worn by Casas Grandes warriors. Unfortunately, most of the warrior costumes and insignia were made from perishable items such as cotton capes, cloaks, sashes, and headdresses composed of feathers. Excavations recovered several objects manufactured from more durable materials that may have been part of these costumes such as copper back-shield plaques, skewers, and armlets or bracelets.

Overall there is considerable direct and indirect evidence for warfare as an integral aspect of Casas Grandes society during the Medio period. The presence of trophy skulls and the association of objects made from human bone as burial accompaniments suggest that warfare may have played an important role in the emergence of hierarchical social structure. Once a hierarchical social structure was in place as an adaptive choice, warfare may have been reinforced and manipulated by the Casas Grandes elite, because conditions of chronic warfare strengthened their position in the society, maintained internal social cohesion, and facilitated the formation of new political alliances.

CONCLUDING THOUGHTS

The investigation of social hierarchy at Casas Grandes using mortuary data has provided some insights to the organization of that society during the Medio period. The description of the Casas Grandes mortuary program reveals that social distinctions were clearly symbolized by qualitative differences in mortuary treatment. The qualitative variables that symbolized social ranking included varying degrees of postmortem processing, special burial locations, construction of common and elaborate grave facilities, and the presence of "high cost" grave accompaniments. This variability in mortuary treatment was interpreted as supporting the hypothesis that Casas Grandes society was organized on the principles of ascriptive or hereditary inequality.

Clearly the detection of social ranking with mortuary data is a complex process that is based on many assumptions. Assessing the social stability of the society, the length of time during which the burial collection accumulated, and the representativeness of the collection contribute to the difficulties of interpreting mortuary data. Nevertheless, I hope that this study demonstrates the potential uses of mortuary data for the archaeological study of prehistoric social organization and that it contributes to the theoretical and methodological approaches developed elsewhere for the identification of social ranking. The dimensional approach that views social organization as consisting of multidimensional social spaces is a useful perspective with which to investigate hierarchical organization using mortuary data.

In addition, this research has illustrated the potential of principal components factoring using the R-mode procedure, a multivariate technique capable of identifying statistically significant dimensions of variability in mortuary programs, as indicated by the covariation of social variables.

The findings of this research contrast significantly with O'Shea's (1984: 250) recent assertion that vertical social distinctions were marked by the type and variety of grave accompaniments rather than burial location, grave facility, and postmortem processing. It is important to emphasize that this analysis of social ranking using Casas Grandes mortuary data is only a case study that should not be used to make cross-cultural generalizations concerning hierarchical organization. These results, however, do suggest that mortuary studies that have identified the presence of social ranking primarily on the basis of differences in the type and quantity of grave associations may be insufficient.

This study demonstrates the importance of reexamining existing archaeological collections from alternative perspectives, and perhaps it will stimulate further analyses of the Casas Grandes material. Because only one aspect of the community was investigated, clearly this research does not describe and explain the total complexity of the organizational structure at Casas Grandes. Additional components of the Casas Grandes social system must be studied to provide a more complete picture of this society and its role within the Greater Southwest.

Grave Associations
(* = Artifacts associated with multiple burials)

Ravesloot Analysis Number	Casas Grandes Burial Number	Provenience	Age	Gender	Accompaniments
192	2–1	Room 3	Young Adult 18–35	Female	Pigment IVB (faceted lumps-hematite clay), IIIG (dished-kaolin); Mined Deposit Material XXI (calcite); Stone Beads I (6 flat disk-gray slate); Fine Coil Bone Awl IIIA (Mule Deer); Coarse Coil Bone Awl II (Mule Deer)
193	3–1	Room 3	Old Adult 50+	Female	Playas Red Jar; Villa Ahumada Poly Jar; C. G. Plain Ware Bowl; Ramos Poly Miniature Bowl; Babicora Poly Miniature Bowl; Ramos Poly Miniature Dipper; Ramos Poly Miniature Bowl; Ramos Plain Ware Miniature Bowl; Textile IA1; Pigment IIF (5 cake limonite clay), IIIA (raw cal), IVE (cake hematite kaolin), VIF (cake silicate?), IB1 (reed formed crayons clay), IIIC (8 reed formed crayons kaolin), IIC1 (6 reed formed crayons limonite clay?); Concretions I (1 chert, 1 jasper, 1 chert); Mined Deposit Materials XIXA (3 quartz crystals), VII (1 mica), XVI (7 fluorite), XXI (8 calcite), XXA (selenite); Stone Pendant IIA1 (ovoid selenite); Pigment IVC (unknown material reed formed crayons); Cordage III
194	4–1	Room 3	Mid-Adult 36–50	Male	Ramos Poly Jar
195	6–1	Room 3	Infant 2		4 Corncobs
197	8A–1	Room 3	Mid-Adult 36–50	Female	Canada Goose
2	9–1	Room 2A	Old Adult 50+	Female	Ramos Poly Jar
199	10–1	Room 2A	Infant		Ramos Black Jar; Ramos Poly Jar; Concretion II (jasper)
3	12–1	Room 2A	Mid-Adult 36–50	Male	Ramos Poly Jar; Shell Tinkler IA (C. perplexus)
8	24–1	Room 5	Young Adult 18–35	Female	C. G. Plain Ware Jar; Ramos Poly Miniature Jar; Ramos Black Miniature Bowl; Unidentified food remains
205	25–1	Room 8	Child 2–5		Hammerstone IA (tuff); Ramos Poly Jar; Ramos Poly Bowl; Ramos Black Jar
206	26–1	Room 8	Adolescent 13–17	Indet.	*With CG 26–1 and 27–1: 4 C. G. Plain Ware Miniature Bowls; Ramos Poly Jar; Mined Deposit Materials XXA (3 selenite); Unidentified stone ornament blank (selenite);
207	27–1	Room 8	Old Adult 50+	Male	Stone Pendant XIVC (eccentric-selenite); Stone Pendant XIVC (eccentric-mica); Shell Bead IVA2 (disk-unidentified); Stone Ball IV (agate); Debitage IVB (1 chert); IIIB (1 chalcedony); Mined Deposit Material XVI (fluorite); Unidentified stone ornament blank (dacite); Debitage IVB (1 chert); Hammerstone IA (3 dacite); Hammerstone IB

Ravesloot Analysis Number	Casas Grandes Burial Number	Provenience	Age	Gender	Accompaniments
					(dacite); Concretion II (chalcedony); Polishing Stone II (dacite); Pigment IIA (raw-limonite); Abrading Stone IVB (fine-grained marl); Raw Material VIII (marl); Debitage IA (rhyolite); Debitage IA (basalt); Knife XID (chert); Debitage IB (chalcedony); Mined Deposit Material XXA (2 selenite)
9	28–1	Plaza 2	Mid-Adult 36–50	Male	Ramos Poly Jar; C. G. Plain Ware Jar; Bone Tube IB (*Grus canadensis*); Shell Tinkler 1A (*C. regularis*); Mined Deposit Material XIXA (quartz crystals); Shell Tessera I (unidentified shell); Mined Deposit Material XXA (selenite); Mined Deposit Material X (sulfur crystals); Debitage IVB (silicate flakes, chalcedony); Unidentified food remains; 2 Corncobs
215	2–4	Burial Vault 1–4	Old Adult 50+	Male	Ramos Poly Jar; Shell Beads IVA 2 (2 flat disk *L. elatum*), IVA 3 (3 *L. elatum*)
216	3–4	Burial Vault 2–4	Mid-Adult 36–50	Female	Ramos Poly Jar
217	4–4	Burial Vault 2–4	Mid-Adult 36–50	Male	Ramos Poly Jar; Shell Bead IA1 (1 tubular vermetid)
11	1–6	Room 21	Infant 2		Ramos Black Jar
16	13–6	Room 9B	Young Adult 18–35	Male	Corralitos Poly Jar; C. G. Tool Punched Jar
8	14–6	Room 9B	Child 3–4		Unidentified red ware jar
12	15–6	Room 9B	Child 2–3		C. G. Plain Ware Jar
223	16A–6	Room 9B	Child 3–4		Ramos Poly Jar
226	18–6	Room 9B	Young Adult 18–35	Female	Ramos Poly Jar
17	19–6	Room 9B	Infant 9–18 mo.		C. G. Plain Ware Jar; Axe IVB1 (straight blade dacite)
19	21–6	Room 10	Infant 2		C. G. Plain Ware Jar; Villa Ahumada Poly Jar
34	22–6	Room 20	Infant 15–18 mo.		Shell Bead IA1 (tubular vermetid); Stone Bead I (flat disk-turquoise, flat disk-apophylite); Shell Beads IVA2 (disk 1 *C. echinata*, 1 *L. elatum*)
229	23A–6	Room 20	Infant 15–18 mo.		Ramos Poly Jar; Shell Beads IIIB1 (6 whole *Olivella dama*); Stone Beads I (flat disk, 183 red slate, 3 gray slate); Stone Beads I (184 flat disk gray slate); Shell Pendant IIIA1a (centrally perforated *Glycymeris gigantea*); Shell Beads IIIB1 (8 whole *Olivella dama*)
231	25–6	Room 20	Young Adult 18–35	Male	2 Ramos Poly Jars
232	26A–6	Room 20	? Adult 18+	Indet. Indet.	*With CG 26A–6 and 26B–6: Shell Beads IIIB1 (220 whole *Nassarius* sp.); Stone Beads I (flat disk, 61 gray slate, 1 red slate, 35 gray slate); Stone Beads I (flat disk, 101 gray slate, 1 red slate); C. G. Plain Ware Jar
233	26B–6	Room 20	?Sub-Adult ?–18		
234	27A–6	Room 20	Mid-Adult 36–50	Male	Ramos Poly Jar; Playas Red Bowl
236	28A–6	Room 20	Young Adult 18–35	Female	Matting IIA; C. G. Plain Ware Jar
20	30–6	Room 21	Child 2–5		C. G. Plain Ware Bowl

Ravesloot Analysis Number	Casas Grandes Burial Number	Provenience	Age	Gender	Accompaniments
22	34–6	Plaza 2	? Adult 18+	Indet.	Stone Raw Material XVI (felsite); Shell Beads IIIA1 (*Nassarius* sp.); Unidentified stone ornament blank (unknown material); Knife X (edge retouch knives, obsidian); Sherd Disk IB (Playas Red); Chipped Preform (obsidian); Debitage IVD (1 chert), VB (2 obsidian), VII (2 obsidian), IC (1 obsidian), IIC (1 obsidian), IB (1 chert), IIA (1 felsite), IVB (4 chert); Knife XID (irregular flakes, chert)
23	35–6	Plaza 2	Young Adult 18–35	Female	Unworked Shell IB
24	36–6	Plaza 2	Infant		Babicora Poly Bowl
246	39–6	Plaza 2	? Adult 18+	Indet.	Knife XIF (rhyolite); Eccentric Worked Sherd VI (Villa Ahumada Poly)
29	46–6	Room D	Infant 6–18 mo.		Ramos Black Jar
30	7–6	Room D	Young Adult 18–35	Female	C. G. Plain Ware Jar
33	51–6	Room 5	?Sub-Adult ?–18	Indet.	Ramos Black Jar; Corralitos Poly Jar
34	1–8	Room 3B	Mid-Adult 36–50	Male	Ramos Poly Effigy Jar
35	5–8	Room 13	Infant 2		C. G. Plain Ware Bowl; Jornada Poly Jar
36	6–8	Room 13	Child		Ramos Black Jar
256	9A–8	Plaza 1	? Adult 18+	Female	C. G. Plain Ware Bowl
259	14–8	Room 19 (Plaza)	Mid-Adult 36–50	Male	2 Military Macaws; 5 Scarlet Macaws
40	17–8	Room 19 (Plaza)	Young Adult 18–35	Female	Cordage IIB
262	22–8	Room 19 (Plaza)	Juvenile 9–10	Indet.	Mined Deposit Materials XXA (2 selenite)
45	24–8	Room 21C	Infant 9 mo.		C. G. Plain Ware Bowl
50	35–8	Plaza 2	Mid-Adult 36–50	Male	C. G. Plain Ware Jar
51	39–8	Room 27	Infant 2		Ramos Black Jar
53	41–8	TT, Block 109–C	? Adult 18+	Indet.	Sherd Pendant IIB2a (centrally perforated, *G. gigantea*); Unidentified Red Ware Jar
267	43A–8	TT, Block 109–C	Mid-Adult 36–50	Male	*With CG 43A–D–8: C. G. Plain Ware Effigy Jar; Ramos Black Bowl; Corralitos Poly Double Jar
268	43B–8	TT, Block 109–C	?Adult 18+	Male	
269	43C–8	TT, Block 109–C	Juvenile 9–11		
270	43D–8	TT, Block 109–C	Child 2–5		
56	2–11	Room 2	Child 5		Stone Pendants IIA2 (pendants with convex faces, sepiolite), IVA (subrectangular plain, gray slate); Shell Tinkler IIA (*C. regularis*)
58	25–11	Room 16	Old Adult 50+	Male	C. G. Plain Ware Jar; C. G. Plain Ware Bowl
48	27–11	Room 17	Infant 2		C. G. Plain Ware Jar; Stone Pendant IXA (trianguloid with apex perforation, feldspar); Matting IIA; Unidentified plant remains
282	29–11	Room 17	Child 2–3		C. G. Plain Ware Eccentric Jar; Unidentified food remains; Matting IIA

Ravesloot Analysis Number	Casas Grandes Burial Number	Provenience	Age	Gender	Accompaniments
284	33–11	Room 15	Young Adult 18–35	Female	Corralitos Poly Jar; Shell Bead IA1 (tubular vermetid); Stone Bead I (flat disk, apophylite); Shell Beads IVA1 (5 disk, unidentified)
285	34–11	Room 15	Child 2–3		C. G. Plain Ware Jar; Unidentified plant remains
63	38–11	Room 26	Mid-Adult 36–50	Female	Mined Deposit Materials XXI (32 calcite), XXA (1 selenite), IV (1 pitchstone); Pigments IIA (11 raw limonite), VIA (1 raw malachite); Raw Material XXII (1 fluorite); Concretion I (agate)
77	54–11	Plaza 3	Mid-Adult 36–50	Male	Unclassified Bone Awls IIB (1 *Ovis canadensis* cf. *mexicana*, 1 *Odocoileus virginianus* cf. *couesi*); Turkey Burial; Unidentified food remains
78	55–11	Plaza 3	Mid-Adult 36–50	Male	Mined Deposit Materials XXXIV (23 azurite), XXXIII (10 malachite), XXII (2 copper ore); Pigment VB (3 faceted lumps azurite)
80	2–12	Room 4	Child 2–3		Corralitos Poly Effigy Jar
81	3–12	Room 4	Juvenile 9–12	Indet.	C. G. Plain Ware Jar
294	6A–12	Room 9	Young Adult 18–35	Female	Playas Red Jar
83	7–12	Room 13	Old Adult 50+	Female	C. G. Plain Ware Bowl; Shell Beads IA1 (1 tubular vermetid), IVA1 (635 disk unidentified shell); Corralitos Poly Double Jar
297	8–12	Room 14	Young Adult 18–35	Female	Ramos Black Jar
299	10A–12	Room 14	?Adult 18+	Female	Ramos Black Bowl
304	20–12	Room 18	Child 2–3		Shell Beads IIIA1 (1 whole *nassarius* sp., 1 *P. bandera*); Stone Pendant IXA (1 trianguloid felsite); Shell Pendants XVIC (fragmentary *D. ponderosa*), V (1 tabular *D. ponderosa*); Stone Bead Pendant I (tabular turquoise); Shell Tinklers IVA (3 *Conus* sp.)
305	21–12	Room 18	?Adult 18+	Female	Ramos Black Bowl; Pigment VIIF (aluminum silicate cakes)
87	19–12	Room 20	Mid-Adult 36–50	Female	Ramos Poly Effigy Jar; Unidentified food remains
309	22–12	Room 14	Young Adult 18–25	Female	Shell Tinklers IA (2 *C. princeps*, 2 *C. perplexus*); Stone Bead Pendant I (tabular turquoise)
311	26–12	Room 29	Mid-Adult 36–50	Male	Shell Pendant XVII (unfinished *P. mazatlanica*); Shell Tinkler IIA (*C. perplexus*); Debitage IVA (basalt)
313	34–12	Room 25	Mid-Adult 36–50	Male	Ramos Poly Jar; Ramos Black Jar; Ramos Black Jar
314	35–12	Room 25	Mid-Adult 36–50	Male	Shell Beads IIIA1 (608 whole *Nassarius* sp.), IVA1 (638 disk unidentified)
90	36–12	Plaza 6	Young Adult 18–35	Male	Ramos Poly Jar
317	7–13	Room 9	Adolescent 14–16	Indet.	Ramos Black Jar; Unidentified seed cotyledon; Unidentified food remains
318	8–13	Room 9	Child 2–3		Ramos Poly Miniature Jar; Ramos Black Jar; Unidentified food remains
					*With CG 7–13 and 8–13: Bone Rasp I (*A. americana*); Raw Material IV (altered felsite)
96	13–13	Room 9	Young Adult 18–35	Male	Hammerstone IA (Chert); Concretion I (chert); Rubbing Stone IIB (vesicular basalt), IIA

Ravesloot Analysis Number	Casas Grandes Burial Number	Provenience	Age	Gender	Accompaniments
					(rhyolite), IIA (vesicular basalt); Concretions III (2 chalcedony); Stone Beads I (2 flat disk red slate); Concretions III (2 quartz); Stone Beads I (14 flat disk turquoise); Shell Beads IVA1 (4 disk unidentified shell); Pigment IB1 (reed formed crayons ash clay); Cordage IB; Debitage IB (1 chalcedony, 1 chert), IA (1 rhyolite), IIB (chalcedony), IIIB (1 chert), IVB (1 chalcedony, 1 jasper, 1 basalt, 8 chert), VIIB (1 chert); Knives XID (2 chert); Chipped Scraper XD (chalcedony); Core IB (1 chert); Ramos Poly Jar; 2 Copper Pendants
326	28–13	Room 8	Young Adult 18–35	Female	C. G. Plain Ware Jar; Ramos Black Jar; Unidentified food remains
103	24–13	Room 7	Child 2		Unclassified worked wood fragments; Pigment VD (azurite); Stone Bead Pendants I (6 tabular turquoise), XIVC (1 eccentric sepiolite); Shell Beads IIIA1 (7 whole *G. maculata,* 27 whole *P. bandera,* 108 whole *Nassarius* sp.), IIIB1 (14 whole *O. dama*), IVA1 (disk, 6 unidentified shell); IA1 (tubular vermetid); Stone Bead I (flat disk, felsite); Mined Deposit Material X (2 sulfur crystals), XI (specular hematite), XIXA (quartz crystals), XXI (calcite), XXVIII (2 molybdenite); Debitage IVB (chert); C. G. Plain Ware Jar; Fossil IF2; Stone Pendant XIVC (sepiolite); Unidentified food remains
327	26–13	Room 4	Juvenile 7–8	Indet.	*With CG 26–13 and 27–13: Ramos Poly Jar; Ramos Black Bowl; Playas Red Bowl; Playas Red Jar; Ramos Black Jar; Shell Beads IIIB1 (9 whole *O. dama*); 3 Lilac-crowned parrots; Unidentified food remains
328	27–13	Room 4	Child 3		
109	33–13	Plaza 2	Mid-Adult 36–50	Female	Stone Bead Pendant I (tabular turquoise), XIVA (dentate turquoise); Stone Beads I (flat disk, 1 turquoise, 2 gray slate)
329	37–13	Room 8	Adolescent 17–18	Female	*With CG 37–13 and 38–13: Polishing Stone IA (dacite); Ceramic Handdrum IIC
330	38–13	Room 8	?Adult 36+	Male	Stone Tesserae I (30 turquoise), II (4 turquoise); Mined Deposit Materials IX (10 turquoise), XXIII (5 malachite); Stone Pendant XVII (fragment, turquoise)
114	40–13	Room A	Old Adult 50+	Indet.	Ramos Black Bowl; Playas Red Jar; Stone Beads I (23 flat disk ricolite, 9 turquoise); Stone Pendant IVA (subrectangular calcite); Unidentified stone ornament blanks (1 dacite, 1 selenite, 1 calcite); Shell Bracelet VII (*L. elatum*); Shell Beads IIIA1 (90 whole *Nassarius* sp.), IIIB1 (13 whole *O. dama*), IA1 (3 tubular vermetid), IVA1 (4 disk unidentified), IVA1 (4 disk unidentified), IVA2 (2 disk unidentified); Shell Armlet IIIB1 (*D. ponderosa*); Polishing Stone III (dacite); Concretion I (2 chert, 1 agate); Enigmatic Sepiolite Object II; Unidentified food remains
331	41A–13	Room 3	Juvenile 7		*With CG 41A–13, 41B–13, and 42–13: Pigment IA (1 faceted lump ash), IB1 (1 reed formed crayon, ash), VIF (19 green cakes celadonite); Shell Armlet IC (incised zoomorphic *G. gigantea*); Shell Beads IA1 (7 tubular vermetid), IB2 (tubular vermetid), IIIB1 (48 whole *Nassarius* sp., 21 whole *O. dama*), IVA2 (4 disk *L. elatum*); Shell Pendants IXA (2 tapered unidentified); Stone Beads I (flat disk, 1 apophylite, 2 turquoise, 2 gray slate); Stone Tessera I (turquoise); Ramos Poly Bowl fragment
332	41B–13	Room 3	Child 3		
333	42–13	Room 3	Infant 2		

Ravesloot Analysis Number	Casas Grandes Burial Number	Provenience	Age	Gender	Accompaniments
115	43–13	Room 3	Infant 2		Bone Plaiting Tool IA (species unknown); Bone Hair Ornament III B (Artiodactyla); Stone Pendant XVII (fragment, selenite); Shell Spangle IB1 (discoidal, *P. mazatlanica*); Shell Bead Pendants I (6 whole *C. albonodosa*)
334	44A–13	Room 3	Old Adult 50+	Male	Villa Ahumada Poly Jar; Ramos Black Bowl; Ramos Poly Jar; Ramos Black Jar; C. G. Tool Punched Effigy Jar; Concretion III (chert); Shell Tinkler IIA (*C. regularis*), IA (2 *C. regularis, C. ximenes*); Shell Bead Pendants I (2 whole *C. albonodosa*); Shell Beads IA1 (2 tubular vermetid), IIB1a (truncated *C. regularis*), IIIA1 (4 whole *Nassarius* sp., 1 *dama*), IVA1 (4 disk, unidentified); Stone Finger Ring I (incised red slate); Stone Tessera I (turquoise); Projectile Point IC (unclassified obsidian fragment); Concretion I (chalcedony); Debitage IIB (chalcedony), IIA (rhyolite), IVA (felsite); Mined Deposit Material XXIII (malachite); Common turkey; Unidentified food remains; Ceramic handdrum
335	44B–13	Room 3	Mid-Adult 36–50	Female	Stone Pendant IIIC (tabular malachite); Stone Bead IVA1 (36 disk, unidentified); Concretion I (chert); Stone Bead Pendant I (tabular turquoise)
336	44C–13	Room 3	Mid-Adult 36–50	Female	
337	44D–13	Room 3	Mid-Adult 36–50	Female	
338	44E–13	Room 3	Mid-Adult 36–50	Male	C. G. Plain Ware Jar; Madera Black-on-red Bowl; Playas Red Bowl; Ramos Poly Jar; Shell Tinklers IA (1 *C. regularis*, 2 *C. perplexus*); IIA (1 *C. regularis*, 1 *C. perplexus*); Stone Pendant VIIB (square siltstone); Unidentified food remains
339	44F–13	Room 3	Mid-Adult 36–50	Female	Miniature Plain Ware Ceramic Ladle
440	44G–13	Room 3	Young Adult 18–35	Female	*With CG 44F–13 and 44G–13: Stone Beads I (flat disk, 21 felsite, 4 red slate, 14 ricolite); Stone Bead Pendant I (tabular turquoise); Shell Beads IIIB1 (whole, 6 *O. dama*), IIB1a (truncated *C. regularis*), IVA1 (31 disk, unidentified), IVA2 (disk, *L. elatum*); Shell pendant IB1a (whole *G. gigantea*); Shell Tinklers IA (8 *C. perplexus*, 4 *C. regularis*), IIA (5 *C. regularis*, 1 *C. perplexus*); Pestle IB (rhyolite); Ramos Poly Jar; Matting IIA
341	44H–13	Room 3	Mid-Adult 36–50	Indet.	
342	44I–13	Room 3	Adolescent 16–18	Indet.	
343	44J–13	Room 3	Adolescent 13–15	Indet.	
344	44K–13	Room 3	Adolescent 13–14	Indet.	
345	44L–13	Room 3	Adolescent 13–15	Indet.	
346	45 13	Room 9	?Adult 18+	Indet.	*With CG 45, 46, 47A–B, 48–13: Ramos Black Jar; C. G. Plain Ware Jar; Ramos Poly Bowl; Ramos Poly Jar; Angiosperm fragments; Unidentified food remains
347	46–13	Room 9	?Adult 18+	Indet.	

Ravesloot Analysis Number	Casas Grandes Burial Number	Provenience	Age	Gender	Accompaniments
348	47A–13	Room 9	Young Adult 18–35	Female	
349	47B–13	Room 9	Old Adult 50+	Indet.	
350	48–13	Room 9	Child 5		
353	51–13	Room 9	Mid-Adult 36–50	Female	Madera Black-on-red Jar; Unidentified food remains
116	52–13	Room 6	?Adult 18+	Female	Textiles IA1; Matting IIIA
117	53–13	Room 6	Juvenile 12	Indet.	C. G. Plain Ware Jar; Unidentified food remains
354	54A–13	Room 6	Mid-Adult 36–50	Male	*With CG 54A–13 and 54B–13: Ramos Poly Bottle; Hammerstone IB (dacite)
355	54B–13	Room 6	Old Adult 50+	Female	
356	55–13	Room 6	Young Adult 18–35	Male	Matting III A

*With CG 54A–13, 54B–13, and 55–13: Ramos Poly Bowl; Ramos Poly Jar; Mined Deposit Material XXIII (5 malachite); Pigment IIA (raw limonite), IID (unclassified worked limonite), IVA (3 raw hematite); IIC1 (reed formed crayons, limonite clay), VID (unclassified worked aluminum silicate), VIF (3 cakes celadonite); Shell Tinkler IA (*C. perplexus*), IVA (*Conus* sp.); Debitage IVB (chalcedony); Hammerstone IA (dacite); Polishing Stone IA (dacite); Rubbing Stone IB (sandstone); Stone Beads I (25 flat disk, 24 ricolite, 1 turquoise); Unidentified food remains |
| 118 | 56–13 | Room 6 | Adolescent 13–17 | Indet. | Ramos Black Bowl |
| 357 | 58–13 | Room 10 | Child 2–3 | | Corralitos Poly Jar; Ramos Poly Miniature Bowl; Stone Pendants IIA3 (1 tabular unknown material; 1 turquoise); Stone Bead Pendants I (1 tabular turquoise, 1 malachite); Stone Beads I (301 flat disk gray slate, 1 fluorite, 1 siltstone, 1 granite, 5 ricolite, 14 red slate, 8 felsite, 1 unknown material), VIC (multifaceted turquoise), II (cylindrical ricolite) |
| 358 | 59–13 | Room 10 | Infant | | Ramos Black Miniature Bowl

*With CG 58–13 and 59–13: Stone Pendant XIIIA (Zoomorphic effigy, ricolite); Shell Pendant IB2b (whole *Conus ximenes*), IIIE2 (centrally perforated fresh water mussel); Shell Tinklers IA (40 incrassata, 1 *C. regularis*, 4 *C. perplexus*) |
361	62A–13	Room 11	Young Adult 18–35	Male	Escondida Poly Jar; C. G. Plain Ware Jar
362	62B–13	Room 11	Young Adult 18–35	Female	*With CG 62A–13 and 62B–13: Madera Black-on-red Bowl; Unidentified food remains
363	62C–13	Room 11	Old Adult 50+	Female	*With CG 62B–13 and 62C–13: Escondida Poly Bowl; C. G. Plain Ware Bowl; C. G. Plain Ware Jar
120	63–13	Room 11	Child 5		C. G. Plain Ware Jar; Shell Pendants IIA (2, modified *A. circularis*); Stone Beads I (61 flat disk turquoise); Mined Deposit Material IX (4 turquoise); Stone Tesserae II (4 turquoise)
364	64A–13	Room 11	Mid-Adult 36–50	Male	

Ravesloot Analysis Number	Casas Grandes Burial Number	Provenience	Age	Gender	Accompaniments
365	64B–13	Room 11	Old Adult 50+	Female	*With CG 64A–13 and 64B–13: Corralitos Poly Jar; 2 Escondida Poly Bowls, Ramos Poly Bowl; 2 Playas Red Jars; Ramos Black Bowl; Ramos Black Jar; Copper Beads I (3 disk); Stone Beads I (flat disk, 1 ricolite, 13 silicate, 5 turquoise, 1 pyrite); Stone Bead Pendants I (tabular fluorite, 13 turquoise); Shell Bead Pendant II (ovoid, unidentified); Shell Bead Pendant IV (dentate, unidentified); Stone Pendant IIA3 (taper turquoise); Shell Beads IVA1 (523 disk, unidentified); Shell Tinklers IVA (2 *Conus* sp.); Axe IV (full-grooved, dacite), IVA1 (straight blade, dacite); Mined Deposit Material IX (turquoise), XXIII (malachite); Unidentified food remains
368	66A–13	Room 16	Old Adult 50+	Female	Ramos Black Jar; C. G. Plain Ware Jar
369	66B–13	Room 16	Young Adult 18–35	Female	
370	66C–13	Room 16	Adolescent 14–17	Indet.	C. G. Plain Ware Jar; Ramos Poly Bowl
371	66D–13	Room 16	Infant Newborn		Eccentric Worked Sherd V (Plain Ware) *With CG 66A–D–13: Shell Pendant IA1 (whole *Natica chemnitzii*); Mined Deposit Material XI (2 specular hematite); Pigment IIIE (powder kaolin); Unidentified food remains
372	68A–13	Room 14	Infant 2		*With CG 68A–13 and 68B–13: Carretas Poly Jar; Pigment IVF (cakes, aluminum silicate); Cucurbit Rind Fragments; Grass Matting
373	68B–13	Room 14	Infant 2		
125	74–13	Plaza 3	Child 2–4		Stone Beads I (3 flat disk ricolite); Shell Beads IVA1 (3 disk, unidentified)
127	76–13	Room A	Mid-Adult 36–50	Female	C.G. Plain Ware Miniature Bowl; Ramos Poly Jar
131	80–13	Plaza 2	Young Adult 18–35	Male	C.G. Plain Ware; Ramos Poly Jar; Unidentified food remains
376	1–14	Plaza 1 Center	Mid-Adult 36–50	Male	Rubbing Stone III (andesite)
378	3A–14	Plaza 1 South	Young Adult 30–32	Female	Escondida Poly Bowl; Rubbing Stone IA (vesicular basalt); Unidentified food remains; Cotton seed coats
140	8–14	Plaza 1	Juvenile 8	Indet.	Sherd Scoop III (fragment, Ramos Poly); Maul IIB (full-grooved, felsite porphyry)
141	9–14	Plaza 2	Mid-Adult 36–50	Female	Stone Pendant XVII (fragment, turquoise)
142	12–14	Room 6	Child 3		Escondida Poly Jar; Playas Red Miniature Bowl; Matting IIA
143	13–14	Room 7	Child 3		Ramos Poly Jar; C.G. Plain Ware Jar; Debitage IVB (2 chert, 1 chalcedony); Unidentified food remains
384	15A–14	Room 15	Infant 7 mo.		*With CG 15A–14 and 15B–14: Ramos Poly Bowl; 2 Escondida Poly Bowls; 2 Ramos Poly Jars; Ramos Poly Miniature Bowl; Corralitos Poly Effigy Jar; Unidentified Stone Ornament (specular hematite); Pigment IB2 (hand formed crayons, ash); Wood paho fragment; 2 Copper Tinklers I; Unidentified plant remains; Textile IA1; Stone Beads I (flat disk, 54 jet, 850 gray slate, 8 red slate, 14 turquoise, 7 unknown, 13 felsite, 33 siltstone,
385	15B–14	Room 15	Infant 6 mo.		

Ravesloot Analysis Number	Casas Grandes Burial Number	Provenience	Age	Gender	Accompaniments
					1 ricolite); Shell Beads IVA1 (disk, 2,321 unidentified), IIIA1 (whole, 875 *Nassarius* sp.)
144	18–14	Room 25B	Young Adult 18–35	Male	C.G. Plain Ware Bowl; Unidentified food remains
390	33–14	Room 27C	Infant		*With CG 33–14 and 34–14: Unidentified food remains; Matting IIIA; Stone Bead Pendant V (tabular turquoise); Projectile Point IC (unclassified fragment, obsidian)
391	34–14	Room 27C	Mid-Adult 36–50	Female	
145	36–14	Room 38B	Young Adult 18–35	Female	Shell Beads IIB1a (truncated, 2 *C. regularis*), IA1 (tubular, 6 vermetid), IIIA1 (whole, 8 *G. maculata*), IVA3 (disk, 2 *L. elatum*); Stone Pendant IIC (stemmed fluorite); Stone Bead Pendant I (tabular fluorite); Rubbing Stone IIA (vesicular basalt)
394	43–14	Room 32B	Mid-Adult 36–50	Female	C.G. Plain Ware Bowl; C.G. Plain Ware Jar; Ramos Poly Bowl; Debitage IVA (felsite); Unidentified food remains
397	46–14	Room 38B	Infant 0–4 mo.		Mined Deposit Material XXI (calcite, 3), XIXA (quartz crystals, 2)
398	47–14	Room 38B	Infant 0–2 mo.		*With CG 47–14 and 49–14: Corralitos Poly Jar
399	48–14	Room 38B	Infant 20–24 mo.		
400	49–14	Room 38B	Child 2–3		
401	53–14	Room 41B	Juvenile 7–9	Indet.	*With CG 53–14, 54–14, and 55–14: Shell Bead IA1 (tubular vermetid); Bone Wand VIC (fragment, Artiodactyla sp.); Bone Hair Ornament I (long bone, Mammalia sp.); Cordage IB; Pigment IB1 (reed formed crayons, ash); Shell Pendant IIIC1 (centrally perforated, *A. circularis*); Playas Red Miniature Bowl; Escondida Poly Bowl; Ramos Black Miniature Bowl; Matting IA; Unidentified food remains
402	54–14	Room 41B	Adolescent 13–15	Indet.	
403	55–14	Room 41B	Young Adult 18–35	Female	
					With CG 55–14: Stone Beads I (flat disk, 69 turquoise); Cordage IIA; Copper Beads II (234); Ramos Black Bowl; Unidentified plant remains
151	56–14	Plaza 3	Young adult 18–35	Female	Corncobs
410	2–16	Room 7	Old Adult 50 +	Male	*With CG 2–16 and 3–16: Ramos Poly Effigy Jar; Stone Pendant XIVC (eccentric limestone); Stone Bead I (flat disk, 2 turquoise); Stone Tessera I (56 turquoise); Shell Pendant IIIA1a (whole *G. gigantea*); Shell Beads IIIA1 (whole, 133 *Nassarius* sp.); Ramos Black Miniature Bowl; Ramos Poly Jar; Escondida Poly Bowl; Unidentified plant remains
411	3–16	Room 7	Mid-Adult 36–50	Male	
					With CG 2–16: Bone Wand IIA (Artiodactyla sp.)
412	4–16	Room 7	Infant 9–14 mo.		Ramos Black Jar; Unidentified plant remains
154	1–15	Plaza 1	Fetus		Drill V (chert); Ramos Black Bowl
404	6A–15	Room 2	?Adult 18 +	Female	*With CG 6A–15 and 6B–15: C. G. Plain Ware Jar; Polishing Stone IA (dacite); Debitage IVB (chert)
405	6B–15	Room 2	?Adult 18 +	Male	
156	7–16	Room 5	Infant		Stone Beads I (flat disk, 84 gray slate)

Ravesloot Analysis Number	Casas Grandes Burial Number	Provenience	Age	Gender	Accompaniments
157	8–16	Plaza 1	Young Adult 18–35	Male	Shell Beads IIIA1 (whole, 1,122 *Nassarius* sp.)
158	10–16	Room 25	Young Adult 18–35	Male	Matting IIIA; Textile IA1; Stone Bead Pendants I (tabular, 4 turquoise); Shell Beads IVA1 (disk, 30 unidentified); Cotton Seeds; Ramos Black Bowl; Ramos Poly Bowl; Villa Ahumada Poly Eccentric Jar; Madera Black-on-red Bowl; Ramos Poly Jar; Matting IIA; Unidentified plant and food remains
161	21–16	Room 29B	Child 5		Pigment IB1 (reed formed crayons, charcoal); Shell Pendant IIA (modified *A. circularis*); Shell Bead Pendant I (whole *T. leucostoma*); Shell Bead IA1 (tubular vermetid), IVA2 (disk, unidentified), IIIB1 (whole, 35 *O. dama*, 1 *O. undatella*); Chipped Scraper VIII (quartz); Debitage IVC, VIIC (13 quartz); Unidentified Stone Ornaments (8 selenite); Playas Red Jar; Unidentified food remains
414 415	22–16 23–16	Room 29B Room 29B	Young Adult 18–35 Child 2–4	Male	*With CG 22–16 and 23–16: Matting IIB; Cotton Seeds; Gymnosperm remains; C.G. Plain Ware Miniature Bowl; Ramos Black Bowl; Ramos Poly Jar; Unidentified plant remains With CG 23–16: Shell Beads IIIA1 (whole, 157 *Nassarius* sp.); Stone Beads I (flat disk, 29 gray slate, 5 ricolite, 1 turquoise); Stone Bead Pendant I (tabular turquoise); Shell Tinklers IA (7 *C. perplexus*, 2 *C. regularis*); Shell Beads IVA1 (2 disk, unidentified)
162	25–16	Room 28	Young Adult 18–35	Female	Matting IA; Cordage IB; Pigment IIIG (dished kaolin), IIIB (5 faceted kaolin), IB1 (reed formed crayons, ash clay); Shell Tinklers IA (9 *C. perplexus*, 4 *C. regularis*, 2 *C. ximenes*, 3 *O. incrassata*), IVA (2 *Conus* sp.); Shell Bead IIB1b (truncated *Conus* sp.), IVA3 (disk, unidentified); Stone Pendant IA (discoidal, 1 felsite, 1 unknown material); Mined Deposit Material XIXA (2 quartz crystals), 2 Ramos Poly Miniature Bowls; Ramos Poly Jar; C.G. Plain Ware Miniature Jar; Unidentified plant remains; Corncob
163	1–19	TT, Block 118–A	Infant 14–20 mo.		C.G. Plain Ware Miniature Bowl; Ramos Poly Jar; Corralitos Poly Jar
417	3–19	TT, Block 118–A	Mid-Adult 18–50	Female?	C.G. Plain Ware Jar; Pigment VID (5 green, unclassified); Unidentified Stone Ornament (malachite)
164	5–19	Room 2B	Adolescent 13–14	Indet.	C.G. Plain Ware Jar; Unidentified food remains
422	5–20	Unit 20, TT	Mid-Adult 36–50	Female	Corncob
171	1–21	Unit 21, NW Entryway	Young Adult 18–35	Male	Ramos Poly Jar; Unidentified food remains
172	3–21	Unit 21, NW Entryway	Juvenile 6–12	Indet.	Ramos Black Bowl
173	4–21	Unit 21, TT	Young Adult 18–35	Female	Common Turkey (2); Scarlet Macaw (2)
174	1–22	Unit 22, TT	Young Adult 18–20	Indet.	Shell Tinkler IA (*C. perplexus*)
426	4–22	Unit 22, TT	Infant		*With CG 4–22 and 5–22: Unworked Shell XXIVB
427	5–22	Unit 22, TT	Newborn		With CG 4–22: Ramos Black Jar; Shell Pendant IIIA1b (incised zoomorphic, *G. gigantea*); Stone Bead I (flat disk, red slate); Shell Beads IVA3, IVA1, IVB (disk, 1 *L. elatum*, 9 unidentified, 1 unidentified)

Ravesloot Analysis Number	Casas Grandes Burial Number	Provenience	Age	Gender	Accompaniments
179	4–23	Unit 23, TT	?Adult 18+	Indet.	C.G. Plain Ware Jar; Ramos Poly Jar
180	5–23	Unit 23, TT	?Adult 18+	Indet.	C.G. Incised Jar; Shell Beads IIIA1 (390 whole *Nassarius* sp.)
181	6–23	Unit 23, TT	?Adult 18+	Indet.	Ramos Black Bowl
182	7–23	Unit 23, TT	Infant		C.G. Plain Ware Bowl
430	1–CP	Under Platform 2	Young Adult 18–35	Male	C.G. Plain Ware Bowl; Shell Beads IVA1 (2 disk, unidentified); Stone Bead Pendants I (6 tabular turquoise); Stone Bead VID (triangular turquoise); Knife V (chert); Projectile Point 1A1 (chert); Mined Deposit Material XIXA (quartz crystal), XXII (copper ore); Debitage IIIB (chalcedony), IVB (chert), IVA (2 rhyolite), IA (rhyolite)
431	2–CP	Under Platform 2	?Adult 18+	Indet.	Hammerstone IA (dacite)
441	10–CP	Under Platform 2	Mid-Adult 36–50	Male	Shell Pendant IIIA1C (whole *G. gigantea*); Shell Bead IVA3 (disk, *L. elatum*); Corncobs

Burial Analysis Numbers for the Casas Grandes Burials

Analysis Number	Casas Grandes Burial Number	Analysis Number	Casas Grandes Burial Number	Analysis Number	Casas Grandes Burial Number	Analysis Number	Casas Grandes Burial Number
001	5 – 1	057	13 – 11	113	39 – 13	169	7 – 20
002	9 – 1	058	25 – 11	114	40 – 13	170	8 – 20
003	12 – 1	059	26 – 11	115	43 – 13	171	1 – 21
004	16 – 1	060	28 – 11	116	52 – 13	172	3 – 21
005	18 – 1	061	35 – 11	117	53 – 13	173	4 – 21
006	22 – 1	062	37 – 11	118	56 – 13	174	1 – 22
007	23 – 1	063	38 – 11	119	57 – 13	175	2 – 22
008	24 – 1	064	39 – 11	120	63 – 13	176	3 – 22
009	28 – 1	065	40 – 11	121	67 – 13	177	6 – 22
010	29 – 1	066	42 – 11	122	69 – 13	178	3 – 23
011	1 – 6	067	43 – 11	123	70 – 13	179	4 – 23
012	6 – 6	068	44 – 11	124	71 – 13	180	5 – 23
013	7 – 6	069	45 – 11	125	74 – 13	181	6 – 23
014	8 – 6	070	46 – 11	126	75 – 13	182	7 – 23
015	12 – 6	071	47 – 11	127	76 – 13	183	8 – 23
016	13 – 6	072	48 – 11	128	77 – 13	184	9 – 23
017	19 – 6	073	49 – 11	129	78 – 13	185	11 –CP
018	21 – 6	074	50 – 11	130	79 – 13	186	12 –CP
019	29 – 6	075	51 – 11	131	80 – 13	187	13 –CP
020	30 – 6	076	52 – 11	132	81 – 13	188	14 –CP
021	33 – 6	077	54 – 11	133	82 – 13	189	20 –CP
022	34 – 6	078	55 – 11	134	83 – 13	190	23 –CP
023	35 – 6	079	56 – 11	135	84 – 13	191	1 –EP
024	36 – 6	080	2 – 12	136	85 – 13	192	2 – 1
025	37 – 6	081	3 – 12	137	86 – 13	193	3 – 1
026	42 – 6	082	4 – 12	138	87 – 13	194	4 – 1
027	43 – 6	083	7 – 12	139	88 – 13	195	6 – 1
028	45 – 6	084	14 – 12	140	8 – 14	196	7 – 1
029	46 – 6	085	15 – 12	141	9 – 14	197	8A– 1
030	47 – 6	086	16 – 12	142	12 – 14	198	8B– 1
031	48 – 6	087	19 – 12	143	13 – 14	199	10 – 1
032	50 – 6	088	24 – 12	144	18 – 14	200	13 – 1
033	51 – 6	089	25 – 12	145	36 – 14	201	17A– 1
034	1 – 8	090	36 – 12	146	37 – 14	202	17B– 1
035	5 – 8	091	37 – 12	147	38 – 14	203	11A– 1
036	6 – 8	092	38 – 12	148	41 – 14	204	11B– 1
037	7 – 8	093	40 – 12	149	50 – 14	205	25 – 1
038	12 – 8	094	41 – 12	150	51 – 14	206	26 – 1
039	16 – 8	095	9 – 13	151	56 – 14	207	27 – 1
040	17 – 8	096	13 – 13	152	57 – 14	208	30A– 1
041	18 – 8	097	17 – 13	153	59 – 14	209	30B– 1
042	19 – 8	098	18 – 13	154	1 – 15	210	30C– 1
043	20 – 8	099	19 – 13	155	6 – 16	211	30D– 1
044	23 – 8	100	20 – 13	156	7 – 16	212	30E– 1
045	24 – 8	101	21 – 13	157	8 – 16	213	30F– 1
046	25 – 8	102	22 – 13	158	10 – 16	214	30G– 1
047	26 – 8	103	24 – 13	159	19 – 16	215	2 – 4
048	27 – 8	104	25 – 13	160	20 – 16	216	3 – 4
049	33 – 8	105	29 – 13	161	21 – 16	217	4 – 4
050	35 – 8	106	30 – 13	162	25 – 16	218	9A– 6
051	39 – 8	107	31 – 13	163	1 – 19	219	9B– 6
052	40 – 8	108	32 – 13	164	5 – 19	220	9C– 6
053	41 – 8	109	33 – 13	165	6 – 19	221	14 – 6
054	42 – 8	110	34 – 13	166	7 – 19	222	15 – 6
055	46 – 8	111	35 – 13	167	1 – 20	223	16A– 6
056	2 – 11	112	36 – 13	168	2 – 20	224	16B– 6

Analysis Number	Casas Grandes Burial Number	Analysis Number	Casas Grandes Burial Number	Analysis Number	Casas Grandes Burial Number	Analysis Number	Casas Grandes Burial Number
225	17 – 6	292	53A– 11	359	60 – 13	426	4 – 22
226	18 – 6	293	53B– 11	360	61 – 13	427	5 – 22
227	20 – 6	294	6A– 12	361	62A– 13	428	1 – 23
228	22 – 6	295	6B– 12	362	62B– 13	429	2 – 23
229	23A– 6	296	6C– 12	363	62C– 13	430	1 –CP
230	23B– 6	297	8 – 12	364	64A– 13	431	2 –CP
231	25 – 6	298	9 – 12	365	64B– 13	432	3 –CP
232	26A– 6	299	10A– 12	366	65A– 13	433	4 –CP
233	26B– 6	300	10B– 12	367	65B– 13	434	5A–CP
234	27A– 6	301	13A– 12	368	66A– 13	435	5B–CP
235	27B– 6	302	13B– 12	369	66B– 13	436	6A–CP
236	28A– 6	303	17 – 12	370	66C– 13	437	6B–CP
237	28B– 6	304	20 – 12	371	66D– 13	438	7 –CP
238	28C– 6	305	21 – 12	372	68A– 13	439	8 –CP
239	31A– 6	306	18A– 12	373	68B– 13	440	9 –CP
240	31B– 6	307	18B– 12	374	72 – 13	441	10 –CP
241	31C– 6	308	18C– 12	375	73 – 13	442	15 –CP
242	31D– 6	309	22 – 12	376	1 – 14	443	16 –CP
243	32A– 6	310	23 – 12	377	2 – 14	444	21A–CP
244	32B– 6	311	26 – 12	378	3A– 14	445	21B–CP
245	32C– 6	312	17 – 12	379	3B– 14	446	21C–CP
246	39 – 6	313	34 – 12	380	7 – 14	447	21D–CP
247	40 – 6	314	35 – 12	381	4 – 14	448	1A– 1
248	41 – 6	315	42A– 12	382	5 – 14	449	1B– 1
249	44A– 6	316	42B– 12	383	6 – 14	450	14 – 1
250	44B– 6	317	7 – 13	384	15A– 14	451	15 – 1
251	49A– 6	318	8 – 13	385	15B– 14	452	19A– 1
252	49B– 6	319	10 – 13	386	29 – 14	453	19B– 1
253	4A– 8	320	11 – 13	387	30 – 14	454	19C– 1
254	4B– 8	321	12 – 13	388	31 – 14	455	20A– 1
255	4C– 8	322	23 – 13	389	32 – 14	456	20B– 1
256	9A– 8	323	14 – 13	390	33 – 14	457	20C– 1
257	9B– 8	324	15 – 13	391	34 – 14	458	20D– 1
258	10 – 8	325	16 – 13	392	39 – 14	459	20E– 1
259	14 – 8	326	28 – 13	393	40 – 14	460	21A– 1
260	15 – 8	327	26 – 13	394	43 – 14	461	21B– 1
261	21 – 8	328	27 – 13	395	44 – 14	462	31 – 1
262	22 – 8	329	37 – 13	396	45 – 14	463	32 – 1
263	34A– 8	330	38 – 13	397	46 – 14	464	1 – 4
264	34B– 8	331	41A– 13	398	47 – 14	465	5 – 4
265	36 – 8	332	41B– 13	399	48 – 14	466	2 – 6
266	37 – 8	333	42 – 13	400	49 – 14	467	3 – 6
267	43A– 8	334	44A– 13	401	53 – 14	468	4 – 6
268	43B– 8	335	44B– 13	402	54 – 14	469	5A– 6
269	43C– 8	336	44C– 13	403	55 – 14	470	5B– 6
270	43D– 8	337	44D– 13	404	6A– 15	471	10A– 6
271	44 – 8	338	44E– 13	405	6B– 15	472	10B– 6
272	45 – 8	339	44F– 13	406	7 – 15	473	11 – 6
273	3 – 11	340	44G– 13	407	8 – 15	474	24 – 6
274	12 – 11	341	44H– 13	408	9A– 15	475	38 – 6
275	15 – 11	342	44I– 13	409	9B– 15	476	2A– 8
276	16 – 11	343	44J– 13	410	2 – 16	477	2B– 8
277	17A– 11	344	44K– 13	411	3 – 16	478	3 – 8
278	17B– 11	345	44L– 13	412	4 – 16	479	8 – 8
279	20 – 11	346	45 – 13	413	5 – 16	480	11 – 8
280	21 – 11	347	46 – 13	414	22 – 16	481	13A– 8
281	27 – 11	348	47A– 13	415	23 – 16	482	13B– 8
282	29 – 11	349	47B– 13	416	2 – 19	483	28A– 8
283	30 – 11	350	48 – 13	417	3 – 19	484	28B– 8
284	33 – 11	351	49 – 13	418	4A– 19	485	28C– 8
285	34 – 11	352	50 – 13	419	4B– 19	486	28D– 8
286	31 – 11	353	51 – 13	420	3 – 20	487	29 – 8
287	32 – 11	354	54A– 13	421	4 – 20	488	31 – 8
288	36A– 11	355	54B– 13	422	5 – 20	489	32 – 8
289	36B– 11	356	55 – 13	423	6 – 20	490	1A– 11
290	41A– 11	357	58 – 13	424	2A– 21	491	1B– 11
291	41B– 11	358	59 – 13	425	2B– 21	492	4 – 11

Analysis Number	Casas Grandes Burial Number	Analysis Number	Casas Grandes Burial Number	Analysis Number	Casas Grandes Burial Number	Analysis Number	Casas Grandes Burial Number
493	5A– 11	513	11 – 12	533	91 – 13	553	2B– 15
494	5B– 11	514	12 – 12	534	10 – 14	554	2C– 15
495	6 – 11	515	28 – 12	535	11 – 14	555	3 – 15
496	7 – 11	516	29 – 12	536	16 – 14	556	4 – 15
497	8 – 11	517	30 – 12	537	17 – 14	557	5 – 15
498	9 – 11	518	31 – 12	538	19 – 14	558	1 – 16
499	10 – 11	519	33 – 12	539	20 – 14	559	9 – 16
500	11A– 11	520	32 – 12	540	21 – 14	560	11 – 16
501	11B– 11	521	43 – 12	541	22 – 14	561	12 – 16
502	11C– 11	522	1A– 13	542	23 – 14	562	14 – 16
503	11D– 11	523	1B– 13	543	24 – 14	563	15 – 16
504	14 – 11	524	1C– 13	544	25 – 14	564	16 – 16
505	18 – 11	525	2 – 13	545	26 – 14	565	18 – 16
506	19 – 11	526	3 – 13	546	27 – 14	566	24 – 16
507	22 – 11	527	4 – 13	547	35 – 14	567	1 – 18
508	23 – 11	528	5A– 13	548	42A– 14	568	8 – 19
509	24A– 11	529	5B– 13	549	42B– 14	569	17 –CP
510	24B– 11	530	6A– 13	550	58 – 14	570	18 –CP
511	1 – 12	531	6B– 13	551	60 – 14	571	19 –CP
512	5 – 12	532	90 – 13	552	2A– 15	572	22 –CP

Component Scores by Burial

Burial Analysis Number	Dimension			Burial Analysis Number	Dimension			Burial Analysis Number	Dimension		
	I	II	III		I	II	III		I	II	III
001	−0.600	0.137	−0.503	057	−0.663	0.118	−0.507	113	−0.801	−0.000	0.585
002	−0.233	0.761	−0.411	058	−0.285	0.738	−0.709	114	0.463	2.676	−0.381
003	0.076	1.063	−0.339	059	−0.663	0.118	−0.507	115	0.678	0.955	0.753
004	−0.687	0.177	−0.392	060	−0.766	0.097	−0.042	116	−0.342	0.809	0.045
005	−0.573	−0.061	0.245	061	−0.963	0.079	1.655	117	−0.177	1.169	−0.600
006	−0.300	0.848	−0.348	062	−0.633	0.116	−0.460	118	−0.319	0.715	−0.334
007	−0.801	−0.009	0.669	063	−0.092	0.722	0.161	119	−0.741	−0.020	0.845
008	0.002	1.455	−0.670	064	−0.421	−0.059	0.527	120	−0.092	1.452	−0.047
009	0.777	2.756	1.074	065	−0.719	0.156	−0.349	121	−0.673	0.049	−0.036
010	−0.470	0.481	−0.433	066	−0.798	0.070	−0.022	122	−0.706	0.056	−0.543
011	−0.256	0.736	−0.633	067	−0.729	0.138	0.001	123	−0.761	0.111	0.021
012	−0.764	0.041	0.628	068	−0.687	0.177	−0.392	124	−0.424	−0.393	0.600
013	−0.516	−0.065	0.382	069	−0.754	−0.174	2.077	125	−0.263	0.705	0.774
014	−0.422	−0.243	0.190	070	−0.389	−0.296	−0.026	126	−0.539	0.067	−0.455
015	−0.483	−0.044	0.339	071	−0.720	0.147	−0.265	127	−0.048	1.009	−0.603
016	−0.181	1.000	−0.268	072	−0.729	0.138	0.001	128	−0.600	0.137	−0.503
017	−0.030	0.904	0.261	073	−0.589	−0.162	1.459	129	−0.764	0.032	0.712
018	−0.047	1.019	−0.687	074	−0.272	−0.534	1.215	130	−0.424	−0.393	0.600
019	−0.720	0.147	−0.265	075	−0.403	−0.363	1.749	131	0.106	1.253	0.108
020	−0.097	0.441	−0.275	076	−0.281	−0.561	2.058	132	−0.875	−0.060	0.503
021	−0.828	−0.001	0.196	077	0.554	1.153	2.074	133	−0.828	−0.001	0.196
022	0.339	1.659	1.183	078	−0.226	0.636	1.175	134	−0.731	0.063	0.585
023	−0.368	0.720	0.406	079	−0.930	0.110	1.528	135	−0.523	−0.267	1.115
024	−0.059	0.466	0.813	080	−0.272	0.746	−0.107	136	−0.793	0.044	0.582
025	−0.610	−0.187	0.937	081	−0.352	0.758	−0.201	137	−0.828	−0.001	0.196
026	−0.518	−0.180	1.177	082	−0.719	0.156	−0.249	138	−0.754	0.059	0.278
027	−0.802	0.078	−0.081	083	0.046	1.362	0.001	139	−0.793	0.044	0.582
028	−0.754	0.059	0.278	084	−0.272	−0.534	1.215	140	−0.201	0.458	1.094
029	−0.352	0.758	−0.201	085	−0.767	0.088	0.043	141	−0.050	0.462	1.366
030	−0.288	0.708	−0.643	086	−0.389	−0.296	−0.026	142	−0.246	0.786	−0.417
031	−0.633	0.106	−0.376	087	−0.150	1.077	−0.192	143	1.473	2.299	−0.034
032	−0.645	−0.043	0.383	088	−1.320	0.181	1.913	144	−0.090	1.129	−0.711
033	0.113	0.903	0.064	089	−1.391	0.174	2.088	145	0.230	1.295	0.632
034	−0.262	0.763	−0.457	090	−0.064	0.443	0.947	146	−1.330	0.163	2.263
035	0.209	0.880	−0.397	091	−0.528	−0.224	1.226	147	−0.963	0.079	1.655
036	−0.223	0.757	−0.706	092	−0.706	0.077	0.218	148	−0.813	−0.131	1.821
037	−0.355	0.438	−0.498	093	−0.424	−0.393	0.600	149	−1.353	0.225	2.046
038	−0.840	0.037	−0.124	094	−0.754	0.059	0.278	150	−1.367	0.122	2.220
039	−0.875	−0.060	0.503	095	−0.439	−0.042	−0.174	151	−0.357	0.715	0.499
040	−0.397	0.732	0.275	096	1.463	2.609	0.862	152	−0.719	0.156	−0.349
041	−0.766	0.097	−0.042	097	−0.690	−0.279	1.027	153	−0.796	0.014	0.648
042	−0.953	0.097	1.305	098	−0.424	−0.393	0.600	154	−0.067	0.630	0.397
043	−0.764	0.032	0.712	099	−0.796	0.014	0.648	155	−0.796	0.099	−0.088
044	−0.636	−0.072	0.502	100	−0.831	0.002	0.539	156	−0.249	0.856	−0.077
045	−0.384	0.731	−0.181	101	−0.100	0.692	1.009	157	−0.240	0.414	1.686
046	−0.802	0.078	−0.081	102	−0.833	−0.027	0.605	158	0.855	2.094	0.619
047	−0.633	0.116	−0.460	103	0.462	2.667	−0.297	159	−0.543	−0.063	0.291
048	−0.389	−0.296	−0.026	104	−0.731	0.063	0.585	160	−0.342	0.800	0.129
049	−0.729	0.138	0.001	105	−0.833	−0.027	0.605	161	0.347	2.230	−0.368
050	−0.387	0.661	0.425	106	−0.382	0.692	0.586	162	0.657	2.921	−0.140
051	−0.352	0.758	−0.201	107	−0.801	−0.000	0.585	163	0.700	−0.033	−0.245
052	−0.802	0.078	−0.081	108	−0.831	−0.019	0.546	164	−0.177	1.169	−0.600
053	−0.197	0.982	0.652	109	−0.124	1.082	0.730	165	−0.477	−0.039	0.508
054	−0.764	0.041	0.628	110	−0.424	−0.393	0.600	166	−0.761	0.111	0.021
055	0.114	−0.936	−0.018	111	−0.764	0.041	0.628	167	−0.597	−0.131	0.078
056	−0.027	1.133	0.017	112	−0.731	0.063	0.585	168	−0.793	0.096	−0.431

Burial Analysis Number	Dimension I	II	III	Burial Analysis Number	Dimension I	II	III	Burial Analysis Number	Dimension I	II	III
169	0.114	−0.936	−0.018	237	0.043	−0.642	−0.488	305	0.411	0.667	−0.359
170	−0.793	0.096	−0.431	238	0.043	−0.642	−0.488	306	−0.030	−0.354	−0.240
171	−0.054	1.054	−0.653	239	−0.297	−0.208	−0.460	307	0.333	−0.778	0.062
172	−0.319	0.715	−0.334	240	0.043	−0.642	−0.488	308	0.333	−0.778	0.062
173	0.244	0.278	1.067	241	0.043	−0.642	−0.488	309	0.672	0.712	−0.111
174	−0.311	0.581	0.991	242	0.043	−0.642	−0.488	310	−0.045	−0.395	0.131
175	−0.480	−0.288	0.685	243	−0.228	−0.335	−0.177	311	0.592	0.565	−0.184
176	−0.699	−0.055	0.278	244	0.008	−0.739	0.139	312	0.836	−1.419	0.070
177	−0.833	−0.027	0.605	245	0.008	−0.739	0.139	313	0.642	0.509	−0.578
178	−0.528	−0.224	1.226	246	0.339	0.046	0.183	314	0.525	0.249	−0.163
179	−0.050	0.943	−0.103	247	−0.309	−0.387	−0.377	315	0.512	−1.380	0.147
180	−0.132	0.885	0.302	248	−0.203	−0.306	−0.338	316	0.512	−1.380	0.147
181	−0.354	0.618	0.292	249	−0.309	−0.366	0.384	317	1.173	0.549	−0.403
182	−0.453	0.622	0.336	250	0.008	−0.739	0.139	318	1.381	0.832	−0.427
183	−0.833	−0.027	0.605	251	−0.332	−0.314	0.251	319	−0.274	−0.290	−1.004
184	−0.314	−0.351	0.517	252	0.008	−0.739	0.139	320	−0.201	−0.240	−0.834
185	−0.801	−0.000	0.585	253	0.546	−1.282	−0.480	321	−0.230	−0.228	−0.968
186	−0.828	−0.001	0.196	254	0.546	−1.282	−0.480	322	−0.233	−0.258	−0.902
187	−0.635	0.040	0.124	255	0.546	−1.282	−0.480	323	1.378	−1.507	0.205
188	−0.424	−0.393	0.600	256	0.139	0.267	−0.030	324	1.378	−1.507	0.205
189	−0.764	0.041	0.542	257	0.008	−0.739	0.139	325	1.378	−1.507	0.205
190	−0.769	0.021	0.542	258	0.008	−0.739	0.139	326	1.921	−0.494	−0.046
191	−0.796	0.014	0.648	259	0.226	0.265	0.509	327	0.004	0.032	−1.042
192	0.427	1.281	−0.591	260	−0.442	−0.406	0.042	328	0.004	0.032	−1.042
193	0.867	1.880	−1.198	261	−0.068	−0.085	0.303	329	1.367	−1.048	−0.382
194	0.185	0.378	−0.607	262	0.072	0.356	0.254	330	1.088	0.524	0.413
195	0.403	0.344	−0.558	263	0.546	−1.282	−0.480	331	0.611	−0.456	0.024
196	−0.050	−0.429	0.089	264	0.546	−1.282	−0.480	332	0.611	−0.456	0.024
197	0.468	0.431	−0.370	265	−0.287	−0.190	−0.810	333	0.239	−0.049	0.072
198	0.043	−0.642	−0.488	266	−0.111	−0.409	−0.170	334	2.396	2.501	0.707
199	0.399	1.139	−0.782	267	0.287	−0.417	0.101	335	1.967	0.791	0.291
200	0.010	−0.459	−0.073	268	0.287	−0.417	0.101	336	1.129	0.023	0.048
201	−0.317	−0.188	−0.856	269	0.287	−0.417	0.101	337	2.609	0.261	1.038
202	0.043	−0.642	−0.488	270	0.287	−0.417	0.101	338	3.335	2.295	0.246
203	−0.168	−0.209	−0.964	271	−0.366	−0.276	−0.483	339	1.394	0.345	−0.193
204	0.043	−0.642	−0.488	272	−0.370	−0.268	−0.542	340	1.286	−0.004	−0.275
205	0.652	0.726	−0.679	273	0.546	−1.282	−0.480	341	1.939	−1.008	0.162
206	0.078	0.092	−0.959	274	−0.201	−0.230	−0.921	342	1.939	−1.008	0.162
207	0.110	0.113	−1.002	275	0.546	−1.282	−0.480	343	1.939	−1.008	0.162
208	0.512	−1.380	0.147	276	0.546	−1.282	−0.480	344	1.939	−1.008	0.162
209	0.512	−1.380	0.147	277	0.546	−1.282	−0.480	345	1.939	−1.008	0.162
210	0.512	−1.380	0.147	278	0.546	−1.282	−0.480	346	0.338	−0.042	−0.456
211	0.512	−1.380	0.147	279	−0.168	−0.209	−0.964	347	0.461	−0.093	−0.404
212	0.512	−1.380	0.147	280	−0.145	−0.345	−0.921	348	0.461	−0.093	−0.404
213	0.512	−1.380	0.147	281	0.812	1.347	−0.470	349	0.611	−0.456	0.024
214	0.512	−1.380	0.147	282	0.634	0.905	−0.334	350	0.611	−0.456	0.024
215	2.662	−0.716	0.229	283	0.074	−0.637	0.438	351	0.546	−1.282	−0.480
216	2.863	−0.688	0.507	284	0.604	1.052	−0.118	352	0.546	−1.282	−0.480
217	3.052	−0.367	0.733	285	0.469	0.636	−0.294	353	0.246	0.806	−0.711
218	−0.028	−0.525	−0.079	286	−0.319	−0.217	−0.790	354	0.078	0.083	−0.875
219	0.043	−0.642	−0.488	287	−0.264	−0.186	−0.503	355	0.825	−0.960	−0.517
220	0.043	−0.642	−0.488	288	−0.334	−0.249	−0.503	356	0.228	−0.107	0.051
221	0.200	0.328	−0.907	289	0.043	−0.642	−0.488	357	0.623	1.153	−0.728
222	0.209	0.411	−1.167	290	−0.140	−0.407	−0.217	358	0.530	−0.037	−0.549
223	0.286	0.375	−0.983	291	0.043	−0.642	−0.488	359	−0.317	−0.188	−0.856
224	0.043	−0.642	−0.488	292	−0.061	−0.530	0.536	360	−0.297	−0.208	−0.460
225	−0.334	−0.258	−0.419	293	0.160	−0.880	0.753	361	0.298	0.713	−1.036
226	0.286	0.365	−0.899	294	0.420	−0.022	−0.690	362	−0.009	0.132	−0.848
227	−0.334	−0.258	−0.419	295	0.043	−0.642	−0.488	363	−0.082	0.072	−0.930
228	0.733	0.358	0.635	296	0.043	−0.642	−0.488	364	0.078	0.092	−0.959
229	0.871	0.934	−0.511	297	0.145	0.362	−1.104	365	0.078	0.092	−0.959
230	0.321	−0.320	−0.525	298	−0.274	−0.290	−1.004	366	−0.287	−0.190	−0.810
231	0.199	0.406	−0.788	299	0.177	0.390	1.124	367	−0.287	−0.190	−0.810
232	0.014	0.071	−0.631	300	0.043	−0.642	−0.488	368	0.136	0.298	−0.662
233	0.321	−0.320	−0.525	301	0.160	−0.880	0.753	369	0.321	−0.320	−0.525
234	0.298	0.704	−0.952	302	0.160	−0.880	0.753	370	0.321	0.652	−0.820
235	0.043	−0.642	−0.488	303	0.546	−1.282	−0.480	371	0.271	0.233	−0.016
236	0.176	0.380	−1.040	304	0.358	0.728	−0.137	372	0.047	0.018	−0.848

Burial Analysis Number	Dimension I	Dimension II	Dimension III	Burial Analysis Number	Dimension I	Dimension II	Dimension III	Burial Analysis Number	Dimension I	Dimension II	Dimension III
373	0.047	0.018	−0.848	440	−0.424	−0.393	0.600	507	0.412	−1.201	0.757
374	−0.369	−0.346	0.124	441	−0.131	1.068	0.852	508	0.412	−1.201	0.757
375	−0.322	−0.287	−0.183	442	−0.754	0.059	0.278	509	0.412	−1.201	0.757
376	0.407	0.205	0.038	443	−0.574	−0.030	0.172	510	0.412	−1.201	0.757
377	−0.336	−0.325	0.081	444	0.512	−1.380	0.147	511	−0.021	−0.855	1.219
378	0.471	1.081	−0.255	445	0.512	−1.380	0.147	512	−0.021	−0.855	1.219
379	0.008	−0.739	0.139	446	0.512	−1.380	0.147	513	−0.021	−0.855	1.219
380	−0.203	−0.306	−0.338	447	0.512	−1.380	0.147	514	−0.021	−0.855	1.219
381	0.512	−1.380	0.147	448	0.412	−1.201	0.757	515	−0.021	−0.855	1.219
382	0.512	−1.380	0.147	449	0.412	−1.201	0.757	516	0.061	−1.012	1.086
383	−0.369	−0.346	0.124	450	−0.021	−0.855	1.219	517	0.061	−1.012	1.086
384	0.321	−0.320	−0.525	451	−0.021	−0.855	1.219	518	0.061	−1.012	1.086
385	0.321	−0.320	−0.525	452	0.412	−1.201	0.757	519	0.061	−1.012	1.086
386	−0.045	−0.385	0.047	453	0.412	−1.201	0.757	520	−0.021	−0.855	1.219
387	0.035	−0.305	−0.303	454	0.412	−1.201	0.757	521	−0.021	−0.855	1.219
388	−0.056	0.073	−0.541	455	0.412	−1.201	0.757	522	0.412	−1.201	0.757
389	0.321	−0.320	−0.525	456	0.412	−1.201	0.757	523	0.412	−1.201	0.757
390	0.128	−0.128	−0.206	457	0.412	−1.201	0.757	524	0.412	−1.201	0.757
391	−0.082	0.072	−0.930	458	0.412	−1.201	0.757	525	−0.021	−0.855	1.219
392	−0.568	−0.308	1.151	459	0.412	−1.201	0.757	526	−0.371	−0.666	1.547
393	−0.531	−0.267	1.194	460	0.412	−1.201	0.757	527	−0.021	−0.855	1.219
394	0.499	1.395	−1.086	461	0.412	−1.201	0.757	528	0.412	−1.201	0.757
395	−0.361	−0.250	−0.892	462	−0.021	−0.855	1.219	529	0.412	−1.201	0.757
396	−0.274	−0.269	−0.243	463	−0.021	−0.855	1.219	530	0.412	−1.201	0.757
397	0.344	0.387	−0.130	464	−0.021	−0.855	1.219	531	0.412	−1.201	0.757
398	0.825	−0.960	−0.517	465	−0.021	−0.855	1.219	532	−0.021	−0.855	1.219
399	0.546	−1.282	−0.480	466	−0.021	−0.855	1.219	533	−0.371	−0.666	1.547
400	0.825	−0.960	−0.517	467	−0.021	−0.855	1.219	534	−0.021	−0.855	1.219
401	0.611	−0.456	0.024	468	−0.021	−0.855	1.219	535	−0.304	−0.535	1.246
402	0.271	−0.022	0.052	469	0.412	−1.201	0.757	536	0.043	−0.616	1.198
403	1.211	1.316	0.108	470	0.412	−1.201	0.757	537	0.053	−0.589	0.763
404	0.942	−1.199	0.724	471	0.412	−1.201	0.757	538	−0.021	−0.855	1.219
405	0.942	−1.199	0.724	472	0.412	−1.201	0.757	539	−0.021	−0.855	1.219
406	−0.264	−0.251	−0.593	473	−0.021	−0.855	1.219	540	−0.021	−0.855	1.219
407	−0.311	−0.310	−0.286	474	−0.021	−0.855	1.219	541	−0.021	−0.855	1.219
408	0.546	−1.282	−0.480	475	−0.021	−0.855	1.219	542	−0.021	−0.855	1.219
409	0.546	−1.282	−0.480	476	0.412	−1.201	0.757	543	−0.021	−0.855	1.219
410	1.064	0.420	0.306	477	0.412	−1.201	0.757	544	0.412	−1.201	0.757
411	0.651	0.133	−0.416	478	−0.021	−0.855	1.219	545	0.412	−1.201	0.757
412	0.177	0.390	−1.124	479	−0.740	−0.352	0.969	546	0.648	−0.184	1.685
413	0.043	−0.642	−0.488	480	−0.021	−0.855	1.219	547	−0.021	−0.855	1.219
414	0.651	0.133	−0.416	481	0.412	−1.201	0.757	548	0.370	−1.017	0.060
415	0.840	0.453	−0.189	482	0.412	−1.201	0.757	549	0.370	−1.017	0.060
416	0.546	−1.282	−0.480	483	0.412	−1.201	0.757	550	−0.371	−0.666	1.547
417	0.080	0.885	−1.146	484	0.412	−1.201	0.757	551	−0.021	−0.855	1.219
418	0.420	−0.022	−0.690	485	0.412	−1.201	0.757	552	0.061	−1.012	1.086
419	0.043	−0.642	−0.488	486	0.412	−1.201	0.757	553	0.061	−1.012	1.086
420	−0.264	−0.251	−0.593	487	−0.021	−0.855	1.219	554	0.061	−1.012	1.086
421	−0.114	−0.427	−0.631	488	−0.371	−0.666	1.547	555	−0.021	−0.855	1.219
422	0.180	0.529	−0.589	489	−0.021	−0.855	1.219	556	−0.021	−0.855	1.219
423	0.546	−1.282	−0.480	490	0.412	−1.201	0.757	557	−0.021	−0.855	1.219
424	0.546	−1.282	−0.480	491	0.412	−1.201	0.757	558	−0.343	−0.418	1.623
425	0.546	−1.282	−0.480	492	−0.021	−0.855	1.219	559	−0.021	−0.855	1.219
426	0.405	1.004	0.171	493	0.412	−1.201	0.757	560	−0.021	−0.855	1.219
427	−0.030	−0.044	0.346	494	0.412	−1.201	0.757	561	−0.021	−0.855	1.219
428	−0.309	−0.366	0.384	495	0.412	−1.201	0.757	562	−0.021	−0.855	1.219
429	−0.299	−0.283	0.124	496	0.412	−1.201	0.757	563	−0.021	−0.855	1.219
430	0.390	1.338	0.657	497	0.412	−1.201	0.757	564	−0.021	−0.855	1.219
431	−0.377	0.712	0.671	498	0.412	−1.201	0.757	565	−0.021	−0.855	1.219
432	−0.453	0.385	0.547	499	0.412	−1.201	0.757	566	−0.021	−0.855	1.219
433	−0.754	0.059	0.278	500	0.412	−1.201	0.757	567	−0.021	−0.855	1.219
434	−0.332	−0.305	0.167	501	0.412	−1.201	0.757	568	−0.021	−0.855	1.219
435	0.008	−0.739	0.139	502	0.412	−1.201	0.757	569	−0.371	−0.666	1.547
436	−0.369	−0.346	0.124	503	0.412	−1.201	0.757	570	−0.371	−0.666	1.547
437	0.008	−0.739	0.139	504	−0.021	−0.855	1.219	571	−0.371	−0.666	1.547
438	−0.764	0.041	0.628	505	0.412	−1.201	0.757	572	−0.371	−0.666	1.547
439	−0.424	−0.393	0.600	506	0.412	−1.201	0.757				

Factor Score Coefficients

Factor Score Coefficients

	FACTOR 1	FACTOR 2	FACTOR 3	FACTOR 4	FACTOR 5	FACTOR 6	FACTOR 7	FACTOR 8	FACTOR 9	FACTOR 10
VAR05	0.00143	0.00115	0.04133	−0.17244	0.10204	0.12838	−0.01419	0.02435	0.11878	−0.09941
VAR06	0.00433	0.01203	0.04221	−0.14037	0.03814	0.11862	0.10626	−0.09899	−0.20038	0.23251
VAR07	−0.10108	0.10307	−0.07809	0.25034	−0.04604	−0.08515	0.01157	0.02836	0.09780	−0.04438
VAR08	0.09321	0.05945	0.05879	−0.07500	0.21960	−0.15603	−0.13392	−0.04294	0.00280	−0.09608
VAR09	−0.03224	0.04543	0.07654	−0.07535	0.14162	−0.08979	−0.15242	−0.05527	0.33259	0.03853
VAR10	0.00792	−0.01721	0.07674	−0.04331	0.10613	0.17870	0.12997	0.02202	−0.07620	−0.31946
VAR11	−0.02523	0.04691	−0.05990	0.03396	−0.05483	−0.06432	0.08501	0.32488	−0.01830	−0.06044
VAR12	−0.04115	0.02458	0.05095	0.02992	−0.07417	0.08690	−0.01021	0.03411	−0.14405	0.29049
VAR13	0.00654	0.03285	−0.10294	0.11152	0.00919	0.01621	0.09976	−0.29755	−0.10132	−0.08885
VAR14	−0.08408	0.10697	−0.00133	0.03967	0.12912	0.09604	0.00714	−0.07131	−0.05185	−0.08011
VAR15	0.08408	−0.10697	0.00134	−0.03968	−0.12910	−0.09605	−0.00718	0.07129	0.05195	0.08012
VAR16	0.11193	−0.02497	0.10569	−0.04731	−0.28055	−0.10935	0.04986	−0.07420	0.05449	−0.10863
VAR17	0.09810	0.01887	0.04364	0.12551	0.13036	0.00074	−0.00643	0.04571	−0.05185	−0.09812
VAR18	−0.03749	0.02752	−0.27183	−0.19867	0.00159	−0.05944	0.08958	0.04431	0.00821	−0.01464
VAR19	0.05366	−0.02033	0.00149	0.14364	0.06526	0.04005	0.06396	−0.06866	0.01755	0.21079
VAR20	0.00706	−0.03084	0.11714	−0.02671	0.05036	0.04227	0.06609	−0.04250	−0.27164	0.05299
VAR21	−0.05066	−0.01940	0.03830	0.02806	−0.09553	0.26913	−0.35571	0.00671	0.10008	−0.08935
VAR22	−0.07339	0.01486	0.15763	0.07393	0.00103	−0.24442	0.04682	0.17784	−0.14715	−0.02002
VAR23	−0.04352	0.00076	0.14466	0.01722	0.03900	−0.08278	0.20797	−0.15211	0.27183	0.13861
VAR24	−0.10763	0.08615	0.11482	−0.08723	−0.06893	−0.03192	0.00421	−0.04753	−0.05819	−0.03550
VAR25	0.10763	−0.08615	−0.11483	0.08723	0.06893	0.03194	−0.00422	0.04752	0.05819	0.03550
VAR26	0.00637	0.01109	0.00096	0.12267	0.00890	0.18673	0.08845	−0.09311	−0.06791	−0.09516
VAR27	−0.00958	0.01541	0.06330	0.01324	0.09314	−0.08636	−0.00115	0.25890	−0.10328	−0.11037
VAR28	−0.02134	0.02112	0.00483	0.01062	0.00343	0.06570	−0.02556	−0.02113	0.17457	0.16938
VAR29	−0.02072	0.02833	−0.01126	−0.05809	−0.02348	0.01495	0.17569	−0.10926	−0.14441	−0.12828
VAR30	−0.03422	0.01440	−0.02181	0.03177	−0.03197	0.00258	0.05003	0.01589	0.09577	−0.21893
VAR31	−0.00680	0.04001	−0.01263	−0.00214	0.00355	0.02884	−0.05976	−0.12364	0.12160	−0.03941
VAR32	−0.02192	0.04489	−0.02664	0.01862	−0.00118	−0.12951	−0.27218	−0.02967	−0.17775	0.08563
VAR33	−0.01599	0.03000	0.02408	0.02483	0.02419	−0.00572	0.24491	−0.06780	0.21126	0.11123
VAR34	−0.13813	−0.15980	0.01876	−0.00374	0.03368	−0.06649	0.02179	0.03558	0.01235	0.02706
VAR35	0.11212	−0.01824	0.02800	0.08202	0.16748	−0.03083	0.02404	0.06864	0.02522	0.03852
VAR36	0.05414	0.09166	0.06478	−0.00828	−0.09061	0.08731	0.04391	0.11974	0.15070	−0.04272
VAR37	0.04461	0.08750	−0.00882	−0.02854	−0.00371	0.10992	0.10084	0.23916	0.09721	−0.02593
VAR38	0.06330	0.08602	−0.00731	−0.04628	−0.12730	−0.17753	0.02891	−0.15874	0.00169	−0.16598
VAR39	0.03619	0.10904	−0.06025	−0.03664	0.03162	−0.09372	−0.04597	−0.05467	−0.04910	0.13451
VAR40	0.02995	0.09623	0.02246	−0.03431	−0.01730	0.14155	−0.04508	0.04066	−0.05525	0.10093
VAR41	0.02957	0.09358	−0.01037	−0.02535	−0.04277	0.10831	0.09320	0.23122	0.01770	0.20486
VAR42	0.04204	0.09989	−0.01234	−0.01359	0.04226	−0.10334	−0.05723	−0.07051	−0.08046	0.09671
VAR43	0.06319	0.05653	0.08175	0.07580	−0.15833	0.07697	−0.07162	−0.06018	−0.04164	−0.02153

References

Aberle, David F.
  1968   Comments. In *New Perspectives in Archaeology*, edited by Sally R. Binford and Lewis R. Binford, pp. 353–359. Chicago: Aldine.

Akins, Nancy J.
  1986   A Biocultural Approach to Human Burials from Chaco Canyon, New Mexico. *Reports of the Chaco Center* 9. Santa Fe: Division of Cultural Research, National Park Service.

Allen, William L., and James B. Richardson III
  1971   The reconstruction of kinship from archaeological data: the concept, the methods, the feasibility. *American Antiquity* 36(1): 41–53.

Anderson, Arthur J. O., and Charles E. Dibble, translators and editors
  1950–   Florentine Codex: General History of the Things of
  1955   New Spain. By Bernardino de Sahagún, O.F.M. Book 1, The Gods; Book 2, The Ceremonies; Book 3, The Origin of the Gods; Book 7, The Sun, Moon and Stars, and the Binding of the Years; Book 8, Kings and Lords; Book 12, The Conquest of Mexico. *School of American Research and Museum of New Mexico Monographs* 14, Parts II–IV, VII–IX, XIII.

Ashby, W. Ross
  1962   Principles of the self-organizing system. In *Principles of Self-Organization*, edited by Heinz von Foerster and George W. Zopf, pp. 255–278. New York: Pergamon Press.

Bandelier, Adolph F.
  1892   Final Report of Investigations Among the Indians of the Southwestern United States, Carried Out Mainly in the Years from 1880 to 1885, Part II. *Papers of the Archaeological Institute of America, American Series*, Vol. 4.

Barth, Fredrik
  1967   On the study of social change. *American Anthropologist* 69: 661–669.

Beals, Ralph L.
  1932   Comparative ethnology of northern Mexico before 1750. *Ibero-Americana* 2.

Benfer, Robert A., Jr.
  1968   An Analysis of a Prehistoric Skeletal Population, Casas Grandes, Chihuahua, Mexico. MS, doctoral dissertation, University of Texas at Austin.

Berry, David R.
  1985   Aspects of paleodemography of Grasshopper Pueblo, Arizona. In "Health and Disease in the Prehistoric Southwest," edited by Charles F. Merbs and Robert J. Miller, pp. 43–64. *Arizona State University Anthropological Research Papers* 34. Tempe: Arizona State University.

Bertalanffy, Ludwig Von
  1968   *General Systems Theory*. New York: George Braziller.

Binford, Lewis R.
  1962   Archaeology as anthropology. *American Antiquity* 28: 217–225.
  1965   Archaeological systematics and the study of culture process. *American Antiquity* 31: 203–210.
  1968   Archaeological perspectives. In *New Perspectives in Archaeology*, edited by Sally R. Binford and Lewis R. Binford, pp. 5–32. Chicago: Aldine.
  1971   Mortuary practices: their study and potential. In "Approaches to the Social Dimensions of Mortuary Practices," edited by James A. Brown, pp. 6–29. *Memoirs of the Society for American Archaeology* 25.

Blau, Peter M.
  1968   The hierarchy of authority in organizations. *American Journal of Sociology* 73: 453–467.
  1970   A formal theory of differentiation in organizations. *American Sociological Review* 35(2): 201–218.
  1977   *Inequality and Heterogeneity: A Primitive Theory of Social Structure*. New York: The Free Press.

Blau, Peter M., and Richard A. Schoenherr
  1971   *The Structure of Organizations*. New York: Basic Books.

Braniff, Beatris
  1986   Ojo de Agua, Sonora and Casas Grandes, Chihuahua: a suggested chronology. In *Ripples in the Chichimec Sea, New Considerations of Southwestern-Mesoamerican Interactions*, edited by Frances Joan Mathien and Randall H. McGuire, pp. 70–80. Carbondale: Southern Illinois University Press.

Braun, David P.
  1977   Middle Woodland-(Early) Late Woodland Social Change in the Prehistoric Central Midwestern U.S. MS, doctoral dissertation, University of Michigan, Ann Arbor.
  1979   Illinois Hopewell burial practices and social organization: a reexamination of the Klunk-Gibson Mound Group. In *Hopewell Archaeology, the Chillicothe Conference*, edited by David S. Brose and N'omi M. B. Greber, pp. 66–79. Kent: Kent State University Press.
  1981   A critique of some recent North American mortuary studies. *American Antiquity* 46(2): 398–416.

Braun, David P., and Stephen E. Plog
  1982   Evolution of tribal social networks: theory and prehistoric North American evidence. *American Antiquity* 47(3): 504–525.

Brown, James A.
1971   (Editor) Approaches to the Social Dimensions of Mortuary Practices. *Society for American Archaeology Memoir* 25: 92–112.
1975   Spiro art and its mortuary contexts. In *Death and the Afterlife in Pre-Columbian America*, edited by Elizabeth P. Benson, pp. 1–32. Washington: Dumbarton Oaks.
1979   Charnel houses and mortuary crypts: disposal of the dead in the Middle Woodland period. In *Hopewell Archaeology, The Chillicothe Conference*, edited by David S. Brose and N'omi M. B. Greber, pp. 211–219. Kent: Kent State University Press.
1981   The Search for Rank in Prehistoric Burials. In *The Archaeology of Death*, edited by Robert Chapman, I. Kinnes, and Klaus Randsborg, pp. 25–37. Cambridge: Cambridge University Press.

Buikstra, Jane E.
1976   Hopewell in the Lower Illinois Valley: A Regional Approach to the Study of Human Biological Variability and Prehistoric Behavior. *Northwestern University Archaeological Program Scientific Papers* 2. Evanston: Northwestern University.
1977   Biocultural Dimensions in Archaeological Study: A Regional Perspective. In "Biocultural Adaptation in Prehistoric America," edited by Robert L. Blakely, pp. 67–84. *Southern Anthropological Society Proceedings* 11. Athens: University of Georgia Press.

Butler, Barbara H.
1971   The People of Casas Grandes: Cranial and Dental Morphology Through Time. MS, doctoral dissertation, Southern Methodist University of Dallas, Texas.

Carlson, Roy L.
1982   The polychrome complexes. In "Southwestern Ceramics: A Comparative Review," edited by Albert H. Schroeder. *The Arizona Archaeologist* 15: 201–234.

Carzo, Rocco, Jr., and John N. Yanouzas
1969   Effects of flat and tall organization structure. *Administrative Science Quarterly* 14: 178–191.

Champion, Dean J.
1975   *The Sociology of Organizations*. New York: McGraw-Hill.

Chang, Kwang C.
1958   Study of the Neolithic social groupings: examples from the New World. *American Anthropologist* 60(2): 298–334.

Chapman, Robert, and Klaus Randsborg
1981   Approaches to the archaeology of death. In *The Archaeology of Death*, edited by Robert Chapman, I. Kinnes, and Klaus Randsborg, pp. 1–24. Cambridge: Cambridge University Press.

Chapman, Robert, I. Kinnes, and Klaus Randsborg
1981   *The Archaeology of Death*. Cambridge: Cambridge University Press.

Clark, Geoffrey A.
1967   A Preliminary Analysis of the Burial Clusters at the Grasshopper Site, East-Central Arizona. MS, master's thesis, Department of Anthropology, University of Arizona, Tucson.

Clarke, David L.
1972   Models and paradigms in contemporary archaeology. In *Models in Archaeology*, edited by David L. Clarke, pp. 1–160. London: Methuen.

Cole, L. C.
1949   The measurement of interspecific association. *Ecology* 30: 411–424.

Cordell, Linda S.
1984   *Prehistory of the Southwest*. Orlando: Academic Press.

Cordell, Linda S., Steadman Upham, and Sharon L. Brock
1987   Obscuring cultural patterns in the archaeological record: a discussion from southwestern archaeology. *American Antiquity* 52(3): 565–577.

Crotty, Helen K. (editor)
1983   Honoring the Dead: Anasazi Ceramics from the Rainbow Bridge-Monument Valley Expedition. *Museum of Cultural History Monograph Series* 22. Los Angeles: University of California.

Crozier, Michel
1964   *The Bureaucratic Phenomenon*. Chicago: University of Chicago Press.

Cushing, Frank H.
1896   Outlines of Zuni Creation Myths. *13th Annual Report of the Bureau of American Ethnology*, pp. 325–447. Washington.

Davis, John C.
1973   *Statistics and Data Analysis in Geology*. New York: John Wiley.

Dean, Jeffrey S.
1970   Aspects of Tsegi phase social organization: a trial reconstruction. In *Reconstructing Prehistoric Pueblo Societies*, edited by William A. Longacre, pp. 140–176. Albuquerque: University of New Mexico Press.

Deetz, James
1965   *The Dynamics of Stylistic Change Among the Arikara*. Urbana: University of Illinois Press.

Deuel, Thorne
1952   The Hopewellian community. In "Hopewellian Communities in Illinois," edited by Thorne Deuel, pp. 249–270. *Illinois State Museum Scientific Papers* 5. Springfield: Illinois State Museum.

Dibble, C. E., and A. J. O. Anderson, translators and editors
1957–   Florentine Codex: General History of the Things of
1969   New Spain, by Bernardino de Sahagún, O.F.M. Book 4, The Soothsayers; Book 5, The Omens; Book 6, Rhetoric and Moral Philosophy; Book 9, The Merchants; Book 10, The People; Book 11, The Earthly Things. *School of American Research and Museum of New Mexico Monographs* 14, Parts V–VII, X–XII.

Di Peso, Charles C.
1968a   Casas Grandes and the Gran Chichimeca. *El Palacio* 75(4): 45–61.
1968b   Casa Grandes, a fallen trading center of the Gran Chichimeca. *The Masterkey* 42(1): 20–37.
1974   *Casas Grandes, A Fallen Trading Center of the Gran Chichimeca*. Vol. 1–3. Flagstaff: Northland Press.
1976   Gila Polychrome in the Casas Grandes region. *The Kiva* 42(1): 57–64.

Di Peso, Charles C., John B. Rinaldo, and Gloria J. Fenner
1974   *Casas Grandes, A Fallen Trading Center of the Gran Chichimeca*. Vol. 4–8. Flagstaff: Northland Press.

Doolittle, William E.
1988   Pre-Hispanic Occupance in the Valley of Sonora, Mexico. *Anthropological Papers of the University of Arizona* 48. Tucson: University of Arizona Press.

Doran, J. E., and F. R. Hodson
1975 *Mathematics and Computers in Archaeology.* Edinburgh: Edinburgh University Press.

Doyel, David E.
1976 Classic period Hohokam in the Gila River Basin, Arizona. *The Kiva* 42(1): 27–38.

Driver, Harold E.
1961 *Indians of North America.* Chicago: University of Chicago Press.

Durkheim, Emile
1933 The Division of Labor in Society. Translation of *De la Division du Travail Social* (1893). 1964 edition. New York: Free Press.

Ekholm, Gordon F.
1942 Excavations at Guasave, Sinaloa, Mexico. *Anthropological Papers of the American Museum of Natural History* 38(2).

Fewkes, J. Walter
1896 The prehistoric culture of Tusayan. *American Anthropologist* 9: 151–174.
1900 Tusayan Migration Myths. *19th Annual Report of the Bureau of American Ethnology*, pp. 573–633. Washington.

Flannery, Kent V.
1972 The cultural evolution of civilizations. *Annual Review of Ecology and Systematics* 3: 399–426.
1976 Contextual analysis of ritual paraphernalia from Formative Oaxaca. In *The Early Mesoamerican Village*, edited by Kent V. Flannery, pp. 333–345. New York: Academic Press.

Foster, George M.
1960 Culture and Conquest: America's Spanish Heritage. *Viking Fund Publications in Anthropology* 27.

Fried, Morton H.
1967 *The Evolution of Political Society: An Essay in Political Society.* New York: Random House.

Frisbie, Theodore R.
1978 High status burials in the Greater Southwest: an interpretive synthesis. In *Across the Chichimec Sea*, edited by Carroll L. Riley and Basil C. Hedrick, pp. 202–227. Carbondale: Southern Illinois University Press.

Gardner, B., and D. G. Moore
1963 Status and Status Hierarchies. In *Organization: Structure and Behavior*, edited by J.A. Litterer, pp. 171–178.

Gibson, James L., and John M. Ivancevich
1976 *Organizations Behavior, Structure, Processes.* Dallas: Business Publication.

Goldstein, Lynne
1976 Spatial Structure and Social Organization: Regional Manifestations of Mississippian Society. MS, doctoral dissertation, Northwestern University, Evanston, Illinois.
1980 Mississippian Mortuary Practices: A Case Study of Two Cemeteries in the Lower Illinois Valley. *Northwestern University Archaeological Program, Scientific Papers* 4. Evanston: Northwestern University.
1981 One-dimensional archaeology and multidimensional people: spatial organization and mortuary analysis. In *The Archaeology of Death*, edited by Robert Chapman, I. Kinnes, and Klaus Randsborg, pp. 39–52. Cambridge: Cambridge University Press.

Goodenough, Ward H.
1965 Rethinking status and role: toward a general model of cultural organization of social relationships. In "The Relevance of Models for Social Anthropology," edited by M. Banton, pp. 1–24. *ASA Monographs* 1. New York: Praeger.

Griffin, P. Bion
1967 A high status burial from Grasshopper Ruin, Arizona. *The Kiva* 33(2): 37–53.

Haas, J. Eugene, and Thomas E. Drabeck
1973 *Complex Organizations: A Sociological Perspective.* New York: Macmillan.

Hammond, George R., and Agapito Rey (trans., eds., and annots.)
1940 *Narratives of the Coronado Expedition 1540–1542.* Coronado Cuarto Centennial Publications, 1540–1940, Vol. 2. Albuquerque: University of New Mexico Press.

Harris, Marvin
1968 Comments. In *New Perspectives in Archaeology*, edited by Sally R. Binford and Lewis R. Binford, pp. 359–361. Chicago: Aldine.

Haury, Emil W.
1956 Speculations on prehistoric settlement patterns in the Southwest. In "Prehistoric Settlement Patterns in the New World," edited by Gordon R. Willey, pp. 3–10. *Viking Fund Publications in Anthropology* 23. New York: Wenner-Gren Foundation for Anthropological Research.

Hayes, Alden C.
1981 Excavation of Mound 7. Gran Quivira National Monument, New Mexico. *National Park Service Publication* 16. Washington.

Hewett, Edgar L.
1905 A General View of the Archaeology of the Pueblo Region. *Annual Report of the Smithsonian Institution*, 1904, pp. 583–605. Washington.

Hill, James N.
1970 Broken K Pueblo: Prehistoric Social Organization in the American Southwest. *Anthropological Papers of the University of Arizona* 18. Tucson: University of Arizona Press.
1977 Systems theory and the explanation of change. In *Explanation of Prehistoric Change*, edited by James N. Hill, pp. 59–103. Santa Fe: School of American Research.

Hodge, Frederick W. (editor)
1907 The Narrative of Alvar Nuñez Cabeza de Vaca and the Narrative of the Expedition of Coronado, by Pedro de Castaneda. In *Spanish Explorers in the Southern United States, 1528–1543*, edited by Frederick W. Hodge and T. H. Lewis, pp. 1–26, 273–387. New York: Charles Scribner's Sons.

Hohmann, John W.
1983 Sinagua Social Differentiation: Inferences Based on Prehistoric Mortuary Practices. *The Arizona Archaeologist* 17. Phoenix: Arizona Archaeological Society.

Jackson, John H., and Cyril P. Morgan
1978 *Organization Theory: A Macroperspective for Management.* New York: Prentice-Hall.

Jacobs, Jane
1969 *The Economy of Cities.* New York: Random House.

Johnson, Gregory A.
1978   Information Sources and the Development of Decision-making Organizations. In *Social Archaeology*, edited by Charles L. Redman, and others, pp. 87–112. New York: Academic Press.
1981   Monitoring complex system integration and secondary phenomena with settlement size data. In *Archaeological Approaches to the Study of Complexity*, edited by Sander E. van der Leeuw, pp. 143–188. Amsterdam.
1982   Organization of Structure and Scalar Stress. In *Theory and Explanation in Archaeology: The Southampton Conference*, edited by Colin Renfrew, M. J. J. Rowlands, and B. Abbott Segraves, pp. 389–421. New York: Academic Press.

Katz, Daniel, and Robert L. Kahn
1966   *The Social Psychology of Organizations*. New York: Wiley.

Kelley, Ellen A.
1978   The Temple of the Skulls at Alta Vista, Chalchihuites. In *Across the Chichimec Sea: Papers in Honor of J. Charles Kelley*, edited by Carroll L. Riley and Basil C. Hedrick, pp. 102–126. Carbondale: Southern Illinois University Press.

Kelley, J. Charles
1966   Mesoamerica and the southwestern United States. In *Handbook of Middle American Indians*, Vol. 4, edited by Gordon F. Ekholm and Gordon R. Willey, pp. 95–110. Austin: University of Texas Press.
1980   Discussion of papers by Plog, Doyel and Riley. In "Current Issues in Hohokam Prehistory," edited by David Doyel and Fred Plog, pp. 49–71. *Anthropological Research Papers* 23. Tempe: Arizona State University.

Kelley, J. Charles, and Ellen A. Kelley
1975   An alternative hypothesis for the explanation of Anasazi culture history. In "Collected Papers in Honor of Florence Hawley Ellis," edited by T. R. Frisbie, pp. 178–223. *Papers of the Archaeological Society of New Mexico* 2. Norman, Oklahoma: Hooper Publishing Co.

King, Thomas F.
1970   The Dead at Tiburon: Mortuary Customs and Social Organization on Northern San Francisco Bay. *Northwestern California Archaeological Society Occasional Papers* 2.
1978   Don't that beat the band? Nonegalitarian political organization in prehistoric central California. In *Social Archaeology*, edited by Charles L. Redman and others, pp. 225–248. New York: Academic Press.

Las Casas, Fr. B.
1967   *Apologética Historia Sumaria*. 2 Vol., edited by E. O'Gorman. Mexico: Universidad Nacional Autonoma de Mexico, Instituto de Investigaciones Historica.

Lawrence, Paul R., and Jay W. Lorsch
1967   Differentiation and integration in complex organizations. *Administrative Science Quarterly* 12: 1–47.

LeBlanc, Steven A.
1980   The dating of Casas Grandes. *American Antiquity* 45(4): 799–806.
1986   Aspects of southwestern prehistory: A.D. 900–1400. In *Ripples in the Chichimec Sea: New Considerations of Southwestern-Mesoamerican Interactions*, edited by Frances Joan Mathien and Randall H. McGuire, pp. 105–134. Carbondale: Southern Illinois University Press.

Lekson, Stephen H.
1984   Dating Casas Grandes. *The Kiva* 50(1): 55–60.

Lightfoot, Kent G.
1984   *Prehistoric Political Dynamics: A Case Example from The American Southwest*. DeKalb: Northern Illinois University Press.

Lightfoot, Kent G., and Gary M. Feinman
1982   Social differentiation and leadership development in early pithouse villages in the Mogollon region of the American Southwest. *American Antiquity* 47(1): 64–86.

Linton, Ralph
1936   *The Study of Man*. New York: Meredith.

Litterer, Joseph A.
1963   *Organization: Structure and Behavior*. New York: Wiley.
1965   *The Analysis of Organizations*. New York: Wiley.
1969   *Organizations*. 2nd edition. New York: Wiley.

Longacre, William A.
1970   Archaeology as Anthropology: A Case Study. *Anthropological Papers of the University of Arizona* 17. Tucson: University of Arizona Press.

March, James G., and Herbert A. Simon
1958   *Organizations*. New York: Wiley.

Martin, Paul S., and John B. Rinaldo
1950   Sites of the Reserve Phase, Pine Lawn Valley, Western New Mexico. *Fieldiana: Anthropology* 38(3). Chicago: Chicago Natural History Museum.

Mathein, Joan Frances, and Randall H. McGuire, editors
1986   *Ripples in the Chichimec Sea: New Considerations of Southwestern-Mesoamerican Interactions*. Carbondale: Southern Illinois University Press.

McGuire, Randall H.
1980   The Mesoamerican connection in the Southwest. *The Kiva* 46(1–2): 3–38.

Miller, James G.
1965   Living systems: basic concepts. *Behavioral Science* 19(3): 192–237.
1978   *Living Systems*. New York: McGraw-Hill.

Milner, George R.
1984   Social and temporal implications of variation among American Bottom Mississippian Cemeteries. *American Antiquity* 49(3): 468–488.

Mindeleff, Cosmos
1897   The Cliff Ruins of Canyon de Chelley, Arizona. *16th Annual Report of the Bureau of American Ethnology*, pp. 79–198. Washington.
1900   Localization of Tusayan Clans. *19th Annual Report of the Bureau of American Ethnology*, pp. 635–653. Washington.

Mindeleff, Victor
1891   A Study of Pueblo Architecture: Tusayan and Cibola. *8th Annual Report of the Bureau of American Ethnology*, pp. 12–228. Washington.

Mintzberg, Henry
1979   *The Structuring of Organizations. A Synthesis of the Research*. Englewood Cliffs: Prentice-Hall.

Moser, Christopher L.
1973   *Human Decapitation in Ancient Mesoamerica*. Washington: Dumbarton Oaks.

Nie, Norman H., and C. Hadlai Hull, Jean G. Jenkins, Karin
Steinbrenner, and Dale H. Bent
1975   *Statistical Package for the Social Sciences*. 2nd edition.
New York: McGraw-Hill.

Olsen, Marvin E.
1968   *The Processes of Social Organization*. New York: Holt,
Rinehart, Winston.

Orser, Charles E.
1980   An Archaeological and Ethnohistorical Socioeconomic
Analysis of Arikara Mortuary Practices. MS, doctoral
dissertation, Southern Illinois University at Carbondale, Illinois.

Osborn, R. N., J. G. Hunt, and L. R. Jauch
1980   *Organization Theory: An Integrated Approach*. New
York: Wiley

O'Shea, John M.
1981   Social configurations and the archaeological study of
mortuary practices: a case study. In *The Archaeology
of Death*, edited by Robert Chapman, I. Kinnes, and
Klaus Randsborg, pp. 39–52. Cambridge: Cambridge
University Press.
1984   *Mortuary Variability: An Archaeology Investigation*.
Orlando: Academic Press.

Pailes, Richard A.
1972   An Archaeological Reconnaissance of Southern Sonora
and Reconsideration of the Rio Sonora Culture. MS,
doctoral dissertation, Southern Illinois University at
Carbondale, Illinois.
1978   The Rio Sonora culture in prehistoric trade systems. In
*Across the Chichimec Sea: Papers in Honor of J. Charles
Kelley*, edited by Carroll L. Riley and Basil C. Hedrick,
pp. 134–143. Carbondale: Southern Illinois University
Press.
1980   The upper Rio Sonora Valley in prehistoric trade. In
"New Frontiers in the Archaeology and Ethnology of
the Greater Southwest," edited by Carroll L. Riley and
Basil C. Hedrick, pp. 20–39. *Transactions of the Il-
linois State Academy of Science* 72(4).

Palkovich, Ann M.
1980   *The Arroyo Hondo Skeleton and Mortuary Remains*.
Santa Fe: School of American Research Press.

Parsons, Talcott
1951   *The Social System*. Glencoe, Illinois: Free Press.

Peebles, Christopher S.
1971   Moundville and surrounding sites: some structural considerations of mortuary practices. In "Approaches to
the Social Dimensions of Mortuary Practices," edited
by James A. Brown, pp. 68–91. *Society for American
Archaeology Memoir* 25.
1974   Moundville: The Organization of a Prehistoric Community and Culture. MS, doctoral dissertation, University of California, Santa Barbara.
1978   Determinants of Settlement Size and Location in the
Moundville Phase. In *Mississippian Settlement Patterns*, edited by Bruce D. Smith, pp. 369–416. New
York: Academic Press.

Peebles, Christopher S., and Susan M. Kus
1977   Some archaeological correlates of ranked societies. In
"Essays on Archaeological Problems," edited by Brian
Fagan and Barbara Voorhies. *American Antiquity* 42(3):
421–448.

Pickering, Robert B.
1985   Human Osteological Remains from Alta Vista Zaca-

tecas: An analysis of the Isolated Bone. In *The Archaeology of West and Northwest Mesoamerica*, edited
by Michael S. Foster and Phil C. Weigand, pp. 289–
325. Boulder and London: Westview Press.

Plog, Fred T.
1974   *The Study of Prehistoric Change*. New York: Academic
Press.

Plog, Fred T., and Steadman Upham
1979   The analysis of prehistoric political organization. In
*Proceedings of the American Ethnological Society of
1979*, edited by Morton H. Fried and F. Findlow. New
York: Columbia University.

Plog, Fred T., Steadman Upham, and Phil C. Weigand
1982   A Perspective on Mogollon-Mesoamerican Interaction.
In *Papers from the 1980 Mogollon Conference*, edited
by Patrick H. Beckett, pp. 227–237. Ramona, California: Acoma Books.

Plog, Stephen
1976   Measurement of prehistoric interaction between communities. In *The Early Mesoamerican Village*, edited
by K. V. Flannery, pp. 225–271. New York: Academic
Press.
1978   Social interaction and stylistic similarity: a reanalysis.
In *Advances in Archaeological Method and Theory*,
Vol. 1, edited by M. Schiffer, pp. 143–182. New York:
Academic Press.
1980   *Stylistic Variation in Prehistoric Ceramics: Design
Analysis in the American Southwest*. Cambridge: Cambridge University Press.

Pugh, D. S., D. J. Hickson, R. Hinings, and C. Turner
1968   Dimensions of organizational structure. *Administrative
Science Quarterly* 13: 65–105.

Randsborg, Klaus C.
1975   Social dimensions of early Neolithic Denmark. *Proceedings of the Prehistoric Society* 41: 105–118.

Rathje, William L.
1970   Sociopolitical implications of Lowland Maya burials:
methodology and tentative hypotheses. *World Archaeology* 1: 359–374.
1973   Models for mobile Maya: a variety of constraints. In
Explanation of Culture Change: Models in Prehistory,
edited by Colin Renfrew, pp. 731–757. London: Duck-
worth.

Ravesloot, John C.
1979   The Animas Phase: Post-Classic Mimbres Occupation
of the Mimbres Valley, New Mexico. MS, master's
thesis, Southern Illinois University at Carbondale, Illinois.
1984   Social Differentiation at Casas Grandes, Chihuahua,
Mexico: An Archaeological Analysis of Mortuary Practices. MS, doctoral dissertation, Southern Illinois University at Carbondale, Illinois.
1987   Files in the Archives of the Arizona State Museum
Library, University of Arizona, Tucson.

Ravesloot, John C., and Patricia M. Spoerl
1987   The Role of Warfare in the Development of Status
Hierarchies at Casas Grandes, Chihuahua, Mexico. Paper presented at the 20th Annual Chacmool Conference,
University of Calgary, Alberta, Canada.

Ravesloot, John C., Jeffrey S. Dean, and Michael S. Foster.
1986   A New Perspective on the Casas Grandes Tree-Ring
Dates. Paper presented at the Fourth Mogollon Conference, University of Arizona, Tucson.

Renfrew, Colin
1974   Beyond a subsistence economy: the evolution of social
        organization in prehistoric Europe. In "Reconstructing
        Complex Societies," edited by C. Moore, pp. *Bulletin
        of the American Schools of Oriental Research* 20.

Reyman, Jonathan E.
1971   Mexican Influence on Southwestern Ceremonialism.
        MS, doctoral dissertation, Southern Illinois University
        at Carbondale, Illinois.
1978   Pochteca Burials at Anasazi Sites? In *Across the Chi-
        chimec Sea*, edited by Carroll L. Riley and Basil C.
        Hedrick, pp. 242–259. Carbondale: Southern Illinois
        University Press.

Riley, Carroll L.
1979   Casas Grandes and the Sonoran Statelets. Paper Pre-
        sented at the Chicago Anthropological Society.
1982   The Frontier People: The Greater Southwest in the Pro-
        tohistoric Period. *Center For Archaeological Investi-
        gations Occasional Paper* 1. Carbondale: Southern
        Illinois University Press.

Ritchie, William A.
1955   Recent Discoveries Suggesting an Early Woodland
        Burial Cult in the Northwest. *New York State Museum
        Circular* 40. Albany.

Rothschild, Nan A.
1979   Mortuary behavior and social organization at Indian
        Knoll and Dickson Mounds. *American Antiquity* 44(4):
        658–675.

Rummel, R. J.
1967   Understanding factor analysis. *Conflict Resolution* 11:
        444–480.
1970   *Applied Factor Analysis*. Evanston: Northwestern Uni-
        versity Press.

Saxe, Arthur A.
1970   Social Dimensions of Mortuary Practices. MS, doctoral
        dissertation, University of Michigan, Ann Arbor,
        Michigan.

Sanders, William T., and Barbara J. Price
1968   *Mesoamerica: The Evolution of a Civilization*. New
        York: Random House.

Schiffer, Michael B.
1972   Archaeological context and systemic context. *American
        Antiquity* 37: 56–65.
1987   *Formation Processes of the Archaeological Record*.
        Albuquerque: University of New Mexico Press.

Scott, William G.
1961   Organizational theory: an overview and an appraisal.
        Academy of Management Journal 4: 7–27.
1975   Organization structure. *Annual Review of Sociology* 1:
        1–20.

Scott, William G., and Terence R. Mitchell
1972   *Organizational Theory: A Structural and Behavioral
        Analysis*. Homewood, Illinois: Richard D. Irwin Inc.
        and the Dorsey Press.

Sears, William H.
1954   The sociopolitical organizations of Pre-Columbian cul-
        tures on the gulf coastal plain. *American Anthropologist*
        56(3): 339–346.

1958   Burial mounds on the gulf coastal plain. *American An-
        tiquity* 23(3): 274–284.
1961   The study of social and religious systems in North
        American archaeology. *Current Anthropology* 2(3):
        223–246.

Service, Elman R.
1962   *Primitive Social Organization*. New York: Random
        House.
1971   *Primitive Social Organization*. 2nd edition. New York:
        Random House.

Simon, Herbert A.
1944   Decision-making and administrative organization. *Pub-
        lic Administrative Review* 4: 16–30.
1947   *Administrative Behavior*. New York: Macmillan.
1957   *Models of Man*. New York: Wiley.
1962   The architecture of complexity. *Proceedings of the
        American Philosophical Society* 106: 467–469.

Spaulding, Albert
1952   The origin of the Adena culture of the Ohio Valley.
        Southwestern Journal of Anthropology 8: 260–268.

Speth, John D., and Gregory A. Johnson
1976   Problems in the use of correlation for the investigation
        of tool kits and activity areas. In *Cultural Change and
        Continuity*, edited by Charles E. Cleland, pp. 35–57.
        New York: Academic Press.

Spicer, Edward H.
1962   *Cycles of Conquest: The Impact of Spain, Mexico, and
        the United States on the Indians of the Southwest, 1533–
        1960*. Tucson: University of Arizona Press.

Steponaitis, Vincas P.
1978   Location theory and complex chiefdoms: a Mississip-
        pian example. In *Mississippian Settlement Patterns*,
        edited by Bruce D. Smith, pp. 417–451. New York:
        Academic Press.
1981   Settlement hierarchies and political complexity in non-
        market society—the Formative period of the Valley of
        Mexico. *American Anthropologist* 83(2): 320–363.
1983   *Ceramics, Chronology, and Community Patterns: An
        Archaeological Study at Moundville*. New York: Ac-
        ademic Press.

Stickel, E. Gary
1968   Status differentiation at the Rincon Site. *Archaeological
        Survey Annual Report* 10: 209–261. Los Angeles: Uni-
        versity of California.

Sutherland, John W.
1975   *Systems: Analysis, Administration and Architecture*.
        New York: Van Nostrand-Reinhold.

Synenki, Alan T., and David P. Braun
1980   Organizational Theory and Social Inference. Paper Pre-
        sented in the Symposium "Regional Social Networks:
        Measurement, Theory, and Examples" at the 45th An-
        nual Meeting of the Society for American Archaeology,
        Philadelphia, Pennsylvania.

Tainter, Joseph A.
1975   The Archaeological Study of Social Change: Woodland
        Systems in West-Central Illinois. MS, doctoral disser-
        tation, Northwestern University, Evanston, Illinois.
1977   Modeling Change in Prehistoric Social Systems. In *For
        Theory Building in Archaeology*, edited by Lewis R.

Binford, pp. 327–351. New York: Academic Press.

1978   Mortuary practices and the study of prehistoric social systems. In *Advances in Archaeological Method and Theory*, edited by Michael B. Schiffer, pp. 105–141. New York: Academic Press.

1980   Behavior and status in a Middle Woodland mortuary population from the Illinois Valley. *American Antiquity* 45(2): 280–313.

1981   Reply to "A Critique of Some Recent North American Mortuary Studies." *American Antiquity* 46(2): 416–420.

1983   Woodland Social Change in the Central Midwest: A Review and Evaluation of interpretive trends. *North American Archaeologist* 4(2): 141–161.

Tainter, Joseph A., and Ross H. Cordy
1977   An archaeological analysis of social ranking and residence groups in prehistoric Hawaii. *World Archaeology* 9: 95–112.

Taylor, Walter W.
1948   A Study of Archaeology. *American Anthropological Association Memoir* 69.

Thompson, James D.
1967   *Organizations in Action*. New York: McGraw-Hill.

Ubelaker, Douglas A.
1984   *Human Skeletal Remains: Excavation, Analysis, Interpretation*. 2nd edition. Taraxcum, Washington.

Upham, Steadman
1982   *Polities and Power: An Economic and Political History of the Western Pueblo*. New York: Academic Press.

Upham, Steadman, Kent G. Lightfoot, and Gary M. Feinman
1981   Explaining socially determined ceramic distributions in the prehistoric plateau Southwest. *American Antiquity* 46(4): 822–833.

Urwick, L. F.
1956   The manager's span of control. *Harvard Business Review* 34: 39–47.

Vivian, R. Gwinn
1970   An inquiry into prehistoric social organization in Chaco Canyon, New Mexico. In *Reconstructing Prehistoric Pueblo Societies*, edited by William A. Longacre, pp. 59–83. Albuquerque: University of New Mexico Press.

Webster, David L.
1975   Warfare and the evolution of the state: a reconsideration. *American Antiquity* 40(4): 464–470.

1977   Warfare and evolution of Maya civilization. In *The Origins of Maya Civilization*, edited by Richard E. W. Adams, pp. 335–372. Albuquerque: University of New Mexico Press.

Weigand, Phil C.
1980   Mining and Mineral Trade in Prehispanic Zacatecas. In *Zacatecas: Anuario de Historia*. Vol. 3, edited by C. E. Sanchez. Departamento de Investigaciones Historicas. Mexico: Universidad Autonoma de Zacatecas.

Weiss, Kenneth M.
1973   Demographic Models for Anthropology. *Memories of the Society for American Archaeology* 27. *American Antiquity* 38(2), Part 2.

Whallon, Robert
1968   Investigations of late prehistoric social organization in New York State. In *New Perspectives in Archaeology*, edited by Sally R. Binford and Lewis R. Binford, pp. 223–244. Chicago: Aldine.

White, Leslie A.
1949   *The Science of Culture*. New York: Farrar

Whittlesey, Stephanie M.
1978   Status and Death at Grasshopper Pueblo: Experiment Toward An Archaeological Theory of Correlates. MS, doctoral dissertation, University of Arizona, Tucson, Arizona.

1984   The uses and abuses of Mogollon mortuary data. In "Recent Research in Mogollon Archaeology," edited by Steadman Upham, Fred Plog, David G. Batcho, and Barbara Kauffman, pp. 276–284. *Occasional Papers* 10. Las Cruces: University Museum, New Mexico State University.

Wilcox, David R.
1986   A historical analysis of the problems of Southwestern-Mesoamerican connections. In *Ripples in the Chichimec Sea: New Considerations of Southwestern-Mesoamerican Interactions*, edited by Frances Joan Mathien and Randall H. McGuire, pp. 9–44. Carbondale: Southern Illinois University Press.

Wilcox, David, and Lynette O. Shenk
1977   The Architecture of the Casa Grande and its Interpretation. *Arizona State Museum Archaeological Series* 115. Tucson: Arizona State Museum, University of Arizona.

Willey, Gordon R. (editor)
1956   Prehistoric Settlement Patterns in the New World. *Viking Fund Publications in Anthropology* 23. New York.

Wittfogel, Karl A.
1957   *Oriental Despotism: A Comparative Study of Total Power*. New Haven: Yale University Press.

Wobst, H. Martin
1978   The archaeo-ethnology of hunters-gatherers or the tyranny of ethnographic record in archaeology. *American Antiquity* 43(2): 303–309.

Wright, Henry T., and Gregory A. Johnson
1975   Population, exchange, and early state formation in southwestern Iran. *American Anthropologist* 77(2): 267–289.

Index

Abandonment, of Casas Grandes, 75
Accompaniments, with burials
    categories of, 42–48, 50–56, 59–67, 70
    See also Burial treatment, artifact
        accompaniments
Achieved social positions, 13, 16, 17, 19, 67
Adaptation, societal, 8–9, 11–12, 75
Administrative levels, in organizations, 10
Age-based differentiation, 16
Agriculture, 6, 7
Alta Vista, site of, 72
Altar piece, shell, 30
Altars, stone, 24, 25
Amerind Foundation, xii, 3, 5, 25, 73
Animal remains. *See* Antelope bone;
    Artiodactyla bone; Bear bone; Bone
    artifacts, animal; Bovine bone; Crane bone;
    Deer bone; Mountain Lion bone
Antelope bone, 53
    artifacts of, 32, 36, 37
Apophylite, 30
Architecture
    ballcourts, 5, 35, 36, 69
    butterfly-shaped rooms, 35, 36, 69
    ceremonial rooms, 5, 25, 69
    colonnade, 25, 35
    cross-shaped room, 36, 38
    domestic rooms, 5, 25
    multistoried, 5, 25, 32
    nesting boxes, 32
    niches, 30
    platform, 39
    platform mounds, 5, 69
    plazas, 5, 22, 39, 45, 52, 62
    public rooms, 5, 25, 30, 69
    puddled adobe, 5, 24, 25, 32, 35
    single story, 22, 25, 32, 36
    subterranean rooms, 30, 32
    T-shaped doorways, 6
Arizona State Museum, xii
Armlet
    copper, 47, 76
    shell, 30, 45
Arroyo Hondo Pueblo, 3
Articulated inhumations. *See* Burial treatment,
    articulated
Artifact accompaniment categories, 42–48,
    50–56, 59–67, 70. *See also* Jewelry;
    Pottery; Rare accompaniments;
    socioreligious accompaniments; Utilitarian
    accompaniments; Vegetal accompaniments
Artifacts. *See* Burial treatment, artifact
    accompaniments
Artiodactyla bone, artifacts of, 36
Ascribed social positions, 13, 16, 17, 18, 19,
    67
Ascriptive ranking, xi, 10, 17, 18, 20, 48, 56,
    68
    measurement of, 16–19

Attributes of burial treatment. *See* Burial
    treatment
Authority
    centralization of, 10, 14
    decentralization of, 14
    levels of, 3, 13, 68
    See also Symbols of authority
Aviculture, 6, 32
Awl, copper, 47
Axes
    copper, 47
    stone, 24, 30, 37
Aztec society, 6, 7

Backshield plaques, copper, 30, 47, 76
Ballcourts. *See* Architecture
Bands, ethnological, 9
Bead pendants
    shell, 45
    stone, 34
Beads
    copper, 34, 47, 53, 72
    shell, 34, 36, 45, 50
    stone, 24, 34, 36
Bear bone, 37
    artifacts of, 30, 37
Bells. *See* Crotals
Benfer, Robert, 24
Bezel, copper, 47
Binford, Lewis, 8, 9, 15, 16, 19
Birds. *See* Lesser Sandhill Crane; Macaws;
    Parrots; Turkeys
Board planks, 32, 36, 56, 69. *See also* Burial
    treatment, subfloor tomb
Body position. *See* Burial treatment, position
Bone artifacts
    animal, 24, 30, 34, 36, 37, 53, 56, 70
    human, 7, 25, 30, 36, 37, 39, 47, 53, 56,
        70, 71, 76
    See also Rasps; Wands
Bovine bone, artifacts of, 30, 36
Bracelets, shell, 45
Braun, David, xi, 14, 16–19, 42, 48, 57, 68
Brown, James, 14, 16, 69–71, 76
Buena Fé phase, 5, 6, 22, 32, 49
Buena Fé Phase Ranch Style Compound, Unit
    6, 22, 25, 32
Burial treatment
    articulated (primary) inhumations, 21, 32,
        34, 49, 50, 54, 59, 67, 68
    artifact accompaniments, 17–18, 21, 24, 25,
        32, 42–47, 52–56, 70–72
    attributes of, 17–18, 42–44, 47, 50, 68
    corpse processing, 21, 54, 56, 69
    deposition of bodies, 19, 50, 54
    Di Peso types, 21–39
    disarticulated burials, 21, 25, 32, 34, 49,
        56, 69
    facility, 19, 21, 50, 54, 59, 69

multiple interments, 19, 21, 23, 36, 48, 50,
    53, 56, 59, 68, 69
orientation, 21, 50
position, 21, 50, 54, 59
Ravesloot types, 54, 59–67, 68–69
secondary burials, 25, 50, 54, 56, 59, 66,
    68
secondary urn, 36, 56, 66
single interments, 19, 21, 56, 67, 68
subfloor tomb, 32, 36, 50, 51, 54, 56, 66,
    69
variables of, 48, 56, 66–67
vault, 25, 50, 54, 56, 66, 69
Burial types. *See* Burial treatment
Burial vault. *See* Burial treatment
Burros Mountains, 46
Butterfly-shaped rooms. *See* Architecture
Button, copper, 47

Caches
    offertory, 30
    subfloor, 30, 32, 34, 36, 46, 69
Carretas Polychrome, 34
Carter Ranch site, 3
Casas Grandes Plain, 42, 47
Casas Grandes site
    architectural units at, 22–39, 49, 51–54,
        59–63
    burial types at, 22–39, 54–56, 59–67, 68–
        69
    chronology at, 5, 49, 72
    description of, 5, 22–41
Castes, 7. *See also* Social differentiation
Cenote of Sacrifice, Chichen Itza, 30
Central Plaza, 39, 45. *See also* Architecture,
    plazas
Ceramic handdrums, 7, 32, 44, 45, 53, 56, 59
Cerrillos Mountains, 46
Chaco Canyon, New Mexico, 3, 6
Chiefdoms, 9
Chihuahua, Mexico, 5
Chi-square tests, 49, 51–54, 59–67
City water system, at Casas Grandes, 5, 54
Cloisonne. *See* Pseudocloisonne
Component scores, 59–62
Concretions, stone, 34
Conjunctive approach, definition of, 8. *See
    also* Social organization, archaeological
    study of
Container, shell, 30
Contemporary organizations
    definition of, 11–14
    structural dimensions of, 12–14
    See also Formal organizations; Hierarchical
    organizations; Informal organizations
Contextural relationships, 8, 22, 70
Copper, artifacts of, 30, 34, 36, 47, 53, 72,
    76
Copper metallurgy, 6, 47

[109]

ABSTRACT

The prehistoric site of Casas Grandes, Chihuahua, Mexico occupies a unique position within the prehistory of the Greater Southwest. Partial excavations of the site resulted in the recovery of a burial collection consisting of 576 individuals. This study orders and synthesizes the Casas Grandes mortuary data into a format amenable to a variety of analyses, one of which is presented here. The purpose of this study is an attempt to determine the degree to which Casas Grandes society was hierarchically structured during the Medio period (A.D. 1200 to 1450). Specifically, the hypothesis that Casas Grandes society was organized on the basis of ascriptive or hereditary ranking was tested. This hypothesis is evaluated by investigating social differentiation among Casas Grandians using mortuary data.

Mortuary treatment expresses important dimensions of social variation, or differentiation, and thus provides a valuable means for examining status differences among individuals. Social differentiation refers to the differences among individuals, social positions, or groups within a society that evolved through the processes of societal interaction. This study of Casas Grandes mortuary practices defines the dimensions of status differentiation that separated members of Casas Grandes society into different social positions or rank levels. Social ranking is evaluated by identifying symbols of rank and authority (for example, body preparation, burial facility, location of facility, quantity and type of associated grave goods) that may crosscut age and gender. Such qualitative distinctions in mortuary ritual treatment consist of either a single attribute or groups of covarying attributes that segregate burials into discrete groups.

Univariate and multivariate analyses of Casas Grandes burial treatment have demonstrated that the burials cluster into several groups that may reflect social status differences. The Casas Grandes elite were given distinctive mortuary treatment that included characteristics such as secondary urn burial, room subfloor tombs, prominent burial locations, and rare grave goods.

RESUMEN

El sitio prehistórico de Casas Grandes, Chihuahua, México, ocupa una posición única en la prehistoria del Sudoeste Mayor. Excavaciones parciales en aquel sitio han resultado en el descubrimiento de los restos de 576 individuos. Este estudio alinea y sintetiza los datos mortuorios de Casas Grandes en una forma que se presta a una variedad de análisis, una de las cuales se presenta aquí. El motivo para este estudio es el atentar la determinación del grado en que la sociedad Casas Grandes se estructuró según una jerarquía particular durante el Período Medio (A.D. 1200–1450). En detalle, se hizo la prueba de la hipótesis que la organización de Casas Grandes se formaba según niveles hereditarios. Esta hipótesis se puede probar por la investigación de las distinciones sociales entre la gente de Casas Grandians por medio de datos mortuorios.

El tratamiento mortuorio de los cadáveres manifiesta aspectos importantes de variaciones o diferencias sociales y así nos proveé medios útiles para examinar diferencias en el estado legal y social de los varios individuos. La expresión "diferenciación social" se dirige a las diferencias entre individuous, rangos sociales, o grupos, dentro de una sociedad que se había desarrollado por procesos de interacción social. El presente estudio de las costrumbres mortuorias entre la gente de Casas Grandes define las dimensiones de la diferenciación en rango que sirvió para separar los miembros de la socieded de Casas Grandes y para establecer distintas posiciones sociales o niveles de rango. Rangos sociales se pueden evaluar por medio de identificación de símbolos de rango y autoridad (por ejemplo: tratamiento de los cadáveres, lugares y maneras de sepultura, cantidad y tipo de efectos localizados en el sepulcro) que pueden cortar al través de edades y sexos. Tales distinciones en calidad del tratamiento ritual mortuorio pueden consistir en solo un atributo o también en grupos de variaciones conexas que separan las sepulturas en clases discretas.

Analisis uni- y multivariente de agrupaciones de entierros de Casas Grandes han demonstrado que los entierros se ordenan en maneras que pueden ser el resulto de distinciones en el estado social. Los del rango más alto recibían tratamiento mortuorio distintivo, incluyendo tales característicos como entierros secundarios en urnas, sepulturas subsuelas en habitaciones, sepulturas en sitios prominentes, y efectos raros en los sepulcros.